Southern Living®

THE **SLIM DOWN SOUTH** COOKBOOK

Carolyn O'Neil, MS, RD

OXMOOR HOUSE®

FOREWORD

Throughout the many years I've known her, Carolyn O'Neil has been a leader in the food world. As peers and friends, we've served together on committees, organized groups together, and shared countless meals in and beyond our beloved South. What I've particularly admired while at the table with Carolyn is her uncommon knack for eating well and healthfully at every meal, whether we're at the ritziest restaurant or the most down-home potluck.

As a smart dietitian and an award-winning food journalist, Carolyn understands the importance of carefully choosing what we eat each day. In fact, she seems to relish the challenge. With a keen eye and an easy grace—and without wagging her finger or ruling out any foods—she guides us to the best-tasting and healthiest meals, no matter the circumstances.

Having *The Slim Down South Cookbook* in your kitchen is like having Carolyn at your elbow at the grocery store, in the kitchen, and at the dinner table. It chooses as smartly for you as Carolyn does for herself, and shows, with no small amount of pride, that incredibly delicious Southern foods can be good for you. As Carolyn knows well, healthy Southern food is not a new thing. Until very recent times, the South was an agrarian region where vegetables served a primary role in every meal, and meat and fat were used as flavorings or occasional indulgences.

Today, most of us are a little removed from the farm, and many struggle to find healthy choices that our families will eat. Calorie-rich and nutrient-poor prepared foods can seem like the easy solution when time, for both cooking and enjoying meals, is at a premium.

But Carolyn shows that you can find satisfaction and health in Southern foods even when your life is rushed. Carolyn has a busy schedule—we see each other in airports and hotels much more than in our homes—so she understands the importance of go-to recipes that take the guesswork out of creating a healthy meal. She's selected *Southern Living* recipes that have the flavors Southern food-lovers crave and the built-in goodness that comes from using fresh ingredients, savvy cooking tricks, and smart portions. She combines these dishes with clever strategies and secrets for a healthy Southern appetite.

As much for my taste buds as for my waistline, I want this book on my next-to-the-stove bookshelf, and I'm sure you will, too!

Nathalie Dupree
Author of the James Beard Foundation Award-winning cookbook,
Mastering the Art of Southern Cooking

CONTENTS

When I first told friends I was working on a healthy Southern cookbook, they suggested we call it *Kiss My Skinny Grits!* or, as a nod to Scarlett's tight corset, *Gone with the Girdle*. A Southern diet book may seem like a comical oxymoron. But, as a registered dietitian who has lived most of her life in the South, I know it's not.

I wanted to create this book with the editors of *Southern Living* to show that great-tasting Southern foods can and do fit in with modern health and nutrition advice. The stay-slim philosophy of *The Slim Down South Cookbook* starts with wholesome ingredients you should be eating more of, not avoiding. Fresh peaches, pecans, okra, greens, and sweet potatoes fill Southern pantries with good health and great taste. They're now widely available, even if you're not lucky enough to live in the South.

I've learned that the best way to get folks to improve their eating habits is to allow them to embrace foods they love. If your life's not complete without fried chicken, design an eating plan that includes it on occasion. If you crave bacon or beignets or bourbon balls, it's not only OK to indulge a little—it's a healthy habit for the long haul.

Of course it's important to know when to say "whoa!" From macaroni and cheese to mile-high pies, the key to indulging without bulging is portion control. It's also a smart idea to give traditional Southern dishes a healthy makeover. From casual lunches to candlelit affairs and from breakfast to dessert (yes, dessert!), the recipes in *The Slim Down South Cookbook* are both fabulous and figure-friendly.

Southern culture certainly tempts us with deviled eggs and layer cakes. But it also gives us the grit to lace up our running shoes, the grace to say, "No thank you, ma'am" to second helpings, and the good manners to eat slowly and not talk with our mouths full. This cookbook includes scores of secrets from slim Southerners about how to navigate temptation.

The slightly slower rhythm of life in the South helps us to be more mindful of the foods we're eating, to take time to appreciate the china pattern and the flowers and the people we're with, so that when the meal's over we're simply more satisfied.

Let's set the table and start cooking, y'all!

Carolyn O'Neil

Carolyn O'Neil, MS, RD

Chapter One

A HEALTHY SOUTHERN PLATE

Bees buzz, shadows lengthen on the lawn, and the sound of chopping mingles with a little humming in the kitchen. You might be in the French or Italian countryside. But step inside to hear pecan shells cracking, smell sweet onions hitting a hot pan, and watch an armful of collard greens disappearing under a steamy lid, and you'll realize this scene isn't set in Florence or Provence. This is the American South.

Like other iconic regions, the South is much more than just a place on the map. It's a state of mind, complete with front porch swings and backyard hammocks, long tables set with pretty china, and short prayers for another cool breeze. What many don't realize is that when enjoyed in the context of an active yet relaxed Southern lifestyle, **real Southern foods share many of the same delicious and nutritious characteristics of the world's healthiest cuisines.**

Healthy *and* Southern?

I know. When was the last time you heard those two words used in the same sentence? When I began telling folks I was writing a healthy Southern cookbook, some laughed and said, "That'll be a short book!"

The stereotypical Southern meal—fried chicken and biscuits followed by an SUV-sized slice of pecan pie—certainly isn't a dietitian's dream. Add to that vegetables overcooked with handfuls of salt and fatback, grits gussied up with gobs of butter, and iced tea laced with sugar, and you can see why **Southern food has gained a reputation as a culprit in rising rates of obesity. But more often than not it's just a bad rap.** Although the most popularized Southern foods rely on frying and using sugar, fat, and salt to make them taste good, they're only one small corner of the true Southern repertoire.

"When visitors come to Charleston, they want fried chicken. They think that we eat fried chicken every day," says Nathalie Dupree, a Southern food expert and co-author of *Mastering the Art of Southern Cooking.* "It was never that way. **Actually we eat more seafood (than fried chicken)** in Charleston."

In fact, if you look a little more closely at Southern food traditions, you'll see a bounty of vegetables and fruits, modest servings of meat, freshly baked breads, dainty desserts, and a pace that lets you savor every blissful bite. While the countrywide craze for Southern cooking has all eyes on bacon and barbecue, Dupree points out that vegetable cookery is the South's true strength.

"We are essentially agrarian in the South," says Dupree, who has authored more than a dozen Southern cookbooks. "We have our own gardens and grow vegetables. Now we might cook them a long time, but we eat the liquid, too." (This liquid, which we call "pot likker," contains important nutrients that leach out of the vegetables during cooking.

Despite the allure of bacon and barbecue, vegetable cookery is the South's true strength.

No good Southern cook tosses it out.) The South produces some of the nation's finest produce: juicy peaches, mouthwatering tomatoes, sweet-as-sugar peas—you name it, we grow it, eat it, and enjoy it. Even the classic "meat-and-three" option at many Southern restaurants (a meat entrée plus three sides) is designed to fill plates primarily with produce.

Indeed, a lifetime of healthy eating solutions can be found on Southern menus. To enjoy the bounty of good-tasting Southern foods from fried okra to peach cobbler—as well as a lifetime of good health—you need only to adopt a slim Southern approach. As I like to say: The more you know, the more you can eat! So, let's find out how Southern foods fit in with a trim modern lifestyle.

The Big Fat Truth

To be sure, the South is a region of culinary contrasts. While there's a healthy harvest of fresh produce year-round, and the climate is pretty friendly for walking, jogging, cycling, tennis, and other forms of outdoor physical activity, there's no denying the sky-high occurrence of obesity, diabetes, and stroke below the Mason-Dixon line.

In the past, the South has held the dubious honor of being the fattest region in the country. In 2011, according to the Centers for Disease Control and Prevention (CDC), the South had the highest prevalence of obesity (29.5%), followed by the Midwest (29%), the Northeast (25.3%), and the West (25.3%). Of the states, Colorado had the fewest obese residents, and Mississippi had the most folks categorized as obese.

But newer findings reported in the journal *Obesity* suggest that, as the country as a whole is becoming more overweight, the South's status as fattest is sliding: A 2013 study from the University of Alabama at Birmingham, using data from the U.S. Census Bureau and the Reasons for Geographic and Racial Differences in Stroke survey, shows that the region is actually the fifth-fattest out of nine areas in the country, with 34 percent of its population considered obese. (The North-Central region including North and South Dakota, Minnesota, Nebraska, Iowa, Kansas, and Missouri actually tops the list with a 41 percent obesity rate.) Data from the National Health and Nutrition Examination Survey ranked the South even lower on the fat scale, seventh out of eight areas of the country in terms of overall obesity.

Still, before you grab another piece of fried chicken, Dr. George Howard of UAB's School of Public Health notes, "The South still has very bad obesity problems, but not worse than some other regions." **The bottom line is that many Americans all over the map need to slim down to a healthier body weight.** Steps like those taken in Mississippi are bringing the South along to a healthier status. In that state, long considered the heaviest, numbers of obese elementary school children fell by more than 10 percent from 2005 to 2011, according to a report

DISHING UP GOOD HEALTH

The USDA's MyPlate guidelines remind us to build a healthy plate at every meal: Fill half your plate with fruits and vegetables, choose small portions of lean protein, and eat more whole grains. A traditional Southern plate achieves the same balance: Half of this plate is filled with green tomatoes and green beans, there's a 3-ounce portion of grilled tenderloin, and a half cup of couscous. Mozzarella cheese gives you dairy, leaving room for some iced tea.

published by the Center for Mississippi Health Policy. Researchers credit the change to school nutrition and fitness programs. Hopefully the rest of the South—and the country—will soon follow and embrace the healthier side of Southern eating and lifestyle.

Health experts are most worried about the long list of serious consequences connected to being obese or overweight, including heart disease, hypertension, stroke, type 2 diabetes, certain types of cancer, osteoarthritis, sleep apnea, and liver and kidney disease. These weight-related conditions are often preventable through diet and exercise. **The key is finding an eating plan and an exercise regimen you can stick with over the long haul.** Adopting a lifetime of healthy habits can literally save your life.

A Southern Take on Good Health

Real Southern cooking is surprisingly similar to a cuisine long considered among the healthiest in the world: the Mediterranean diet. For decades, nutrition experts have touted the powerful, disease-fighting benefits of the Mediterranean cuisine and lifestyle, and the research continues to pour in. One major clinical trial conducted in Spain and published in *The New England Journal of Medicine* found that a traditional Mediterranean diet can prevent 30 percent of heart attacks, strokes, and deaths from heart disease. Subjects in this study followed a daily diet including at least four tablespoons of olive oil or a quarter cup of nuts, at least three servings of fruit, and at least two servings of vegetables, plus a glass of wine. Participants were asked to eat fish and legumes (peas, beans, and lentils) at least three times a week, and to limit sugary desserts.

But you don't have to travel all the way to the Mediterranean to follow this approach. **The same basic elements are mainstays in the Southern pantry and on many a Southern menu:** bell peppers, black-eyed peas, rice, corn, butter beans, pecans, peanuts, peaches, figs, greens, freshwater fish, and seafood. A vegetable plate featured at The National restaurant in Athens, Georgia, is a state-of-the-art example: Carolina Gold rice with black lentils, fried cauliflower with yogurt and harissa, beets with kumquats and fennel fronds, cabbage and caraway slaw, and marinated carrots with fennel. Close your eyes and you're sitting on a terrace overlooking the Aegean. Open them and you'll see a restaurant full of happy diners in a Southern college town.

And those aren't the only ways true Southern cuisine fits into a healthy lifestyle. **The foods in the Southern market basket also dovetail nicely with the Dietary Guidelines for Americans** (DGA), a set of recommendations established by the federal government after years of vigorous review of scientific evidence on healthy approaches to eating. Here's how a truly Southern diet measures up on the DGA checklist:

Find a Healthy Southern Balance

No discussion of Southern foods past, present, or future would be complete without input from Alabama-born chef Frank Stitt. Since the early 1980s, Stitt has held the reins of the Southern farm-to-table movement, guiding it to elegant heights by blending French technique with farm-fresh local ingredients. Respectfully known as "The Godfather" of contemporary Southern cuisine by his culinary colleagues, Stitt is the owner and executive chef of the critically acclaimed Highlands Bar and Grill, Chez Fonfon, Bottega, and Bottega Café restaurants in Birmingham.

Though Southern plates have evolved, Stitt says some negative stereotypes linger. "We are stuck with old reputations in the South, partially deserved, of having pork fat in everything and a lot of fried foods all eaten together—fried pork chops with fried okra and skillet-fried cornbread," he says. But at Bottega, Stitt balances crispy fried oysters with a refreshing watercress salad.

The Southern table Stitt grew up around in Cullman, Alabama, was piled high with vegetables. His grandmother's garden yielded a gourmet variety of beets, tomatoes, cucumbers, onions, and even asparagus. "We could never leave my grandmother's house," he recalls, "without her loading us down with fresh strawberries and lady peas."

Stitt said his mother often offered a plate of crudités with cottage cheese before dinner, a

Frank Stitt, Birmingham chef and restaurateur

healthy indulgence and a way to prolong the enjoyment of a meal.

After leaving the South for college in Boston, Stitt worked in the Berkeley kitchen of Chez Panisse, the famed Alice Waters's restaurant and birthplace of lighter California cuisine, where his love of cooking fresh ingredients with a balance of French and Southern techniques was confirmed.

"I use some butter and some pork fat, but I want to feel light after a meal," he says. "That's how I build menus, how I build a dish."

"I use some butter and some pork fat, but I want to feel light after a meal."

Is your plate loaded with produce? *Check.* The DGA recommends you fill half your plate with fruits and veggies and reduce meat intake to a three- or four-ounce serving per meal. Since the meaty portion of the meal is often the most expensive, cost-conscious Southerners have long offered a variety of palate-pleasing vegetable dishes to fill up their plates. As with Mediterranean cuisine, traditional Southern plates pile on plant-based foods and pair them with a smaller serving of meat, poultry, or seafood. In the Mediterranean, you might eat a Moroccan tagine of couscous and vegetables served with a small amount of chicken. In the South, you might enjoy a tomato-and-okra gumbo served over rice with a few shrimp. The health benefits of this approach are clear: Fruits and vegetables are relatively low in calories and help fill in common nutrition gaps with potassium, fiber, magnesium, and vitamins A, C, and K. They're also loaded with important phytonutrients, which can help prevent such chronic ailments as cancer, diabetes, and heart disease.

Do you use salt, sugar, and fat with care? *Check.* Good Southern cooks don't gild the lily. They know that salads are drizzled with dressing, not drenched, and that frying at the right temperature and with heart-healthy oils limits the addition of unhealthy fats to food. Good Southern cooks let the natural flavors of ingredients shine, waiting for a peach to ripen to its full sweetness rather than loading it up with sugar, or letting the Vidalia onions add a touch of sweetness to a salad of sliced tomatoes and cucumbers so you need only a little honey in the honey-mustard dressing. Just as Italian cooks add a piece of the rind from Parmesan cheese to enhance soups, stews, and braised vegetables, Southern cooks add a bit of fatback for flavor. Good Southern cooks also use salt-free seasonings—hot peppers in vinegar, cayenne pepper, and freshly squeezed citrus juice—to enhance flavor without adding extra salt.

Do whole grains make up half of your grain consumption? *Check.* Almost every type of whole grain is high in the necessary nutrients that can help fight disease and keep you feeling good. The DGA advises us to make at least half of our grains the whole grain group. And the

THE SKINNY ON SALT

Pepper adds heat, but salt is the seasoning that fans the flames of the dietary debate over sodium.

Government health officials have declared the sodium in table salt a nutrition no-no, advising limited amounts in home cooking, on restaurant menus, and in processed foods and school lunches. That's because many research studies associate too much sodium in the diet with high blood pressure, which can increase the risk for heart attack and stroke.

One recent report published by the American Heart Association predicted we could save up to half a million lives over the next decade simply by scaling back the amount of sodium in our diets.

Current national dietary guidelines recommend that healthy adults consume no more than 2,300 milligrams of sodium (about a teaspoon of salt) per day. A lower limit of 1,500 milligrams per day is recommended for adults with high blood pressure, diabetes, kidney disease, the over-50s, and all African-Americans.

But other studies suggest there's no benefit for most people (and harm for some) when sodium levels drop below 2,300 milligrams per day.

Bottom line: Since the average American consumes 3,400 milligrams of sodium a day, most of us can stand to cut back some to get closer to the 2,300-milligram sweet spot.

FYI: Nearly 80 percent of the sodium in American food comes from food processing rather than from salt added during cooking or at the table or from sodium naturally occurring in foods. So one of the best ways to keep tabs on your sodium intake is to check the label on packaged and convenience foods including canned goods, frozen entrées and pizzas, and condiments. Happily, more and more brands now offer good-tasting reduced-sodium versions.

Southern pantry fits this advice to a T, with a mix of refined grains (such as enriched white flour and long-grain white rice) and whole grains (such as stone-ground grits, cornmeal, and whole wheat flour). While we might enjoy long-grain white rice with jambalaya at dinner, we can try whole grain bread for a sandwich at lunch. And if we prefer white bread for tomato sandwiches? That's fine—as long as we have some stone-ground whole grain grits for breakfast. Soft white Southern flour—including brands such as White Lily or those labeled as cake or pastry flour—makes for tender biscuits and cakes but contains less protein and fewer nutrients than whole wheat and harder-wheat flours (such as durum wheat and standard all-purpose flour). It's OK to enjoy baked goods made with soft white flour as long as we make sure to add breads or rolls made with whole wheat flour to our repertoire, too. (Even better, we can experiment with 100 percent whole grain pastry flour, which can now be found in many grocery stores.) Corn—cooked and eaten straight off the cob with a dab of butter and a dash of salt—is a delicious whole grain, and one that contains more antioxidants than any other grain in the group.

Do you enjoy fried foods in moderation? *Check.* Fried chicken may be the stereotypical Southern entrée, but historically it's only served once a week. And even the act of frying may not be the nutrition demon we once feared: When foods such as okra, potatoes, shrimp, or even pickles are fried in healthy fats such as canola, olive, soybean, or other vegetable oils, they actually contribute a combination of fatty acids that are associated with preventing heart disease. Plus, the oil in fried foods helps the body better absorb fat-soluble vitamins, such as vitamins A and E, which are found in some vegetables. That's another happy reason to toss some fried shrimp on top of a big green salad! Most important, smart Southern cooks know that proper frying with the right oil at the right temperature can limit the total amount of oil absorbed by the food, therefore limiting the total calories. It will be crispier and tastier, too. We're not saying fry everything—in fact, just the opposite. When you have just a sampling of fried fare, you'll appreciate it that much more. It's like nutritionist Sarah-Jane Bedwell, a registered dietitian based in Nashville, Tennessee, says: "You enjoy something like fried food more when you don't have it every day—it feels more special. And you don't need to have more than one fried item at any given meal. Do you really need the fried pickles and the fried chicken and the fried potatoes and the fried okra and the fried pie all at one meal? Didn't think so!"

Do you take part in regular physical activity? *Check.* Because of our mostly temperate weather, Southerners are active year-round in tennis, golf, water sports, walking, running, hiking, and biking. Strolling down Main Street or along the beach after a big meal is a pleasant way to pass the evening with friends and family. Whether it's a walk around the park or a hike in the mountains, physical activity is a key component in weight management and disease

STONE GROUND GRITS

prevention. Study after study concludes that getting more movement in your day (ideally, doing at least 30 minutes of a moderate activity like brisk walking) is one of the single greatest things that you can do to improve your health and prevent chronic disease.

SLIM Secrets Revealed!

It's clear that living—and eating—like a true Southerner can help put you on the path to good health. But before you even begin to think about boiling water for stone-ground grits or grating sharp Cheddar to make macaroni taste like magic, remember that having the right mind-set is vital to helping you stay slim while still enjoying every morsel of delicious Southern fare. If you'd rather look more like a slender green bean than a fluffy buttermilk biscuit, you need the right attitude. When you get right down to it, enjoying great food and good health comes down to four fundamental elements that work whether you're in South Carolina or South Dakota. And they're as easy to remember as the word SLIM:

Savor the South: Discover the healthy variety of Southern foods.
Linger Longer: Take your sweet time to enjoy meals.
Indulge a Little: Incorporate little splurges that keep you satisfied.
Make It Happen: Use Southern grit and grace to stay the course.

So, what do I mean by that? Really, savoring the South is about widening your taste horizons (and keeping your waist) by discovering the delicious bounty of genuine Southern ingredients—from garden-fresh varieties of greens and peas you may have never tried before to new ways to enjoy roasted sweet potatoes and just-caught shrimp. **Go beyond the bacon, and get to know bona fide Southern staples that fill soup bowls and salad plates.** Collard greens, sugar snap peas, black-eyed peas, okra, pole beans, peaches, pecans, and peanuts—the delicious and healthful list goes on and on.

Our temperate climate means there's an endless rotation of fresh fruits and vegetables just bursting with flavor. Along with citrus, strawberries, and apples, the Southern fruit harvest yields sweet figs and blueberries, too. (Fact: Georgia's blueberry crop is now bigger than its harvest for peaches!) They don't just taste good; they're good for you. Pecans are higher in antioxidants than any other tree nut, and sweet potatoes are loaded with beta-carotene, fiber, and potassium. Name a Southern crop and you're sure to find a long list of better-health benefits that even a Northern nutritionist will love.

BRING THE FARM HOME

Farmers' markets are great places to check out what's fresh and fabulous.

From summer's sweet corn, sweet onions, and juicy tomatoes to autumn's pumpkin, squash, and kale—the seasonal parade of produce is exciting. The best thing about a farmers' market is that you can sample and ask the folks who grew the stuff all about it.

If you're not sure what to do with a particular pea or unusual squash, chances are the farmer will share a recipe and a smile.

Supermarkets offer a great selection of local and seasonal produce, too. But you might also consider signing up for a CSA (that's short for Community Supported Agriculture). CSA programs offered in thousands of communities around the country bring the farm to you in the form of boxes, bags, or baskets bursting with seasonal ingredients delivered to your home or a dedicated drop-off each week. And who knows? You might find some Southern comfort in fresh flowers or just-laid eggs brought right to your door.

Variety is the spice of Southern life. Within categories of crops there are different shapes, sizes, colors, and flavors to discover, all with their own unique nutritional benefits. Let's pick peas: We've got lady peas, crowder peas, zipper peas, pink-eyed purple hull peas, black-eyed peas, and many more. Then there are all the Southern ways to prepare produce. Okra, for one, can be fried, grilled, or stewed with tomatoes. Or try it cold, crunchy, and pickled (the perfect garnish for a Bloody Mary).

True Southern cooking embraces the region's range of ingredients, from collards to peaches, squash to sweet potatoes and figs to blackberries. We've long learned to make the most of what's grown right in our own backyards by canning tomatoes and other seasonal delights, pickling green beans, or putting up fruit preserves so we can enjoy their goodness any time of year.

Produce isn't the only option when it comes to filling your plate with Southern flavors. **Pork, popular on Southern menus, is healthier than you might think.** Today's pork actually has 16 percent less total fat and 27 percent less saturated fat than the pork produced in the early '90s. It's also high in protein, B vitamins, and minerals like iron, zinc, and selenium. So go ahead and have it (in moderation) with a side of greens or served up straight from the grill with some peach salsa.

Southerners also eat a lot of fish and shellfish. Whether it's from the Gulf of Mexico or the Georgia coast, sweet and succulent fresh shrimp is perfect for simple peel-and-eat affairs or fancy-pants recipes for company. Trout, grouper, snapper, and bass are all ready to jump into the pan or onto the grill. Maryland crabs, Louisiana crawfish, Mississippi catfish, and North Carolina rainbow trout are all Southern favorites.

To eat like a slim Southerner and follow an important recommendation from the DGA wherever you live, enjoy delicious fish dishes at least twice a week. Eating one to two (three-ounce) servings of fatty fish a week—salmon, herring, mackerel, anchovies, or sardines (which have the highest concentration of heart-healthy omega-3 fats)—reduces the risk of dying from heart disease by 36 percent. That's according to researchers at the Harvard School of Public Health who analyzed 20 studies involving hundreds of thousands of people. Eating fish is literally a smart move because omega-3 fats are connected to boosting cognitive health. Leaner white-fleshed fish such as trout, monkfish, and bass also are super nutritious, offering high-quality protein with fewer calories than fatty fish.

Other Southern staples that offer a harvest of good health include pecans, peanuts, benne (sesame) seeds, corn, stone-ground grits, long-grain rice, sorghum syrup, and tea. We've got honey from beehives tended all over the South and fermented favorites like pickled chowchow or hot peppers in vinegar. And, of course, there are loads of fragrant spices (like ground red pepper, dried crushed red pepper, and ginger) and fresh herbs (such as chives, parsley, cilantro, rosemary, thyme, basil, mint, and lemon verbena) that are an important part of the Southern pantry. Put them together and you've got the makings of meals that are as glorious as a Southern sunrise.

SAVOR THE SOUTH
LINGER LONGER
INDULGE A LITTLE
MAKE IT HAPPEN

There's a leisurely pace to living in the South. Rocking chairs and picnic tables were meant for sitting a spell while sharing lemonade, long talks, and lingering over lunches. But taking the time to sip iced tea with a slice of coconut cake and to truly enjoy the experience isn't just an old-fashioned notion; it fits in with modern nutrition advice to slow down, appreciate flavors, and be more mindful of what we're eating and drinking. **Slow is the way to go according to a bumper crop of studies on weight control and satiety** (the measure of how satisfied we are with what and how much we eat).

In a study of 3,000 people in Japan, those who reported regularly gulping down their meals until they felt full were three times more likely to be overweight. On the flip side, a diet study conducted at the University of Rhode Island found that women who slowed down when they ate not only enjoyed their food more but actually consumed 70 fewer calories per meal. Nutrition researchers theorize that's because it takes time for your brain to register that your belly is full, and when you slow down you have more time to process these signals. British researchers discovered that subjects released more hormones that signaled feelings of fullness when they ate a bowl of ice cream in 30 minutes, compared to when they wolfed down the same serving size in just five minutes.

Bottom line: **Whether your meal is a race or a ritual is an important factor that impacts how much you eat.** When you slow down and appreciate small portions of big tastes, you're practicing cutting-edge habits to improve your health. That doesn't mean every lunch needs to be a two-hour affair. Even if you have only 20 minutes to sit down and eat, I encourage you to stop, look, listen, and pay attention to what you're doing.

On a busy workday, if lunch is a pimiento cheese sandwich with lemonade at your desk, put your phone and computer to sleep, set your work aside for a few minutes, and create a meal-focused environment. You might even set out a place mat to pretty up the setting and keep your papers clean! When it's a night out with friends sharing plates at the latest farm-to-table eatery, set down your fork between bites, take a sip of wine or water, participate in the conversation, and appreciate each mouthful. It's a strategy that helps prevent overeating and lets you enjoy your meal a whole lot more.

There's another reason it pays to take it easy every once in a while: It helps minimize stress, which has damaging health consequences of its own. During times of stress, our body is hardwired to reach for high-calorie fare, the stuff that's loaded with fat, sugar, and salt—whether that's a bag of pork rinds or a chunk of chocolate cake. When it perceives a threat, the brain triggers the release of adrenaline and cortisol, creating a "stress soup" combo that turns on enzymes, which in turn signal the fat cells to become fat-storing machines. As the HBO documentary *Weight of the Nation* explained, this biochemistry served us well when we were hunters and gatherers who needed energy to outrun saber-toothed tigers, but it's not quite so convenient when our biggest stress is a deadline at work or a pileup on the highway. Over time, **chronic levels of stress can trigger excess weight gain,** especially the deep belly fat that has been linked to numerous chronic diseases.

Emerging research also connects getting enough rest with lower cortisol levels and links getting too little sleep (less than five or six hours a night) with a higher risk of being overweight. So, take a moment and enjoy some of that laid-back Southern mind-set, whether you're going for an evening stroll, rocking on the veranda while chatting with your neighbor, or even napping in a hammock.

The Southern expression "gimme some sugar" is usually a request for affection, a little love to keep you going. Your healthy diet needs some of that, too. We Southerners know that you've got to indulge now and then. Your sweet treat of choice might be dessert. Others might crave something creamy or salty like macaroni and cheese. And some may splurge with sweet tea or a cocktail. Nutrition studies show that incorporating personal favorites in a healthy diet reduces the risk of a relapse into unhealthy ways. For instance, if you know you can savor one simply

If you add more activity to your day, you get to add more splurge calories. That's the kind of math I like!

divine praline candy without blowing your diet, you're less likely to give up and dive into the whole batch.

The sweet takeaway: **Whether you dream of chocolate cake, cheese grits, or bourbon on the rocks, there's room for a little indulgence.** In fact, allowing yourself a splurge budget is one of the most surprising secrets to long-term weight management success.

Ever watched a skinny little thing devour a red velvet cupcake and wondered how she stays so trim? Research offers some clues. The National Weight Control Registry tracks the habits of more than 6,000 people who have lost at least 30 pounds and kept it off for more than a year. (The average participant has lost about 70 pounds and has kept it off for six years.) Turns out that these fit folks stick to a routine eating pattern most of the day, even on weekends and holidays, and allow themselves occasional treats and plan their splurges ahead of time.

Even the U.S. government approves of cheating on your diet. According to MyPlate.gov, which the USDA created with input from health experts and stacks of nutrition research, solid fats, added sugars, and other "empty" calories found in sweets and alcohol can be part of a healthy diet "as long as food group recommendations are met and overall calorie needs are not exceeded." The sweet takeaway: If you know you're going to a cocktail party and the hostess with the mostest makes a Parmesan-artichoke dip you just adore, just add a few more minutes to your treadmill routine or dance your socks off to make up for the extra calories. Generally, the allotment for empty or "splurge" calories is about 250 per day for a healthy moderately active adult. If you add more activity to your day, you get to add more splurge calories. That's the kind of math I like!

So give in within reason. Think of the rich ingredients you crave as exciting accessories when you're designing your plate. Though you may want several (Cheddar cheese, fried croutons, and bacon crumbles on your salad), often just one completes the look.

Southerners also have tremendous inner strength. We are known for digging in our heels and setting our mind to things. One of the most powerful secrets to success no matter what your goal, **this famed Southern spirit—a sassy "can-do" attitude—can help you make and stick with healthy lifestyle changes.**

Ever heard the expression that willpower is like a muscle—the more you use it, the stronger it becomes? That fits in nicely with our ingrained Southern sense of politeness. Learning to say "no thanks" to empty calories and high-fat fare, and even to smile through gritted teeth when someone cuts you off on the highway or shuts a door before you have a chance to come in, can also go a long way toward keeping you in good health.

Roy F. Baumeister, Ph.D., a researcher at Florida State University, has shown through numerous studies that willpower isn't a personality trait, skill, or virtue. It's something that can be learned, and even strengthened over time. And other research has revealed that sleeping, laughing, focusing on the positive, and treating yourself right—all of which can be found in some of our favorite Southern pastimes—can work to help boost willpower. When it's time for dessert, we can skip that sundae and go straight for a slice of juicy watermelon or a bowl of sweet strawberries.

It's true that when you're trying to follow a healthier way of eating, you're going to run into some obstacles. It might take some practice, and it's harder for some than others, but you're going to tackle those obstacles with Southern backbone. Nothing ruffles my feathers more than hearing that some people were just born to be fat or thin. Hogwash! Sure, we're all different in so many ways. But **don't let anyone ever tell you that you can't change your dress size or waistline.**

Opposition can come in many forms. It might be a spouse, a friend, a relative, or a really vexing person at work. It's amazing what some folks will say, even when they know you're trying to make healthier choices. "Oh, don't you want another brownie? You know sweet Betty Sue went to so much effort to share her dear aunt's favorite family recipe with us today." Here's what you say: "Those brownies are delicious, and I can't wait to ask for the recipe! Thank you for offering." **Set your boundaries, and throw in a compliment. That's showing them Southern grit with a little grace.**

It turns out if you try to appease everyone, it's really difficult to decline a cookie. Researchers at Case Western Reserve University studying "sociotropy"—the scientific term for having the need to please others—found that excessive niceness could be a recipe for excessive weight gain. It's hard to say no to the sweet sales pitch of an 8-year-old Girl Scout, and even harder to turn down your mother-in-law's "just-for-you" lemon meringue pie. A study on the people-pleasing factor in eating showed that student volunteers who scored higher on the sociotropy scale—a measure of how invested people are in interpersonal relationships—ate more from a passed bowl of M&Ms than students who were less concerned about what others thought. Psychology professor Julie Exline, who directed the study published in the *Journal of Social and Clinical Psychology,* says that recognizing perceived social pressure is the first step to learning **it's OK to say, "No, thank you."**

Another exercise in being your own best cheerleader is forgiving yourself for slipups and realizing tomorrow is another day. So, you ate a haystack of cheese straws or wolfed down the whole plate of bacon and waffles. All is not lost. You simply work in a few extra walks this week and get right back on track at the next meal. Once you've found

When we Southerners hit an obstacle, we tackle it with grace and grit.

what works for you—whether it's downsizing your dinner plate, eating your vegetables first, adding lemon slices to water, trading fried shrimp for steamed and chocolate cake for sorbet, or all of the above—it'll be easier than ever to make it happen.

Georgia dietitian Lanier Dabruzzi says that, **as with all Southern wiles, it's a kind of figuring out that you have to do for yourself.** "The trick lies in having enough to satisfy without overdoing it," she says. "It's just like learning the perfect eye flutter."

Living the SLIM Southern Way

Now that you know **slimming down with Southern foods is just as much about the grit and grace as it is about the groceries,** let's get cooking! This cookbook is organized to provide meal suggestions and recipes throughout the day, from breakfast and lunch to dinner and dessert. Every recipe's designed to support a healthy adult lifestyle in keeping with the USDA's dietary guidelines. Sodium, dietary cholesterol, and saturated fat are kept in check, so you can aim to keep sodium under 2,300 milligrams a day, cholesterol below 300 milligrams, and calories from saturated fat less than 10 percent of your daily calories. As for total calories, if you're a moderately active, normal-weight woman between 31 and 50, aim for about 2,000 calories a day. Moderately active, normal-weight men between 31 and 50 should aim for 2,600 calories a day.

While we've kept calories reasonably low, we've also made sure portion sizes are satisfying, not skimpy. With balance, moderation, and some cooking skills, you can enjoy most any food while being good to your body. Use the nutrition information provided with each recipe to plan and track your meals.

"Chapter 7: Company's Coming" provides entertaining menus that feel special but don't overdo it: Every meal in it is around 700-900 calories, reasonable for an occasional celebratory meal (and much lower in calories than typical feasts). In "Chapter 8: Make-It-Happen Days," you'll see how to meet your most challenging eating days and stay under 2,000 calories a day. Skip a treat, and you'll cut calories without depriving your body of what it needs—or your cravings for Southern eats.

Every day is different, so there are recipes for dishes that come together in a flash and others for times you want to linger in the kitchen and enjoy every minute of chopping, stirring, and whirring. There are menus to help you through unique situations (from tailgating parties to brunches to little black dress days). There are simple recipes for busy weeknights and, of course, fancier spreads for entertaining. It's only natural that you'll want to share your healthy Southern cooking with friends and family. Plus, the food's so good, they'll never know you've trimmed the calories and boosted the nutrition. Bless their hearts!

Sometimes a Little Less Is So Much More

In South Florida, where contemporary cuisine collides with traditional Southern foods, chef Michelle Bernstein dredges chicken in quinoa (a whole grain) before pan-frying and makes cabbage slaws with vinegar-based dressings instead of mayonnaise.

"It's about making smart choices," says Bernstein, who owns Michy's restaurant in Miami. "A pan-seared pompano with peanut sauce and braised greens Is Southern, delicious, and healthy."

Running a restaurant so close to body-conscious South Beach has fueled her efforts to lighten up foods without skimping on flavor. "There's a preconception that 'diet food' is motherless and tasteless," she says. "We need to change people's opinion and get rid of that stigma. People eat my dishes (such as a gorgeous red gazpacho or a filling salad with barley) and ask, 'This is diet food?'"

Bernstein says modest changes can add up to good flavor and good health. When you cook stone-ground grits in vegetable stock and finish them with roasted vegetables, for example, she says, the grits are creamy and satisfying without cream or butter.

Eating better to maintain a healthy weight doesn't have to mean giving up Southern food favorites. Bernstein says succotash made with beans, peas, and corn is both traditional and healthy. And a little bit of flavorful pork can go a long way.

Michelle Bernstein, Miami chef

"I don't agree that you have to leave out the pork fat to create a healthy dish," she says.

"I add a little ham hock to collard greens, and you only need a quarter strip of bacon to add a lot of flavor when cooking vegetables."

> "I don't agree that you have to leave out the pork fat to create a healthy dish."

The 14-Day SLIM Eating Plan

Still not sure how to eat Southern in a healthful way? Just have what I'm having! These two weeks, drawn from my personal food diary, show you one way to have 14 days of slim Southern indulgence.

	SUNDAY **At home in Atlanta**	MONDAY **A writing day**	TUESDAY **Out and about in Atlanta**
MORNING	Cup of coffee (freshly brewed medium-roast with 1% milk and ½ tsp. sugar) while I read the newspaper and watch *CBS Sunday Morning* **BREAKFAST:** *Veggie Frittata* (page 50) with 1 slice whole grain toast and 6-oz. glass grapefruit juice, another cup of coffee Brisk 3-mile walk around the park with friend to talk about life (and our other friends!)	**BREAKFAST:** ½ cup Greek yogurt with ½ cup fresh blueberries, sprinkled with ¼ cup Grape-Nuts cereal, coffee 	**BREAKFAST:** Raisin Bran cereal with 1 cup fat-free milk and a sliced whole banana Pilates class
NOON	**SNACK:** 16 oz. water, 1 banana, and a handful of roasted pecan halves Plant basil, oregano, and mint in pots **LATE LUNCH ON THE BACK TERRACE:** *Chicken Blueberry Salad* (page 90) with unsweetened iced tea garnished with some of my newly planted mint Plant tomato and pepper plants in the back garden	**LUNCH:** Turkey sandwich (2 slices deli turkey on whole grain bread with romaine, sliced cucumbers, sliced tomatoes, 1 tsp. light mayo mixed with 2 tsp. grainy mustard), unsweetened iced tea, peach Think up ideas on 45-minute walk around my hilly Atlanta neighborhood Interview nutrition researcher and write up notes for future feature	**LUNCH AT NEW FARM-TO-TABLE ATLANTA RESTAURANT:** Pasture-raised chicken with three vegetable sides (braised kale, okra with tomatoes, and stone-ground grits), 2 big bites of a shared berry cobbler, and unsweetened peach iced tea Write about the restaurant
NIGHT	Girlfriends over for dinner and new episode of our favorite TV series **COCKTAILS:** *Fig-and-Bourbon Fizz* (page 260) and *Cracker Spoons with Creamy Pimiento Cheese* (page 262) *while we recap episodes so far* **DINNER:** *Glazed Salmon with Stir-fried Vegetables* (page 164) **DESSERT:** *Mocha-Pecan Mud Pie* (page 218) as the suspense builds	**DINNER AND DESSERT:** *Honey-Grilled Pork Tenderloins* (page 183) with 1 cup steamed green beans and 3 boiled red new potatoes with 1 tsp. butter and chopped parsley, water with lemon and lime; *Blackberry-Buttermilk Lemon Sorbet* (page 201)	**LIGHT DINNER AT HOME:** *Lime-Orange Catfish* (page 163), mixed greens salad and *Oregano-Feta Dressing* (page 70), sparkling water  Pack bags and scope out restaurant menus for upcoming trip

WEDNESDAY	THURSDAY	FRIDAY	SATURDAY	
A splurge day in New Orleans	**Heading back to see son, Jack!**	**A home-office day**	**Market-fresh dinner on the patio**	

PACK TRAVEL SNACKS: Nuts, whole wheat crackers, presliced apples, 2% string cheese, coffee to drink in the car on way to airport, carton of lemon Greek yogurt to eat before going through airport security

ON THE PLANE: Ask for half sparkling water, half orange juice (a cheater mimosa with vitamin C!)

Swim in hotel pool

ROOM SERVICE BREAKFAST: 2 eggs scrambled, sliced tomato, 1 slice whole wheat toast with a pat of butter, small grapefruit juice, coffee

Attend meeting of Louisiana registered dietitians

BREAKFAST: *English Muffin French Toast* (page 48), topped with fresh berries; coffee

Body Sculpt class; Work on *Atlanta Journal-Constitution* "Healthy Eating" column

BREAKFAST: Whole grain cereal with 1 cup fat-free milk, sliced banana

Shop the Peachtree Road Farmers Market for fresh produce, cheese, bread, and flowers

LUNCH AT EMERIL'S RESTAURANT: Grilled Niman Ranch pork chop with Louisiana field pea succotash, Southern cooked greens, and mango chowchow. Wow. Tall glass of unsweetened iced tea. Trade wine for dessert: the house-made sorbet

Walk French Quarter, scouting antiques shops for interesting china serving pieces

LUNCH AT CONFERENCE: Green salad, shrimp Creole, rice, buttermilk beignets (just 1 for me), and unsweetened iced tea

Fly home, make *Pecan Sandies* (page 249) for son, Jack, visiting from Austin

LUNCH: *Baby Carrot Soup* (page 68), *Peanut Chicken Pitas* (page 96)

Finish column

LUNCH: Cheese, bread, and sliced tomatoes from market

Plant annual flowers in backyard

One Sazerac cocktail at reception presented by The Museum of the American Cocktail

DINNER AT COMMANDER'S PALACE: Black skillet seared Gulf fish; a light dish of grilled eggplant, Creole tomatoes, roasted garlic, ripped basil, kalamata olives, crispy capers, baby greens, local legumes, and lemon-red chili butter; a glass of suggested white wine from Greece; 2 delicious bites of bread pudding soufflé (a lighter version of the dense classic) shared with a colleague

DINNER AT HOME WITH JACK: *Molasses Glazed Flank Steak Soft Tacos* (page 188), steamed vegetables, baked sweet potato, Pecan Sandies (send extras home with Jack), and peach iced tea

DINNER WITH FRIENDS: Meet at Lydia's house so we can walk 15 minutes to area Italian restaurant; enjoy 1 "spritz" cocktail (Aperol, Prosecco, and soda water with orange slice); share plates of salads, appetizers, pizza; walk back to Lydia's

ALFRESCO DINNER FOR 8: *Pepper Jelly & Goat Cheese Cakes* (page 124), *Summer Salad with Grilled Chicken and Peaches* (page 175), *Farmers' Market Pasta Salad* (page 168), *Key Lime Pie* (page 214), and Spanish white wine (Albarino)

	SUNDAY To the lake!	MONDAY Heading home	TUESDAY Work at home and in the office
MORNING	**BREAKFAST:** Greek yogurt sprinkled with ¼ cup granola, 1 cup chopped cantaloupe Drive to Mom's house on the lake in South Carolina	**BREAKFAST:** Mom's microwave scrambled eggs with sliced tomatoes and English muffin Walk around the lake, pack lunch for the road	**BREAKFAST:** *Fruit-and-Bran Muffins* (page 35), glass of fat-free milk Pilates class Write and conduct phone interviews
NOON	**LUNCH:** Packed road-trip lunch to save time, money, and calories: sandwich with 2 (1-oz.) slices of deli ham, 1 (1-oz.) slice of light Swiss cheese, lettuce, and mustard; grapefruit-flavored sparkling water Swim in the lake	**LUNCH:** Drive home, make business calls, munch on packed sandwich, apple, lemon-flavored sparkling water Check e-mail, write	**LUNCH:** Brown-bag lunch meeting at video production office (for me: leftover Shrimp Risotto, cucumber tomato salad, and a fresh peach)
NIGHT	**DINNER WITH MOM AND HER FRIENDS:** (These retirees are always celebrating something!) *Texas Caviar Rice and Beans* (page 154), *Pork Chops with Grilled Pineapple Salsa* (page 184), 1 light beer	**SIMPLE DINNER AT HOME:** Mixed greens salad with red wine vinegar and olive oil, *Shrimp Risotto* (page 160); glass of Pinot Grigio	**DINNER:** Attend launch party for new Atlanta restaurant; share plates with other food writers, pass on ones I don't like, have another bite of those I do like, make note of healthier menu choices, ask chef about preparation techniques and ingredients

WEDNESDAY Prepping for a show	THURSDAY On-air demo day	FRIDAY Picnic in the park	SATURDAY Leisurely start to the weekend	
BREAKFAST: *Blueberry Smoothie* (page 42) Brisk walk around park, add extra loop to make it 4 miles Grocery shopping, so I don't overbuy, bring water and snack on an apple and a handful of roasted pecan halves in the car	Early-morning TV demonstration on healthy Southern foods; **BREAKFAST:** During the breaks, a few bites of 4 healthy dishes and coffee 	**BREAKFAST:** *Pecan Pancakes* (page 47) topped with fresh orange segments, coffee Cardio Sculpt class Conference call with Academy of Nutrition and Dietetics committee	**BREAKFAST:** 1 piece whole grain toast, 1 hard-cooked egg, 6-oz. glass grapefruit juice 45-minute swim at neighborhood pool	MORNING
LUNCH: Meet friend for soup and salad (for me: vegetable soup and butterbean and chickpea salad, unsweetened iced tea with lemon) Prep foods and props for TV food demonstration	**LUNCH AT HOME:** Avocado and turkey sandwich on whole grain bread, watermelon slices Walk neighborhood hills for 45 minutes **AFTERNOON SNACK:** Hummus, whole grain crackers, orange slices	**LUNCH:** Tuna sandwich (3 oz. canned tuna mixed with 1 Tbsp. light mayo and ¼ cup chopped celery, 2 slices whole grain bread with romaine lettuce and sliced avocado) and lemon-flavored sparkling water Interview Atlanta chef and Georgia farmer at a restaurant for upcoming feature **AFTERNOON SNACK:** Greek yogurt	**LUNCH:** Take out-of-town friends to Atlanta BBQ restaurant Fox Brothers (must arrive early to get a seat!); share an order of fried pickles, plus a pulled pork sandwich with collard greens and coleslaw sides, and unsweetened iced tea with a splash of sweet iced tea 	NOON
DINNER: *Salmon and Vegetable Salad* (page 85), *Lemon-Herb Cornmeal Madeleines* (page 142), glass of Chardonnay Chamomile tea 	**DINNER:** Potluck meeting with fellow Atlanta members of Les Dames d'Escoffier; I bring *Broccoli Slaw with Candied Pecans* (page 134) and a bottle of dry Riesling	**DINNER:** Picnic for 6 taken to 7:30 p.m. concert at Chastain Park. I pack flowers from my garden, tablecloth, candles, pretty paper plates, napkins, and 'silver' plasticware, *Sweet Pea Crostini* (page 116), a beet side salad, *Roasted Red Bliss Potato Salad* (page 150), *Bourbon Balls* (page 202), and sparkling wine	**DINNER:** Invited to Liz's house for cocktails (vodka, club soda, and fresh lime for me) and classy but casual dinner where everyone brings something. I bring cut flowers from my garden for the hostess and bring a dish I know will be a healthy choice: *Marinated Shrimp & Artichokes* (page 127)	NIGHT

Chapter Two

RISE AND SHINE!

Whether your morning begins with a mad dash out the door after dawn or a quiet meditation before 8 o'clock, good Southern breakfast options abound. Our lives are just as rushed in the South as they are in other places. But sunny attitudes tend to prevail when you're savoring scrambled eggs and a buttermilk biscuit, sliced peaches, and a glass of freshly squeezed orange juice. So, up and at 'em! It's breakfast time.

Like your momma always told you, **breakfast really is the most important meal of the day.** And if you're serious about weight control, it's an absolute necessity. Breakfast is more than just a fast fuel-up after a good night's rest. It sets the tone for the rest of your day and puts you on the track to better health and wellness.

Study after study shows that eating a healthy breakfast—not just a gooey cinnamon roll washed down with coffee in the car—helps to boost your metabolism, lowers your cholesterol, provides essential nutrients, and gives you the strength, endurance, and stamina (mental and physical) to power through your day.

Eat Up, Slim Down

It may seem counterintuitive, but **eating breakfast is important to maintaining a healthy weight.** Of the 10,000 successful long-term dieters who make up the National Weight Control Registry, 78 percent report eating breakfast on a regular basis. And a British study of nearly 7,000 men and women found those who ate breakfast the most often had the lowest Body Mass Index (BMI), a measure of height to weight.

You might think that skipping the morning meal helps you save calories, but the truth is that when you go without eating until noon or later, you're far more likely to succumb to a mid-morning doughnut or a chow-down at lunch.

Plus, going for hours and hours without eating (if your last meal was at 8 p.m., that means you're going on a good 16 hours by the time you get to midday) wreaks havoc on insulin levels, which can increase your body's desire to store more calories as fat.

If you've got kids in school, you know how important it is to make sure they don't rush out the door on an empty stomach.

Students who eat breakfast do better in school, scoring higher on math and reading scores and improving their memory skills and cognitive performance.

It only makes sense that what's good for your family is also good for you: Sitting down to a healthy breakfast means **you're less likely to lose steam later,** and keeps you in better shape to take on whatever challenges the day brings.

> Eating a healthy breakfast helps boost your metabolism, lowers cholesterol, provides essential nutrients, and gives you strength.

Protein Power

Fresh fruit and yogurt, or cheesy grits? Pecan pancakes, or a vegetable frittata? Sweet or savory, these Southern breakfast favorites all have one thing in common: In addition to tasting scrumptious and being made with fresh, healthy ingredients, they're all high in protein. And that's especially important when you're starting off your day. Several research studies show that **a breakfast rich in protein is the key to staying slim.**

"Protein stops the production of hunger-inducing hormones in the gut and stimulates the hormones that help you feel full," explains physiologist Heather Leidy, Ph.D., a researcher at the University of Missouri-Columbia who has made it her focus to find out how **eating breakfast affects appetite control.** Her work suggests that eating a protein-rich breakfast blunts hunger, boosts satiety, and even reduces brain responses involved with food cravings, so you're less likely to gorge on junk food at night.

As it turns out, Southern favorites like egg-and-sausage casseroles are actually better for weight management than high-carb bagels or doughnuts or no breakfast at all, says Leidy. She advises choosing eggs and leaner meats such as sausage made from pork loin or Greek yogurt topped with fruit and granola. Skippers should start eating breakfast again, she adds, "but make it healthier."

Another big reason to start your day with some protein: It keeps your muscles moving. Research shows that muscle tissue prefer a steady flow of the nutrient throughout the day rather than one big heaping dose. If your breakfast most often looks like white toast and coffee, adding in some milk, yogurt, cheese, eggs, ham, nut butter, beans, or even a little beef or chicken can help.

Scrambled, over easy, or sunny-side up, **eggs remain one of the healthiest breakfast choices.** One large egg has 75 calories and 6 grams of high-quality protein. Don't skip the yolk, which contains 125 milligrams of choline, a nutrient important for eye and brain health. Choline helps support the brain's messengers, called neurotransmitters. It's also linked to new memory cell production. So an egg is literally a smart way to start the day. Another wise breakfast addition, a cup of milk has 8 grams of protein.

As with any meal, **portions are key.** In the old days, rural Southerners enjoyed big breakfasts. Today, most of us don't have to plow the north 40 before noon. We don't need sky-high piles of bacon and eggs or a visit to the breakfast buffet every Sunday.

Healthy modern breakfasts for a more urban (read: more sedentary!) lifestyle are more about quality than quantity. Of course they should be satisfying. But breakfast is also the perfect time to help you fill in some common nutrition gaps.

The Skinny on Fat

Fat is an important component in any diet, and truth be told, breakfast wouldn't be nearly as tasty without it. But we're not just talking buttery grits or crispy bacon: Fat can be found in a variety of foods, and to some degree, it's a necessity.

While fat improves the taste, texture, and smell of food, it also helps your body absorb fat-soluble vitamins (like A, D, E, and K). It's especially important for infants, toddlers, and children because it helps them grow and develop. Even as an adult, **you need a certain amount of fat in your diet to stay healthy.** Of course, the fat you choose makes a big difference.

There are different categories of fats, and they are all relatively nutrient dense, containing 9 calories per gram compared to 4 calories per gram of protein or carbohydrates. **Monounsaturated fats can be found in foods like olives, olive oil, canola oil, nuts, and avocado.** Their job is to raise "good" (HDL) cholesterol, and lower "bad" (LDL) cholesterol, as well as help keep the linings of your blood vessels smooth and elastic. **Polyunsaturated fats are found in seed oils** such as safflower, soy, and corn, as well as fatty fish like salmon or mackerel, some seeds, and nuts like walnuts and pecans. They are also important in helping to keep a balance of "good" and "bad" cholesterol.

More confusion surrounds saturated fats. They are primarily found in animal products such as beef, pork, and lamb, as well as dairy products like butter, cream, ice cream, and yogurt, and, of course, that Southern cooking favorite, lard. Saturated fat has long been maligned by groups such as the Centers for Disease Control and Prevention (CDC) and the American Heart Association for its perceived role in increasing the risk of heart disease and other chronic ailments. But new evidence, including a 2010 meta-analysis of nearly 350,000 people worldwide, suggests there wasn't a lot of good data to link saturated fat to heart disease. Other research shows that when you take out other risk factors like overall diet and fiber intake, the bad-guy role of saturated fat diminishes a bit.

There is, however, no denying the negative qualities of artificially created trans fats. These fats, which are primarily engineered through food processing and found in products like stick margarine and shortening, were used in greater amounts in packaged baked goods and other snacks in years past. Trans fats have been shown to raise bad cholesterol, lower good cholesterol, and increase the risk of developing heart disease, stroke, and diabetes. Although many manufacturers have phased them out, you can still find them on some store shelves. (Look for the words "partially hydrogenated vegetable oil" on the ingredient list.) **Avoid trans fats whenever possible.**

And what, you may ask, about bacon? It falls into the saturated fat category. And with our "indulge a little" food philosophy, you can add it to breakfast in moderation. **One slice of crispy bacon contains about 45 calories, so it's not a wild splurge.** Fix a pretty plate with one strip

HOW MUCH FAT'S IN THAT?

One tablespoon of . . .

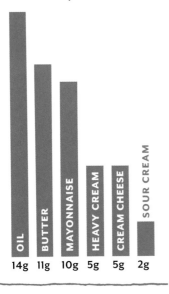

OIL	BUTTER	MAYONNAISE	HEAVY CREAM	CREAM CHEESE	SOUR CREAM
14g	11g	10g	5g	5g	2g

MIND THE GAPS

Most Americans still don't get enough of these important nutrients:

DIETARY FIBER *(20g to 35g per day)*
What it does: Helps you feel fuller faster, aids in digestion, helps reduce risk of diabetes and heart disease **Where you'll find it:** Breads, cereals, granola, nuts, fruits, and vegetables

CALCIUM *(1,000mg to 1,200mg per day)*
What it does: Builds strong bones and teeth, helps muscles move and nerves to fire; helps release hormones and enzymes
Where you'll find it: Milk, yogurt, cheese, plus nondairy products like almonds, kale, and broccoli; sometimes added to breakfast cereals and fruit juices

VITAMIN D *(600 IU to 800 IU per day)*
What it does: Helps your body absorb calcium, important to bone growth and strength; also helps support the immune system **Where you'll find it:** Egg yolks, milk, yogurt, fatty fish, and fruit juice (fortified with vitamin D), plus sunlight

POTASSIUM *(4.7g per day)* **What it does:** Builds proteins and muscles, breaks down carbohydrates, helps control electrical activity in heart and maintain normal body growth **Where you'll find it:** Milk, citrus fruits, fruits, vegetables, pork, beef, chicken, and cereals (fortified with potassium)

of bacon, a two-egg veggie omelet with a half-ounce of shredded sharp Cheddar, and a slice of whole wheat toast with whipped butter, and add a 6-ounce glass of orange juice and you'll still clock in under 500 calories. You'll also be eating vegetables, getting vitamin C and other nutrients from the juice, whole grains from the toast, protein from the eggs, and a whole lot of taste and enjoyment from the butter and bacon. That's what "well balanced" is all about.

Finding Your Morning

Whether you like to take your sweet time getting to breakfast or rush to the morning table to "break the fast," the Southern favorites that follow are sure to wake up your taste buds and provide the good nutrition you need to fuel a fit and fabulous day.

Fruit-and-Bran Muffins

Use uncooked hot cereal as a base, then add some fresh and dried fruit for an easy, fiber-rich muffin that's loaded with flavor and nutrients.

MAKES 12 muffins   HANDS-ON 15 min.   TOTAL 40 min.

1   **cup fat-free milk**
2   **cups O-shaped sweetened oat-and-wheat bran cereal**
1   **large Granny Smith apple, peeled and diced**
1¼ **cups uncooked oat bran hot cereal**
⅓   **cup golden raisins**
¼   **cup firmly packed dark brown sugar**
¼   **cup egg substitute**
1   **Tbsp. baking powder**
½   **tsp. ground cinnamon**
¼   **tsp. ground nutmeg**
3   **Tbsp. applesauce**
Paper baking cups
Vegetable cooking spray

1. Preheat oven to 375°. Bring milk to a boil in a large saucepan; remove from heat, and stir in O-shaped cereal. Let stand 5 minutes or until cereal is softened.

2. Stir in apple and next 8 ingredients until blended.

3. Place paper baking cups in muffin pans, and lightly coat with cooking spray. Spoon batter evenly into cups, filling two-thirds full.

4. Bake at 375° for 18 to 20 minutes or until a wooden pick inserted in center comes out clean. Remove muffins from pans immediately, and cool slightly on a wire rack.

Note: We tested with Cracklin' Oat Bran Cereal for sweetened cereal and Hodgson Mill Oat Bran Hot Cereal for uncooked cereal.

SERVING SIZE 1 muffin CALORIES 109 FAT 1.1g (sat 0.2g, mono 0.4g, poly 0.4g) PROTEIN 3.3g CARB 22.9g FIBER 2.1g CHOL 0.4mg IRON 3.3mg SODIUM 154mg CALC 105mg

Honey Ginger Tea

MAKES 1 serving   HANDS-ON 5 min.   TOTAL 8 min.

1   **(1-inch) piece fresh ginger, peeled**
1   **regular-size green tea bag**
1   **Tbsp. fresh lemon juice**
2   **Tbsp. honey**
1   **cup boiling water**

1. Grate ginger using the large holes of a box grater. Squeeze juice from grated ginger into a small bowl to equal ½ tsp.; discard solids.

2. Place tea bag, lemon juice, and honey into a mug; add boiling water. Cover and steep 3 minutes. Remove and discard tea bag without squeezing.

SERVING SIZE 1 cup CALORIES 133 FAT 0.1g (sat 0g, mono 0g, poly 0g) PROTEIN 0.4g CARB 35.5g FIBER 0.1g CHOL 0mg IRON 0.1mg SODIUM 2mg CALC 3mg

Fruit Salad with Yogurt

Tropical fruits like pineapples and mangoes go perfectly with seasonal ones like grapes, raspberries, and strawberries. Stir in some high-protein Greek yogurt and a touch of maple or sorghum syrup and you've got a healthy, sweet way to kick off the day!

MAKES 7 servings   HANDS-ON 10 min.   TOTAL 10 min.

2   cups cubed fresh
     pineapple
1½ cups fresh
     strawberries, halved
1½ cups seedless
     green grapes
1   mango, peeled and
     chopped
1   (4-oz.) container
     fresh raspberries
1   cup vanilla bean
     2% reduced-fat
     Greek yogurt
3   Tbsp. maple syrup

1. Toss together first 5 ingredients in a large bowl. Stir together yogurt and syrup in a small bowl. Spoon fruit into individual bowls; top with yogurt mixture.

SERVING SIZE 1 cup fruit and about 2 ½ Tbsp. yogurt mixture CALORIES 137 FAT 1.1g (sat 0.5g, mono 0.1g, poly 0.2g) PROTEIN 4g CARB 30.7g FIBER 3.4g CHOL 2mg IRON 0.6mg SODIUM 14mg CALC 54mg

Dried Cherry-Pecan Oatmeal

Do your morning bowl of oatmeal one better: Add dried fruit and chopped pecans for a burst of nutrition along with a sweet and satisfying crunch. Using fat-free milk also provides more calcium, vitamin D, and protein.

MAKES 6 servings   HANDS-ON 10 min.   TOTAL 30 min.

- **3 cups fat-free milk**
- **2 cups whole oats (not instant)**
- **½ cup dried cherries, coarsely chopped**
- **½ tsp. table salt**
- **5 Tbsp. brown sugar, divided**
- **1 Tbsp. butter**
- **¼ tsp. ground cinnamon**
- **¼ tsp. vanilla extract**
- **2 Tbsp. chopped pecans, toasted**

1. Bring 3 cups water, milk, oats, cherries, and salt to a boil; reduce heat, and simmer, stirring occasionally, 20 minutes or until thickened. Remove from heat. Stir in 4 Tbsp. brown sugar and next 3 ingredients. Spoon 1 cup oatmeal in each of 6 bowls. Sprinkle evenly with pecans and remaining 1 Tbsp. brown sugar. Serve immediately.

SERVING SIZE 1 cup CALORIES 259 FAT 5.7g (sat 1.8g, mono 2.1g, poly 1.2g) PROTEIN 8.4g CARB 44.5g FIBER 3.9g CHOL 8mg IRON 1.5mg SODIUM 270mg CALC 169mg

Carrot Cake Muffins

Use canned fruit like crushed pineapple and buy the carrots already shredded to make this recipe even more convenient. When shopping for canned fruit, look on the label for "in juice" instead of "in syrup" to cut total calories and sugar content.

MAKES 18 muffins   HANDS-ON 9 min.   TOTAL 42 min.

1¾ cups all-purpose flour
¾ cup sugar
2 tsp. baking soda
½ tsp. table salt
1½ tsp. ground cinnamon
¼ cup vegetable oil
1 Tbsp. vanilla extract
2 (8-oz.) cans crushed
   pineapple in juice,
   drained
2 large eggs
2 cups shredded carrots
Paper baking cups
Vegetable cooking spray

1. Preheat oven to 350°. Combine first 5 ingredients in a large bowl; make a well in center of mixture.

2. Whisk together oil and next 3 ingredients; add to flour mixture, stirring just until moistened. Fold in carrots. Place paper baking cups in 18 muffin cups, and coat with cooking spray; spoon batter into cups, filling two-thirds full.

3. Bake at 350° for 22 to 25 minutes or until a wooden pick inserted in center comes out clean. Cool in pans on wire racks 10 minutes; remove from pans to wire racks. Serve warm or at room temperature.

SERVING SIZE 1 muffin CALORIES 128 FAT 3.8g (sat 0.5g, mono 1.6g, poly 1.5g) PROTEIN 2.1g CARB 21.5g FIBER 0.9g CHOL 21mg IRON 0.8mg SODIUM 223mg CALC 11mg

Make Breakfast Beautiful

MY STAY-SLIM SECRET
Caroline Stuart, 60, food writer

Is breakfast a bowl of cereal on a cluttered kitchen counter? Not for food writer Caroline Stuart, who grew up in Bartow, Florida. She co-founded the culinary world's prestigious James Beard Foundation, and starts her day with Southern gentility. "If there are two or more of us, I set the table—even for breakfast," she says. "It's about ceremony, taking the time to make what you eat look beautiful." One allowable morning rush: Stuart enjoys orange juice like a true Florida girl. She squeezes it fresh and drinks it quickly right after juicing to make sure the vitamin C is still intact.

Sweet Potato and Edamame Hash

A morning mainstay on many Southern tables, this recipe for hash offers up a new twist with nutrient-packed ingredients like sweet potato and edamame.

MAKES 8 servings   HANDS-ON 42 min.   TOTAL 42 min.

1   **(8-oz.) package diced smoked lean ham**
1   **medium sweet onion, finely chopped**
1   **Tbsp. olive oil**
2   **medium sweet potatoes, peeled and cut into ¼-inch cubes**
1   **garlic clove, minced**
1   **(12-oz.) package frozen shelled edamame (green soybeans)**
1   **(12-oz.) package frozen whole kernel corn**
¼   **cup chicken broth**
1   **Tbsp. chopped fresh thyme**
½   **tsp. kosher or table salt**
½   **tsp. freshly ground black pepper**
4   **cups arugula**
8   **large eggs, poached**

1. Sauté ham and onion in hot oil in a nonstick skillet over medium-high heat 6 to 8 minutes or until onion is tender and ham is lightly browned. Stir in sweet potatoes, and sauté 5 minutes. Add garlic; sauté 1 minute. Stir in edamame and next 3 ingredients. Reduce heat to medium. Cover and cook, stirring occasionally, 10 to 12 minutes or until potatoes are tender. Stir in salt and pepper.

2. Place ½ cup arugula on each of 8 plates. Top each with 1 cup hash. Place 1 poached egg onto each serving. Serve immediately.

Note: We tested with Birds Eye Steamfresh Super Sweet Corn.

SERVING SIZE ½ cup arugula, about 1 cup hash, and 1 poached egg CALORIES 245 FAT 10.3g (sat 2.4g, mono 3.5g, poly 2.2g) PROTEIN 18.2g CARB 21.2g FIBER 4.4g CHOL 198mg IRON 2.9mg SODIUM 630mg CALC 82mg

Corn Muffins

Corn is a whole grain that offers more antioxidants, including vitamin A, than other grains. Look for whole grain cornmeal for this recipe to get the best health benefits.

MAKES 12 muffins   HANDS-ON 13 min.   TOTAL 33 min.

1 **cup all-purpose flour**
1 **cup yellow cornmeal**
1 **(11-ounce) can sweet whole kernel corn, drained**
2 **Tbsp. minced red bell pepper**
1 **Tbsp. baking powder**
½ **tsp. table salt**
¼ **tsp. ground red pepper**
¾ **cup 1% low-fat milk**
½ **cup egg substitute**
2 **large egg whites**
1 **Tbsp. vegetable oil**
Vegetable cooking spray

1. Preheat oven to 375°. Combine first 7 ingredients in a large bowl; make a well in center of mixture.

2. Stir together milk and next 3 ingredients. Add to flour mixture, stirring just until moistened. Spoon into muffin cups coated with cooking spray, filling two-thirds full.

3. Bake at 375° for 20 minutes. Remove muffins from pan immediately, and cool slightly on wire racks.

SERVING SIZE 1 muffin CALORIES 129 FAT 1.7g (sat 0.3g, mono 0.6g, poly 0.6g) PROTEIN 4.5g CARB 22.4g FIBER 1g CHOL 0.8mg IRON 1.1mg SODIUM 299mg CALC 88mg

SAVOR THE SOUTH
LINGER LONGER
INDULGE A LITTLE
MAKE IT HAPPEN

Bacon

It's hard to imagine Southern cooking without a little bacon: BLTs, crispy bacon crumbles on salads, greens braised with bacon, shrimp and grits with bacon, honey-glazed bacon in desserts, and even bacon-infused cocktails. Just a touch of its smoky goodness adds a whole lot of love to many foods.

It might surprise folks that pork fat contains about a third less saturated fat than butter, about twice as much monounsaturated fat (the "good" fat) as butter, and about the same amount of polyunsaturated fat (the other "good" fat) of olive oil.

Because a slice of regular bacon adds about 45 calories and 3 grams of fat, it's smart to use it more as a seasoning in a larger dish (a slice or two crumbled over a dish that serves eight) rather than as the main attraction (four strips on a single sandwich). If you want bacon flavor with a bit less fat and calories, choose leaner center-cut bacon, which at 35 calories and 2 grams of fat per slice is comparable to many brands of turkey bacon.

Blueberry Smoothie

Blueberries are loaded with fiber, vitamin C, and disease-fighting phyto-nutrients. If you can't get 'em fresh, use frozen ones: They actually yield a brighter color and smoother texture. For a dairy-free version, use vanilla soy milk and soy yogurt.

MAKES 4 servings   HANDS-ON 5 min.   TOTAL 5 min.

2 **cups frozen blueberries**
1 **(6-oz.) container
   vanilla low-fat yogurt**
1½ **cups 1% low-fat milk**

1. Process all ingredients in a blender until smooth, stopping to scrape down sides as needed. Serve immediately.

SERVING SIZE 1 cup CALORIES 111 FAT 2g (sat 1g, mono 0.5g, poly 0.1g) PROTEIN 5.3g CARB 19.3g FIBER 2g CHOL 7mg IRON 0mg SODIUM 65mg CALC 177mg

Make Room for New Traditions

If your great-grandfather basted eggs with bacon grease in a cast-iron skillet, chances are it's a lasting food memory. "Southern food holds a very strong connection to the past," says Chadwick Boyd, who modernizes Southern recipes for new generations at his Atlanta-based food and lifestyle company, Lovely and Delicious.

As someone who treasures family food traditions, he understands why change, especially to the diet, can be difficult. "I've been in many kitchens of Southern families, and it's very common to hear, 'This is how my grandmother did it,' or 'I make it like my aunt made it.' There's a fear of dishonoring our loved ones and the past if we make changes to our Southern favorites."

Boyd still believes there's room for fried chicken brined in buttermilk with cayenne, but says he reins it in when his tux gets too tight. When remaking recipes, he keeps the flavor foundations—from mayo to molasses—the same, but adds fresh herbs and uses whole ingredients (like kernels of corn in cornbread) to make a little bit taste a whole lot more filling.

"We're in a different time, and we know better about the foods we eat now," he says. "I see it changing with the younger generations holding the hands of their elders. It's actually quite sweet to watch.

Chadwick Boyd, lifestyle guru

And it's starting to make a difference."

Taking time at the table is a tradition he continues to honor with a little change in format. "Unlike my Southern grandmothers, I make a point to sit at the table and visit with my guests rather than fuss over everyone and spend the majority of the meal going to and from the kitchen," he says. "It slows people down, I've found, and people savor their food more."

"We know better about the foods we eat now. I see it changing with the younger generations."

Oatmeal Scones with Pecans

Scones originated in Scotland and were first made with unleavened oats. Oatmeal remains key in this recipe, and pecans add a Southern touch.

MAKES 8 servings   HANDS-ON 10 min.   TOTAL 31 min.

¾ cup uncooked quick-cooking oats
⅓ cup sugar
1¾ cups all-purpose flour
2 tsp. baking powder
½ tsp. baking soda
¼ tsp. table salt
2 Tbsp. cold butter, cut up
⅔ cup fat-free buttermilk
1 large egg
Vegetable cooking spray
3 Tbsp. sugar
½ tsp. ground cinnamon
1½ Tbsp. fat-free buttermilk
2 Tbsp. chopped pecans, toasted

1. Preheat oven to 400°. Bake oats in a 15- x 10-inch jelly-roll pan at 400° for 6 minutes or until lightly browned. Cool.

2. Combine oats and next 5 ingredients.

3. Cut butter into oats mixture with a pastry blender or fork until crumbly. Stir together ⅔ cup buttermilk and egg. Add to flour mixture, stirring just until dry ingredients are moistened and dough forms.

4. Turn dough out onto a jelly-roll pan coated with cooking spray. Shape dough into a 7 ½-inch circle.

5. Combine 3 Tbsp. sugar and ½ tsp. cinnamon. Brush dough with 1 ½ Tbsp. buttermilk. Sprinkle with sugar mixture and pecans.

6. Bake at 400° for 15 minutes or until a wooden pick inserted in center comes out clean. Cut into 8 wedges; serve immediately.

SERVING SIZE 1 scone CALORIES 238 FAT 5.6g (sat 2.2g, mono 1.8g, poly 0.7g) PROTEIN 5.8g CARB 41.1g FIBER 1.8g CHOL 31mg IRON 2mg SODIUM 311mg CALC 106mg

Escape with Exercise

MY STAY-SLIM SECRET
Nathalie Thomas, 27, fashion designer

Physical activity can be a getaway from the day-to-day, says fashion designer Nathalie Thomas, who makes time for running, cycling, and hot yoga while running a philanthropic-minded clothing business, Cultivation Five, in Atlanta.

"Exercising has become therapeutic for me," says Thomas, whose company donates $5 from the sale of each of its cute cotton T-shirts to the buyer's charity of choice. "It's the chance to escape my busy mind and zone out for a good hour. Even though getting to the gym is the hardest part, I am always thankful and happy I did."

Pecan Pancakes

Bring out the rich, nutty pecan flavor by toasting them first. Simply swirl the nuts around in the bottom of a sauté pan over medium heat for a few minutes. You can also substitute walnuts (another rich source of vitamin E and heart-healthy omega-3 fatty acids) in place of the pecans.

MAKES 5 servings   HANDS-ON 6 min.   TOTAL 16 min.

1   **cup all-purpose flour**
⅓   **cup finely chopped pecans or walnuts, toasted**
1   **tsp. granulated sugar**
1   **tsp. light brown sugar**
½   **tsp. baking powder**
½   **tsp. ground cinnamon**
¼   **tsp. baking soda**
⅛   **tsp. table salt**
1   **cup nonfat buttermilk**
2   **Tbsp. vegetable oil**
1   **large egg**
Vegetable cooking spray

1. Stir together first 8 ingredients until well combined.

2. Whisk together buttermilk, oil, and egg in a bowl; add to flour mixture, stirring just until dry ingredients are moistened.

3. Pour about ¼ cup batter for each pancake onto a hot griddle or large skillet coated with vegetable cooking spray. Cook pancakes 2 to 3 minutes or until tops are covered with bubbles and edges look cooked. Turn and cook other sides. Serve immediately.

Note: Mix the dry ingredients ahead to make breakfast quicker in the morning. Store the mix in an airtight container up to one week.

SERVING SIZE 2 pancakes CALORIES 230 FAT 12.2g (sat 1.4g, mono 5.9g, poly 4.3g) PROTEIN 6.3g CARB 24.8g FIBER 1.5g CHOL 37.2mg IRON 1.6mg SODIUM 227mg CALC 102mg

English Muffin French Toast

French toast doesn't have to be limited to Sunday brunch. Make it as a quick-and-easy midweek meal by using whole grain English muffins.

MAKES 6 servings   HANDS-ON 20 min.   TOTAL 8 hours, 20 min.

4   **large eggs**
1   **cup nonfat buttermilk**
2   **tsp. orange zest**
1   **tsp. vanilla extract**
6   **English muffins, split**
Vegetable cooking spray
1   **cup fat-free Greek yogurt**
2   **Tbsp. maple syrup**
1½ **cups chopped fresh strawberries, blueberries, or nectarines**

1. Whisk together first 4 ingredients in a bowl. Place English muffins in a 13- x 9-inch baking dish, overlapping edges. Pour egg mixture over muffins. Cover and chill 8 to 12 hours.

2. Remove muffins from remaining liquid, discarding liquid.

3. Cook muffins, in batches, in a large skillet coated with cooking spray over medium-high heat 2 to 3 minutes on each side or until muffins are golden. Stir together yogurt and syrup until blended; serve with muffin French toast and fruit toppings.

SERVING SIZE 1 English muffin, 2 Tbsp. yogurt mixture, and ¼ cup fruit CALORIES 249 FAT 4.4g (sat 1.3g, mono 1.5g, poly 1.3g) PROTEIN 13.9g CARB 38.1g FIBER 0.9g CHOL 124mg IRON 1.6mg SODIUM 301mg CALC 211mg

Zucchini-Onion Frittata

One-skillet frittatas are a quick and easy way to get a healthy breakfast on the table. Make this when you've got bumper crops of zucchini in the summer.

MAKES 6 servings   HANDS-ON 17 min.   TOTAL 39 min.

2   **medium onions**
1   **Tbsp. butter**
2   **Tbsp. vegetable oil**
2½ **cups thinly sliced zucchini (2 medium)**
½   **cup grated Parmesan cheese, divided**
8   **large eggs**
¼   **cup 1% low-fat milk**
¾   **tsp. table salt**
½   **tsp. black pepper**
1   **Tbsp. chopped fresh basil**
Garnish: chopped seeded plum tomatoes

1. Preheat oven to 350°. Peel onions; cut in half lengthwise. Cut each half crosswise into thin slices to measure 2 cups.

2. Melt butter with oil in a 10-inch ovenproof skillet over medium-high heat. Add onion and zucchini; sauté 12 minutes or until tender and browned. Remove from heat; stir in ¼ cup grated Parmesan cheese.

3. Whisk together eggs and next 3 ingredients at least 1 minute or until well blended. Pour over vegetable mixture.

4. Bake at 350° for 20 minutes or until set; increase oven temperature to broil, and broil 5 ½ inches from heat 1 to 2 minutes or until edges are lightly browned. Sprinkle evenly with remaining ¼ cup grated Parmesan cheese and basil. Cut into 6 equal wedges and serve hot or at room temperature.

SERVING SIZE 1 wedge CALORIES 219 FAT 15.2g (sat 5.1g, mono 5.5g, poly 3.5g) PROTEIN 12.7g CARB 8.4g FIBER 1.5g CHOL 259mg IRON 1.6mg SODIUM 520mg CALC 149mg

SAVOR THE SOUTH
LINGER LONGER
INDULGE A LITTLE
MAKE IT HAPPEN

For Good Measure

Controlling portion size helps you fit into the size you'd like to be. But it's hard to judge just how much cereal is in the bowl. So get out the measuring cups and get to know what a cup, a half-cup, and a quarter-cup look like.

You won't have to measure your food all of the time, but periodically reviewing what a cup of mashed potatoes looks like on a plate will help you keep track of how much you're eating at home and in restaurants.

If you're somewhere you just can't measure, a few tricks can help you eyeball it: A 3-ounce serving of meat, chicken, or fish is about the size of a deck of cards. A cup of rice is about the size of a tennis ball. And a 2-tablespoon portion of peanut butter or pimiento cheese is about the size of a golf ball.

Veggie Frittata

This easy one-pan frittata is a great way to boost your vegetable intake. We use fresh baby spinach for an added boost of vitamins and minerals, but you can get the same benefits by using frozen chopped spinach, as well. A combination of whole eggs and egg whites helps keep the fat and cholesterol content down.

MAKES 8 servings   HANDS-ON 20 min.   TOTAL 35 min.

1 medium-size yellow onion, chopped
½ (8-oz.) package sliced fresh mushrooms
1 Tbsp. olive oil
1 (6-oz.) bag fresh baby spinach
4 large eggs
6 large egg whites
1 cup (4 oz.) shredded 2% reduced-fat sharp Cheddar cheese
¼ cup freshly grated Parmesan cheese
2 Tbsp. fat-free milk
½ tsp. black pepper
¼ tsp. table salt
¼ tsp. ground nutmeg

1. Preheat oven to 350°. Sauté onion and mushrooms in hot oil in an ovenproof nonstick 10-inch skillet over medium-high heat 10 minutes or until tender. Stir in spinach, and sauté 3 minutes or until water evaporates and spinach wilts. Remove from heat, and set aside.

2. Whisk together eggs, egg whites, Cheddar cheese, and next 5 ingredients.

3. Pour egg mixture into skillet with onion mixture, stirring to combine.

4. Bake at 350° for 12 to 15 minutes or just until set. Let stand 3 minutes. Cut into 8 equal wedges.

SERVING SIZE 1 wedge CALORIES 139 FAT 8.2g (sat 3.3g, mono 3.1g, poly 0.8g) PROTEIN 12.1g CARB 5.2g FIBER 1.4g CHOL 106mg IRON 1.3mg SODIUM 366mg CALC 292mg

Trust Your Jeans

MY STAY-SLIM SECRET
Jill Castle, age 46, dietitian

Even without stepping on a scale, you know it's time to step away from the table when your clothes start to feel snug. Dietitian and family nutrition expert Jill Castle, who has lived in Nashville, Tennessee, lets her wardrobe be her warning. "If the jeans get tight, I know it's time to take a closer look at my eating and exercise behaviors," she says. "It must be working because the other day my daughter asked me, 'How old are those jeans?' I smiled because I've worn them for 13 years!" Now that's worth celebrating, Jill, perhaps with a new pair of jeans.

Baked Cheese Grits

This polenta-like favorite, made from coarsely ground corn, is a breakfast staple throughout the South. The cheese will melt evenly so it's distributed into every delicious bite.

MAKES 7 servings   HANDS-ON 15 min.   TOTAL 55 min.

⅔ **cup quick-cooking grits**

2 **Tbsp. reduced-calorie margarine**

2 **large eggs, lightly beaten**

½ **(8-oz.) package light processed cheese, cut into ½-inch pieces**

¼ **tsp. table salt**

¼ **tsp. ground red pepper**

Vegetable cooking spray

1. Preheat oven to 350°. Bring 2 ⅔ cups water to a boil; add grits, and cook, stirring often, 5 minutes or until thickened. Remove from heat. Add margarine and next 4 ingredients, stirring until blended. Spoon mixture into a 2-qt. baking dish coated with cooking spray.

2. Bake at 350° for 40 minutes or until lightly browned.

Note: Casserole may be made ahead through step 1 and chilled up to 8 hours. Let stand at room temperature 30 minutes; bake as directed.

SERVING SIZE ½ cup CALORIES 141 FAT 6.5g (sat 2.2g, mono 2.1g, poly 1.3g) PROTEIN 6.3g CARB 13.9g FIBER 0.3g CHOL 60mg IRON 0.4mg SODIUM 391mg CALC 101mg

SAVOR THE SOUTH
LINGER LONGER
INDULGE A LITTLE
MAKE IT HAPPEN

Stone-Ground Grits

There are grits, and then there are stone-ground grits. The goopy white instant sort will have you hankering for hash browns. But stone-ground grits are a revelation: They taste like fresh corn and have the pleasing texture of polenta.

The reason for the difference? Instant grits are made from dried corn that's been stripped of its outer layer and inner germ for faster cooking. Those parts contain loads of flavor, nutrition, and texture. Stone-ground grits are made from the whole corn kernel and take a bit longer to cook, but they are so flavorful they're delicious without butter or cheese.

Stone-ground grits can be yellow, white, blue, or a mixture of colors depending on the corn variety used. Anson Mills uses an heirloom corn called Carolina Gourdseed White that dates back to the 1600s.

In addition to being a whole grain, stone-ground grits are a good source of fiber, vitamin A, and antioxidants that are important for eye health.

Migas Tacos

In Tex-Mex cuisine, migas combine scrambled eggs with crunchy tortilla strips, peppers, onions, tomato, and cheese. Enjoy the mix in a soft breakfast taco; some cilantro would be a nice addition.

MAKES 2 servings   HANDS-ON 15 min.   TOTAL 23 min.

⅓ **cup lightly crushed tortilla chips**
¼ **cup chopped onion**
¼ **cup diced tomatoes**
2 **Tbsp. chopped jalapeño peppers**
1 **tsp. vegetable oil**
2 **large eggs, lightly beaten**
1/16 **tsp. table salt**
⅛ **tsp. black pepper**
2 **(8-inch) soft taco-size flour tortillas, warmed**
½ **cup (2 oz.) shredded 2% reduced-fat Mexican four-cheese blend**

1. Sauté first 4 ingredients in hot oil in a medium-size nonstick skillet over medium heat 3 to 4 minutes or just until onion is translucent.

2. Whisk together eggs, salt, and pepper. Add to skillet, and cook, without stirring, 1 to 2 minutes or until eggs begin to set on bottom. Gently draw cooked edges away from sides of pan to form large pieces. Cook, stirring occasionally, 2 minutes or until eggs are thickened and moist. (Do not overstir.) Spoon egg mixture into warm tortillas, and sprinkle each with ¼ cup cheese; serve immediately.

SERVING SIZE 1 taco CALORIES 256 FAT 13.8g (sat 5.7g, mono 2g, poly 1.9g) PROTEIN 10.7g CARB 25g FIBER 2g CHOL 22mg IRON 1.5mg SODIUM 384mg CALC 280mg

Ditch Deprivation

MY STAY-SLIM SECRET
Jennifer Hughes, 39, public relations pro

Traveling for work can be a challenge when you're trying to stay trim, especially when dining out is part of the job. But Jennifer Hughes, director of public relations for Memphis, Tennessee-based Homewood Suites, says trying to be too good is a bad idea. "If you deprive yourself of something that you really want," she says, "you will end up eating more of it later than if you had just taken a few bites in the first place." Her favorite splurge: a breakfast of biscuits and gravy on a day she knows she's going to be very active to help burn off the calories.

Breakfast Sausage Tostadas

Low-fat ground pork sausage, egg whites, and reduced-fat cheese and Greek yogurt slash the calorie and saturated fat count of this satisfying breakfast.

MAKES 6 servings   HANDS-ON 20 min.   TOTAL 33 min.

6 **(6-inch) corn tortillas**
Vegetable cooking spray
⅛ **tsp. table salt**
6 **oz. reduced-fat ground pork sausage**
1 **(8-oz.) package refrigerated prechopped tricolor pepper mix**
½ **cup vertically sliced onion**
½ **tsp. dried crushed red pepper**
6 **large egg whites**
4 **large eggs**
1½ **cups (6 oz.) shredded 2% reduced-fat Mexican four-cheese blend**
½ **cup 2% reduced-fat Greek yogurt**
½ **cup refrigerated prepared salsa**
3 **green onions, chopped**

1. Preheat oven to 425°. Arrange tortillas in a single layer on a baking sheet coated with cooking spray; spray tortillas with cooking spray, and sprinkle with salt. Bake at 425° for 13 minutes or until crisp and lightly golden, turning after 8 minutes.

2. Meanwhile, brown sausage in a large nonstick skillet over medium-high heat, stirring often, 5 minutes or until meat crumbles and is no longer pink. Add pepper mix, onion, and crushed red pepper; sauté 5 minutes or until vegetables are tender.

3. Whisk together egg whites and eggs; pour over sausage mixture. Cook, without stirring, 1 minute or until eggs begin to set on bottom. Gently draw cooked edges away from sides of skillet to form large pieces. Cook, stirring occasionally, 3 to 4 minutes or until eggs are thickened and moist. (Do not overstir.)

4. Spoon about ½ cup egg mixture onto each tortilla; sprinkle each with ¼ cup cheese. Bake at 425° for 2 to 3 minutes or until cheese is melted.

5. Top each tostada with 4 tsp. yogurt and 4 tsp. salsa. Sprinkle green onions evenly over tostadas. Serve immediately.

SERVING SIZE 1 tostada CALORIES 320 FAT 16g (sat 6.2g, mono 5.7g, poly 2.3g) PROTEIN 24.3g CARB 21.2g FIBER 2.3g CHOL 163mg IRON 0.8mg SODIUM 639mg CALC 297mg

Grillades and Grits

Journey to New Orleans and you'll find this popular combo served up at many a breakfast or brunch. Lean cutlets like pork, veal, or beef are cooked alongside fresh vegetables, then served over creamy grits for a hearty meal.

MAKES 4 servings   HANDS-ON 15 min.   TOTAL 50 min.

3   Tbsp. all-purpose flour
1   tsp. Creole seasoning, divided
1   lb. lean breakfast pork cutlets, trimmed
2   tsp. olive oil
1   cup finely diced onion
1   cup finely diced celery
½   cup finely diced green bell pepper
1   (14.5-oz.) can no-salt-added diced tomatoes
1   (14-oz.) can reduced-sodium fat-free chicken broth
Creamy Grits

1. Combine flour and ½ tsp. Creole seasoning in a shallow dish. Dredge pork in flour mixture.

2. Cook pork, in 2 batches, in ½ tsp. hot oil per batch in a large skillet over medium-high heat 2 minutes on each side or until done. Remove from skillet, and keep warm.

3. Add remaining 1 tsp. oil to skillet. Sauté diced onion, celery, and bell pepper in hot oil 3 to 5 minutes or until vegetables are tender. Stir in remaining ½ tsp. Creole seasoning. Stir in diced tomatoes and chicken broth, and cook 2 minutes, stirring to loosen browned bits from bottom of skillet. Simmer 15 to 18 minutes or until liquid reduces to about 2 Tbsp. Serve tomato mixture over Creamy Grits and pork.

SERVING SIZE 2 cutlets, ¾ cup sauce, and ½ cup grits CALORIES 369 FAT 11g (sat 3.4g, mono 5.1g, poly 1.2g) PROTEIN 31.8g CARB 33.7g FIBER 3.2g CHOL 76mg IRON 2.5mg SODIUM 350mg CALC 129mg

Creamy Grits

MAKES 4 servings   HANDS-ON 5 min.   TOTAL 20 min.

Bring **1 (14-oz.) can reduced-sodium fat-free chicken broth** and **1 cup fat-free milk** to a boil in a medium saucepan over medium-high heat; reduce heat to low, and whisk in ½ **cup quick-cooking grits.** Cook, whisking occasionally, 15 to 20 minutes or until creamy and thickened.

SERVING SIZE ½ cup CALORIES 101 FAT 0.6g (sat 0.3g, mono 0.1g, poly 0.2g) PROTEIN 4.9g CARB 18.8g FIBER 0.9g CHOL 2.9mg IRON 0.6mg SODIUM 73mg CALC 76mg

Chapter Three

LET'S DO LUNCH

Don't you just love lunch? It's the halfway point in the middle of a busy day—a time to sit down and chat with colleagues over a bowl of soup and a sandwich and give yourself a well-deserved break. Lunch can be an elegant affair at an upscale restaurant or a quick bite at your desk. But no matter how you approach it, it's an important time to both relax and refuel.

The Midday Meal

Lunchtime in the South was traditionally the day's biggest meal. It gave farmers a chance to come in and cool off, children an opportunity to eat when they came home from school, and even professionals like bankers an occasion to sit down and dine with their families. Not many of us still have time for a long, multicourse meal smack dab in the middle of the day. But taking a few minutes to eat—and digest—without rushing around can still have a big impact, even in our very busy, modern lives.

If you can't be bothered to take time to eat lunch, you're setting yourself up for trouble. The minutes you might spare by skipping lunch can become lost as low blood sugar levels make you more unproductive later in the day. And if you're "saving" calories for later, you're sure to give in to high-fat, high-sugar binges by evening.

Some experts stress the importance of getting your fuel in the earlier part of the day, rather than waiting until nightfall. "I tell my clients that at least 50 to 60 percent of their calories should be consumed by 2 p.m. to avoid overeating at night," says nutritionist Angela Lemond, of Plano, Texas. "I challenge people all the time to make a point of eating more at the front part of the day. In most cases, having this balance of energy helps you make better choices and maximizes your metabolism all day long."

So how do you incorporate some of our Linger Longer principles on days when grabbing more than a few seconds to eat seems like pure luxury? **Start by setting the right environment.** Whether you're stuck in front of your computer or able to sit down at the kitchen table, clear some space for your meal. Some folks even keep a place mat and some nice china and cutlery at their desks to turn a work environment into a fine dining one—at least temporarily!

"If you focus on what you are doing, really slowing down and being mindful of the experience, you appreciate what you are eating more and you end up feeling more satisfied," says registered dietition Constance Brown-Riggs, a spokesperson for the Academy of Nutrition and Dietetics in New York who spent childhood summers in North Carolina. "Really think about the flavors, texture, and tastes. Even dashboard dining can be done mindfully."

Taking a few minutes to eat—and digest—without rushing around can have a big impact in our busy, modern lives.

Knowing just what you're going to eat ahead of time can also help turn lunch into a healthful, happy experience. Serving yourself some colorful Crab-Peach-Avocado Salad (page 81) or a Chopped Chicken Sandwich with Crunchy Pecan Slaw (page 94-95) you prepared ahead of time lets you enjoy all the flavors of a satisfying, healthy meal. Forget takeout: You've got a Chicken BLT Salad (page 89) in the fridge with your name on it!

Sometimes a leisurely lunch with good friends can stretch long into the afternoon. I guess that's when we in the South call it a luncheon. Enjoy the experience of these midday indulgences, then turn dinner into "supper"—a lighter evening meal with small-yet-satisfying portions.

Salad Days

One of the nicest things about lunch is that it can range from a three-course feast to a simple salad, depending on your hunger, time, and preference. In the South, where hot, steamy weather can rule a July or August day, nothing cools you off like a refreshing cold soup or a crisp salad. Even in winter, salads make an appearance on many a Southern lunch menu, whether it's a heaping plate of greens or a classic slaw.

There are really no limits to what a salad can include. Take your lettuce variations. You'll still find a basic wedge salad with iceberg taking center stage at many a restaurant establishment. While it may not be a nutritional powerhouse, iceberg's crisp taste and high crunch means it's full of water, which is terrifically quenching on a hot-as-blazes day.

Even more rewarding is the chance to create your own salad masterpiece: Start with a great foundation, whether it's baby kale, baby spinach, arugula, Bibb lettuce, watercress, dandelion greens, or romaine. **Any mix of leafy greens will give you some fiber, plus calcium, iron, vitamins, and other essential nutrients.** For tougher greens, like kale or collards, try massaging them lightly with a little bit of olive oil, then leaving them to marinate for a few hours or overnight. This softens up the greens so they're less chewy, and the oil adds a bit of healthy fat and flavor.

Once you have your base, personalize it however you wish, adding in crunchy cucumber, sweet onions, juicy tomatoes, petite baby carrots, or whatever else suits your mood. The more varied the color palette on your plate, the more nutrition you'll be getting in every bite. Carrots and leafy greens like spinach, kale, and collards dish up lots of beta-carotene and lutein, important for healthy vision. Tomatoes provide loads of lycopene, linked to lower levels of prostate cancer. Cabbage and broccoli are rich in glucosinolates, which can help fight off numerous other forms of cancer. **As you can see, the more types of vegetables (and fruits!) you add to your salads, the better the taste—and the more nutrients you'll find.**

It's important to note that many of these plant-based nutrients, like carotenoids, are fat-soluble, which means they're more easily absorbed when consumed with fat. That fits right in with the idea of consuming some healthy fats like olive oil- or canola oil-based salad dressings on a regular basis. They not only taste great and help you feel fuller longer, they can also make the other foods you eat more nutritious.

To give your salad some more staying power, don't forget to add some extra protein. Whether it's shrimp, salmon, turkey, or chicken— or eggs, edamame, nuts, or chickpeas—a lean or vegetarian protein source can turn a simple dish into a hearty meal. Serve it with a side of cornbread or a warm pita and you've got a satisfying lunch.

Preserving the Past—and Future

Back in your grandparents' time, almost everyone canned their fruit and vegetables, especially in the South. It was a simple, easy way to ensure you had enough fruits and vegetables to get you through the winter. Canning, pickling, and making preserves like jam and jelly meant you could still get foods like peaches, bell peppers, tomatoes, and other bounties of summer even deep into January or February. Today, of course, you needn't go farther than your closest grocery store for a year-round selection of fresh produce. But that hasn't stopped many Southerners—and others throughout the country—from continuing the tradition of "putting up" foods.

"Canning, pickling, and making preserves is a lot safer today thanks to new techniques and technologies," notes Sheri Castle, a food historian and author of *The New Southern Garden Cookbook*. "It's also a lot easier, because you don't have to put up 20 or 30 quarts at once—you can make small batches with just a couple pints, which makes it much more accessible to people who don't have a lot of storage room."

Canned fruits and vegetables are a great way to liven up a meal any time of year. Try adding some hot peppers or pickles to your favorite sandwich or wrap for some extra spice or crunch. Use preserved fruit like peaches or pears to naturally sweeten a dessert, or stir in some jam to liven up a salad dressing. There's no shortage of ways to use condiments like these—you're limited only by your imagination. If you've always wanted to try making pickled, canned, or preserved fruits and vegetables

HOW TO AVOID SLIM PICKINGS AT LUNCH

1. Plan and make your lunch ahead of time so you have more time to enjoy it, even if it's just for a few minutes.

2. Include a variety of fruits and vegetables partnered with whole grains and lean proteins.

3. Include a little indulgence: Bacon crumbles on a salad or a small cookie for dessert can elevate lunchtime to leisure time.

4. Prepare for the unexpected; have a backup plan (such as a healthy option in the freezer or granola bars and fruit at your desk) in case your lunch plans change.

but have no idea where to start, check out the National Center for Home Food Preservation, which is run through the University of Georgia. There's even a free online course available through the group's Web site at homefoodpreservation.com. Or get a copy of *Little Jars, Big Flavors,* the *Southern Living* cookbook on small-batch jams, jellies, and preserves.

Ready, Set, Lunch!

The beautiful recipes in this chapter serve up a diverse selection of delicious Southern soups, salads, and lunch entrées that satisfy without weighing you down. Try a few small courses and sides together for a longer sit-down, or pack a sandwich or salad for a quick, casual meal. Lunch is on!

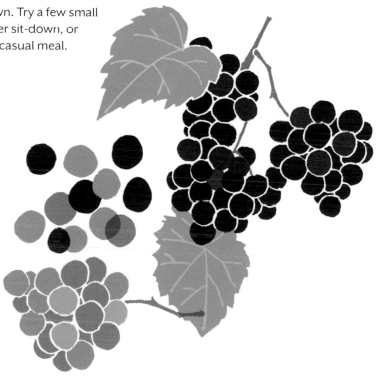

Peach-and-Tomato Gazpacho
with Cucumber Yogurt

When the days grow hot, cool off with this refreshing summertime soup, which highlights some of the best flavors of the season—juicy sweet peaches and fresh tomatoes. The savory yogurt topping adds protein and calcium.

MAKES 5 servings   HANDS-ON 20 min.   TOTAL 1 hour, 20 min.

5   **large peaches, peeled and divided**
3   **large tomatoes, cored and divided**
½   **medium-size sweet onion, coarsely chopped (about ½ cup)**
3   **Tbsp. apple cider vinegar**
⅛   **tsp. kosher salt**
⅛   **tsp. freshly ground white pepper**
¾   **cup finely diced English cucumber**
⅓   **cup plain Greek yogurt**
2   **Tbsp. chopped fresh chives**
1   **garlic clove, minced**
Extra virgin olive oil
Garnish: fresh chives

1. Quarter 4 peaches and 2 tomatoes. Process quartered peaches and tomatoes and next 2 ingredients in a food processor until smooth.

2. Chop remaining peach and tomato. Stir into pureed mixture. Season with kosher salt and freshly ground white pepper. Cover and chill 1 hour.

3. Meanwhile, combine cucumber and next 3 ingredients in a medium bowl. Season with kosher salt and freshly ground white pepper. Cover and chill 1 to 24 hours.

4. Ladle gazpacho into bowls. Spoon cucumber mixture over gazpacho. Drizzle each serving with about 1 tsp. extra virgin olive oil. Serve immediately.

SERVING SIZE about 1 cup CALORIES 150; FAT 5.7g (sat 0.9g, mono 3.8g, poly 0.7g); PROTEIN 4.2g; CARB 23.8g; FIBER 4.3g; CHOL 1mg; IRON 0.8mg; SODIUM 60mg; CALC 40mg

Baby Carrot Soup

Vidalia onions were first grown during the Depression in the sandy soil of Toombs County, Georgia, where farmers were surprised to find they'd cultivated a variety that was sweet, not hot. Their unique taste balances the slightly hot chipotle peppers in this easy-to-make (yet company-worthy!) soup.

MAKES 5 servings   HANDS-ON 10 min.   TOTAL 37 min.

1   (7-oz.) can chipotle peppers in adobo sauce
1   small sweet onion, chopped
1   Tbsp. olive oil
1   (32-oz.) container reduced-sodium fat-free chicken broth
1   (16-oz.) package baby carrots
⅓   cup half-and-half
½   tsp. table salt
5   tsp. reduced-fat sour cream
Toppings: chopped fresh chives, chopped dried chile peppers

1. Remove 2 tsp. adobo sauce from can; reserve peppers and remaining sauce for another use.

2. Sauté onion in hot oil in a Dutch oven over medium heat 3 to 4 minutes or until tender. Stir in broth, carrots, and 2 tsp. adobo sauce; cover, increase heat to medium-high, and bring to a boil. Reduce heat to medium, and simmer, partially covered, 15 to 20 minutes or until carrots are tender. Remove from heat, and cool 10 minutes.

3. Process carrot mixture in a blender or food processor 1 minute or until smooth, stopping to scrape down sides as needed. Return carrot mixture to Dutch oven. Stir in half-and-half and salt. Cook over low heat 2 to 4 minutes or until thoroughly heated. Ladle 1 cup of soup into each of 5 soup bowls. Top each with 1 tsp. sour cream and desired toppings.

SERVING SIZE 1 cup CALORIES 123; FAT 5.8g (sat 2.3g, mono 2.7g, poly 0.4g); PROTEIN 4.3g; CARB 14.3g; FIBER 3.4g; CHOL 12mg; IRON 1.0mg; SODIUM 309mg; CALC 67mg

Halve It Your Way

MY STAY-SLIM SECRET
Susan Irby, 47, author and blogger

Thinking about putting on a bathing suit can be motivation enough to eat the right foods. As author of "The Bikini Chef" blog, Susan Irby thinks about bikinis every day. Born in Marietta, Georgia, Irby spent summers swimming in Alabama lakes and cooking up ways to trim calories without sacrificing taste. "My favorite is equal parts nonfat sour cream and nonfat milk for heavy cream in cream sauces," she says. Thinking in halves works for sandwiches, too: "Use one slice of bread, and make an open-faced sandwich or eat it as a half sandwich."

Fresh Asparagus Soup

One of the first sure signs of spring in the South is the appearance of fresh asparagus. It's high in folic acid and a rich source of potassium, fiber, thiamin, and vitamins A, B6, and C. Enjoy it simply steamed, or in recipes like this soup, which bring out the vegetable's unique flavor.

MAKES 6 servings   HANDS-ON 15 min.   TOTAL 35 min.

1 lb. fresh asparagus
2 cups reduced-sodium fat-free chicken broth
½ cup chopped onion
1 garlic clove, chopped
¾ tsp. fresh thyme, divided
1 Tbsp. all-purpose flour
2 cups 1% low-fat milk
2 tsp. butter
½ tsp. table salt
½ tsp. lemon zest, divided
½ cup reduced-fat sour cream
1 Tbsp. fresh lemon juice
Garnish: fresh thyme sprig

1. Cut asparagus into 2-inch pieces, discarding tough ends.

2. Combine asparagus, broth, onion, garlic, and ½ tsp. thyme in a large saucepan over medium-high heat; bring to a boil. Reduce heat to medium-low; cover and simmer 10 minutes. Remove from heat; let stand 10 minutes. Process asparagus mixture, in batches, in a blender or food processor until smooth. Return to pan.

3. Whisk together flour and milk until smooth. Gradually add flour mixture to asparagus mixture, whisking until blended. Bring to a boil, stirring constantly. Reduce heat; simmer, stirring constantly, 5 minutes. Remove from heat; stir in butter, salt, ¼ tsp. lemon zest, and remaining ¼ tsp. thyme.

4. Combine sour cream, lemon juice, and remaining ¼ tsp. lemon zest. Top each serving with about 3 tsp. sour cream mixture.

Note: Freeze soup after Step 3 for up to one month. When ready to serve, thaw, reheat, and proceed as directed with Step 4.

SERVING SIZE 1 cup soup and about 3 tsp. sour cream mixture
CALORIES 107; FAT 4.8g (sat 3g, mono 1.3g, poly 0.2g); PROTEIN 6.7g;
CARB 10.8g; FIBER 1.9g; CHOL 17mg; IRON 1.8mg; SODIUM 310mg;
CALC 146mg

Oregano-Feta Dressing

Originally named for the milk left over after making butter, buttermilk is prized throughout the South. Nonfat buttermilk keeps this dressing on the creamy yet slender side.

MAKES 8 servings   HANDS-ON 10 min.   TOTAL 10 min.

3   oz. reduced-fat feta cheese, crumbled
¼   cup nonfat buttermilk
3   Tbsp. fresh lemon juice
1   garlic clove
½   tsp. dried oregano*
¼   tsp. freshly ground black pepper
2   Tbsp. olive oil
¼   small green bell pepper, chopped

1. Process first 6 ingredients and 2 Tbsp. water in a food processor until smooth. Gradually add olive oil in a slow, steady stream, processing until smooth. Add bell pepper, and pulse 3 seconds.

***** 1 tsp. chopped fresh oregano may be substituted for the dried oregano.

SERVING SIZE about 2 Tbsp. CALORIES 57; FAT 4.8g (sat 1.4g, mono 2.9g, poly 0.4g); PROTEIN 2.6g; CARB 1.4g; FIBER 0.3g; CHOL 3mg; IRON 0.1mg; SODIUM 155mg; CALC 37mg

Orange-Raspberry Vinaigrette

Many Southern cooks preserve orange marmalade, made with the juice and peel of the fruit, but you can easily sub the store-bought version. Its sweet flavor counters the acidic vinegar, and jalapeño brings the heat.

MAKES 16 servings   HANDS-ON 10 min.   TOTAL 10 min.

½   cup orange marmalade
¼   cup white balsamic-raspberry blush vinegar
1   medium jalapeño pepper, seeded and minced
2   Tbsp. chopped fresh cilantro
2   Tbsp. olive oil

1. Stir together all ingredients.

Note: We tested with Alessi White Balsamic Raspberry Blush Vinegar.

SERVING SIZE 1 Tbsp. CALORIES 45; FAT 1.7g (sat 0.2g, mono 1.2g, poly 0.2g); PROTEIN 0g; CARB 7.9g; FIBER 0.1g; CHOL 0mg; IRON 0mg; SODIUM 6mg; CALC 4mg

Barley-Pine Nut Salad

Barley's chewy texture and nutty flavor are welcome in soups and stews, but it also shines as a key ingredient in this grain-based salad. Enjoy with a green side salad or pita chips.

MAKES 4 servings   HANDS-ON 25 min.   TOTAL 40 min.

2   cups reduced-sodium fat-free chicken broth
1   cup uncooked quick-cooking barley
¾   cup chopped jarred roasted red bell peppers
1   small cucumber, diced
1   Tbsp. chopped fresh dill
1   Tbsp. chopped fresh parsley
3   Tbsp. fresh lemon juice
2   Tbsp. extra virgin olive oil
¾   tsp. sugar
½   tsp. table salt
½   tsp. black pepper
2   Tbsp. pine nuts, toasted
2   Tbsp. crumbled feta cheese

1. Bring 2 cups chicken broth to a boil in a 2-qt. saucepan; stir in barley. Cover, reduce heat, and simmer 10 minutes or until barley is tender. Remove from heat; let stand, covered, 5 minutes. Drain well.

2. Combine cooked barley, roasted red bell peppers, and next 3 ingredients in a large bowl.

3. Whisk together lemon juice and next 4 ingredients. Drizzle over barley mixture, tossing to coat. Sprinkle evenly with toasted pine nuts and crumbled feta cheese; serve immediately.

To make it a Brown Rice-Pine Nut Salad: Substitute 1 cup brown rice for barley. Increase broth to 2¼ cups, and increase cooking time to 45 minutes. Proceed as directed.

SERVING SIZE 1⅛ cups CALORIES 314; FAT 11.8g (sat 2.3g, mono 6.5g, poly 2.4g); PROTEIN 8.5g; CARB 44.8g; FIBER 9.4g; CHOL 7mg; IRON 2.1mg; SODIUM 483mg; CALC 67mg

---

Leave Less Room for Trouble

MY STAY-SLIM SECRET
Kari Pricher, 38, TV producer

Healthy plates take some planning. Kari Pricher, who produces TV programs including *Anderson Cooper 360°* and *The Dr. Oz Show*, has a good trick for "producing" proper portions.

"My secret is to make sure half of my plate has something healthy on it such as salad or vegetables," she says. "That leaves less room for me to get into trouble." Though she's a Manhattanite now, Pricher grew up in

Florida, graduated from the University of Alabama, and loves Southern food. The "trouble" side of her plate might include her dad's fried chicken, her great-aunt's creamed corn, or homemade peach ice cream.

Corn and Black Bean Salad

Golden corn is one of summer's sweetest crops, served up fresh off the cob and bursting with flavor. Pair it with black beans for a balance of essential proteins. To enjoy this recipe year-round, you can substitute frozen corn.

MAKES 8 servings   HANDS-ON 15 min.   TOTAL 37 min.

2 **cups fresh corn kernels (about 3 ears)**
1 **(15-oz.) can black beans, drained and rinsed**
1 **cup chopped tomato**
⅓ **cup lime juice**
¼ **cup finely chopped red onion**
½ **jalapeño pepper, seeded and chopped**
2 **Tbsp. chopped fresh cilantro**
2 **tsp. hot sauce**
½ **tsp. table salt**
½ **tsp. ground cumin**
½ **tsp. ground coriander**
½ **tsp. black pepper**

1. Preheat broiler with oven rack 5 inches from heat. Place corn on an aluminum foil-lined baking sheet.

2. Broil corn 12 minutes or until lightly browned, stirring once. Remove from oven, and let stand 10 minutes.

3. Combine corn and remaining ingredients in a large bowl. Cover and chill until ready to serve.

SERVING SIZE ½ cup CALORIES 69; FAT 0.7g (sat 0.1g, mono 0.2g, poly 0.2g); PROTEIN 3.2g; CARB 14g; FIBER 2.6g; CHOL 0mg; IRON 0.8mg; SODIUM 254mg; CALC 19mg

Tabbouleh Salad

The refreshing scent of mint plays an important role in many Southern recipes, from iced tea to juleps. It's a key ingredient in this tasty side salad. Pair tabbouleh with simply grilled chicken, fish, or lamb.

MAKES 5 servings   HANDS-ON 20 min.   TOTAL 1 hour, 50 min.

1   cup uncooked bulgur wheat*
1   cup boiling water*
2   medium tomatoes, chopped
4   green onions, thinly sliced
¼   cup minced fresh parsley
¼   to ½ cup chopped fresh mint
½   tsp. lemon zest
⅓   cup fresh lemon juice
3   Tbsp. olive oil
½   tsp. table salt
½   tsp. black pepper
20   romaine lettuce leaves

1. Place bulgur in a large bowl, and add boiling water. Cover and let stand 30 minutes.

2. Stir in tomato and next 8 ingredients. Chill 1 hour. Spoon into lettuce leaves just before serving.

* 1 cup instant brown rice, cooked, may be substituted for 1 cup bulgur wheat and 1 cup boiling water.

SERVING SIZE 1 cup salad and 4 lettuce leaves CALORIES 206; FAT 8.7g (sat 1.2g, mono 6.0g, poly 1.1g); PROTEIN 5.6g; CARB 29.6g; FIBER 9.0g; CHOL 0mg; IRON 2.2mg; SODIUM 249mg; CALC 59mg

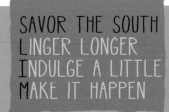

SAVOR THE SOUTH
LINGER LONGER
INDULGE A LITTLE
MAKE IT HAPPEN

Sweet Tea

There's iced tea. And then there's sweet tea. Served all over the South, sweet tea is super-duper sweet. Some joke that you can stand a spoon up in it. All joking aside, a 32-ounce tumbler of sweet iced tea can clock in at 240 calories and 60 grams of sugar.

But a few small adjustments can cut the sugar dramatically. First off, alternate tea with water. Skip the tea refill, and you've just cut 240 calories. Next up: Opt for unsweetened tea with plenty of ice and just a little sweet tea added. To ease into the change, go for a 50-50 mix first (you've just cut 120 calories!), then 80-20 (you've saved nearly 200 calories!) and so on until you only need a splash to get your fix.

Absent added sugar, tea is linked to smaller waistlines,

sharper minds, and healthier hearts. As Jeffrey Blumberg, Ph.D., professor of nutrition science at Tufts University in Boston, puts it: "The many bioactive compounds in tea appear to impact virtually every cell in the body to help improve health outcomes." And, good news for those who wash down their fried chicken with iced tea: Drinking one cup of black tea per day has been shown to help control blood pressure and increase blood flow after high-fat meals.

Thai Noodle Salad

Peanuts combine perfectly with fresh mint, cilantro, sesame oil, and garlic along with the heat from jalapeño.

MAKES 4 servings   HANDS-ON 25 min.   TOTAL 25 min.

1   (8-oz.) package vermicelli
⅓   cup chopped fresh cilantro
2   garlic cloves, minced
1   jalapeño pepper, seeded and chopped
¼   cup fresh lime juice
1   Tbsp. fish sauce*
1   Tbsp. honey
1½ tsp. sesame oil
¼   tsp. table salt
2   carrots, grated
1   cucumber, peeled, seeded, and thinly sliced
1   cup finely shredded cabbage
¼   cup chopped fresh mint
¼   cup chopped dry-roasted peanuts

1. Cook pasta according to package directions. Drain, rinse, and place in a large bowl; set aside.

2. Process cilantro and next 7 ingredients in a food processor until smooth, stopping to scrape down sides.

3. Toss together pasta, cilantro dressing, carrots, and next 3 ingredients. Divide salad mixture evenly among 4 plates. Sprinkle each salad with 1 Tbsp. peanuts, and serve immediately.

* Soy sauce may be substituted for fish sauce.

SERVING SIZE 1 salad CALORIES 326; FAT 7.3g (sat 1.1g, mono 2.9g, poly 2.2g); PROTEIN 11.3g; CARB 56.4g; FIBER 4.6g; CHOL 0mg; IRON 2.5mg; SODIUM 534mg; CALC 52mg

Less Is More

MY STAY-SLIM SECRET
Densie Webb, 59, nutrition writer

The shrimp-and-chicken gumbo, boiled crawfish, red beans and rice, butter beans, snap peas, okra and tomatoes, and turnip greens that Densie Webb grew up eating in Louisiana can still fit happily into a healthy diet. A registered dietitian with a Ph.D. in nutrition, Webb now works as an Austin-based nutrition writer. She says a smarter approach to seasoning favorite dishes that are usually high in fat and salt can keep old favorites in rotation: "You still can get the traditional flavor by using the smallest amount of bacon or lower-fat sausage," she says, "and by sautéing onions in olive oil, rather than bacon fat."

Crab-Peach-Avocado Salad

Succulent crabmeat blends perfectly with sweet peaches, creamy avocado, and a kick of jalapeño in this beautiful layered dish. Lump crabmeat works best to help keep the salad's shape.

MAKES 6 servings   HANDS-ON 30 min.   TOTAL 30 min.

1   lb. fresh jumbo lump crabmeat
2   Tbsp. lemon zest
1   Tbsp. mayonnaise
½   tsp. dry mustard
5   Tbsp. fresh lemon juice, divided
½   jalapeño pepper, seeded and finely diced
¼   cup finely diced celery
2   green onions, finely chopped
⅛   tsp. kosher salt
⅛   tsp. freshly ground white pepper
5   or 6 medium peaches (about 1¾ lb.), unpeeled and coarsely chopped
1   Tbsp. honey
3   medium avocados, diced
6   cups arugula
Garnish: Freshly ground black pepper

1. Chill 6 salad plates.

2. Pick crabmeat, removing any bits of shell. Whisk together lemon zest, next 2 ingredients, and 1 Tbsp. lemon juice. Fold in jalapeño pepper, next 2 ingredients, and crabmeat, using a rubber spatula. Season with kosher salt and freshly ground white pepper to taste.

3. Stir together peaches and remaining 4 Tbsp. lemon juice. Reserve 3 cups peach mixture. Pulse honey and remaining peach mixture in a food processor 8 to 10 times or until smooth. Season pureed peach mixture with kosher salt and freshly ground white pepper.

4. Spoon ¼ cup pureed peach mixture onto a chilled plate. Place a 3½-inch round cutter in center of peach mixture on plate. (A clean, empty tuna can with both ends removed may be used instead.) Spoon one-sixth of diced avocados and ½ cup reserved chopped peach mixture into cutter, packing each layer firmly and sprinkling with kosher salt and freshly ground white pepper to taste. Top with about ½ cup crab mixture. Carefully remove cutter from plate. Repeat procedure with remaining chilled plates, pureed peach mixture, avocado, chopped peach mixture, and crab mixture. Arrange 1 cup arugula around each layered salad; serve immediately.

SERVING SIZE 1 salad CALORIES 287; FAT 14.5g (sat 1.7g, mono 8.4g, poly 2.3g); PROTEIN 18.1g; CARB 26.8g; FIBER 5.3g; CHOL 60mg; IRON 2.1mg; SODIUM 286mg; CALC 104mg

Grilled Shrimp Salad

A dressing made from Southern sweet tea balances the salty and pungent blue cheese; crunchy pecans and juicy peaches also make this salad fun to eat.

MAKES 6 servings   HANDS-ON 16 min.   TOTAL 1 hour, 6 min., including vinaigrette

- 1 **lb. peeled, jumbo raw shrimp**
- 1 **Tbsp. olive oil**
- 2 **large fresh peaches, cut into 8 wedges each**
- 1 **(6-oz.) bag mixed baby salad greens**

Sweet Tea Vinaigrette
- 1/16 **tsp. table salt**
- 1/8 **tsp. black pepper**
- 3/4 **cup crumbled blue cheese**
- 1/2 **cup coarsely chopped toasted pecans**

1. Preheat grill to 350° to 400° (medium-high) heat. Devein shrimp, if desired, and toss with olive oil. Grill shrimp, covered with grill lid, 2 to 3 minutes on each side or just until shrimp turn pink. At the same time, grill peach wedges 1 to 2 minutes on each side or until grill marks appear.

2. Toss salad greens with Sweet Tea Vinaigrette; season with salt and pepper. Divide salad greens evenly among 6 salad plates. Top each salad evenly with grilled shrimp, peaches, blue cheese, and pecans. Serve immediately.

SERVING SIZE 1 salad CALORIES 356; FAT 28.6g (sat 5.2g, mono 15.6g, poly 6.4g); PROTEIN 15.3g; CARB 11.2g; FIBER 1.7g; CHOL 108mg; IRON 1mg; SODIUM 400mg; CALC 140mg

Sweet Tea Vinaigrette

Make the dressing up to a week ahead to allow it to cool; otherwise it'll wilt your salad. Store it in the refrigerator in an airtight container.

MAKES 6 servings   HANDS-ON 10 min.   TOTAL 45 min.

Bring **1 cup sweetened tea** to a boil in a saucepan over medium-low heat; reduce heat to low, and simmer 9 to 10 minutes or until reduced to 1/3 cup. Remove from heat; cool 20 minutes. Whisk in **2 Tbsp. apple cider vinegar, 1/4 tsp. honey, 1/4 tsp. Dijon mustard,** and **a pinch of table salt.** Whisk in **6 Tbsp. canola oil** in a slow, steady stream.

SERVING SIZE 2 Tbsp. CALORIES 137; FAT 14.0g (sat 1.0g, mono 8.9g, poly 3.9g); PROTEIN 0g; CARB 3.3g; FIBER 0g; CHOL 0mg; IRON 0mg; SODIUM 28mg; CALC 0mg

Salmon and Vegetable Salad

The tastes of spring come alive in this simple but satisfying entrée salad, featuring fresh asparagus and sugar snap peas. The Creamy Herb Dressing will keep up to one week in the refrigerator.

MAKES 4 servings   HANDS-ON 17 min.   TOTAL 23 min.

½ **lb. fresh asparagus**
1 **cup sugar snap peas**
1¼ **lb. skinless salmon fillets, cut into 2-inch chunks**
½ **tsp. table salt**
¼ **tsp. black pepper**
6 **cups chopped romaine lettuce hearts**
½ **cup uncooked shelled fresh or frozen edamame, thawed**
¼ **cup sliced radishes**
Creamy Herb Dressing

1. Preheat broiler with oven rack 6 inches from heat. Cut asparagus into 1-inch-long pieces, discarding tough ends, and cook with sugar snap peas in boiling salted water 2 to 3 minutes or until crisp-tender; drain. Plunge into ice water; drain.

2. Sprinkle salmon with salt and pepper; broil on a lightly greased rack in a broiler pan 3 to 4 minutes or to desired degree of doneness.

3. Arrange lettuce, edamame, radishes, asparagus mixture, and salmon evenly on each of 4 plates. Drizzle each salad with 2 Tbsp. dressing.

SERVING SIZE about 2 ⅓ cups salad and 2 Tbsp. dressing CALORIES 358; FAT 17.2g (sat 3.2g, mono 7.7g, poly 4.6g); PROTEIN 36.3g; CARB 12.0g; FIBER 4.1g; CHOL 77mg; IRON 3.6mg; SODIUM 583mg; CALC 83mg

Creamy Herb Dressing

MAKES 8 servings   HANDS-ON 5 min.   TOTAL 35 min.

Whisk together ½ **cup buttermilk, ¼ cup mayonnaise, 3 Tbsp. chopped fresh herbs (such as mint, dill, and chives), 1 Tbsp. fresh lemon juice, ⅛ tsp. salt,** and **⅛ tsp. pepper.** Chill 30 minutes.

SERVING SIZE 2 Tbsp. CALORIES 33; FAT 2.8g (sat 0.3g, mono 1.4g, poly 0.8g); PROTEIN 0.5g; CARB 1g; FIBER 0g; CHOL 2.2mg; IRON 0mg; SODIUM 100mg; CALC 1mg

Sweet-and-Sour Shrimp
with Onion and Red Pepper

Serve this enticing shrimp entrée at an elegant luncheon, or simply enjoy it as a midday treat for yourself.

MAKES 4 servings   HANDS-ON 40 min.   TOTAL 1 hour, 16 min.

1   **lb. unpeeled, medium-size raw shrimp**
1   **Tbsp. dry sherry**
6   **tsp. cornstarch, divided**
3   **tsp. vegetable oil, divided**
4   **thin slices fresh ginger**
4   **green onions, cut into 1-inch pieces**
2   **garlic cloves, minced**
1   **small red bell pepper, cut into thin strips**
1   **(6-oz.) can unsweetened pineapple juice**
1   **Tbsp. apple cider vinegar**
1   **Tbsp. lite soy sauce**
1   **Tbsp. thawed, frozen orange juice concentrate**
2   **cups hot cooked jasmine rice**

1. Peel shrimp, and devein, if desired.

2. Whisk together sherry and 2 tsp. cornstarch in a medium bowl; add shrimp, coating well. Chill 30 minutes, turning occasionally.

3. Heat 2 tsp. vegetable oil in a large nonstick skillet or wok at medium-high 2 minutes. Add ginger and next 3 ingredients; cook 1 minute or until tender. Remove vegetables from skillet; discard ginger.

4. Remove shrimp from marinade, discarding marinade.

5. Heat remaining 1 tsp. vegetable oil in skillet; add shrimp, and cook, stirring often, 2 minutes or until shrimp turn pink. Return vegetables to skillet; stir in pineapple juice and next 3 ingredients.

6. Stir together 2 Tbsp. water and remaining 4 tsp. cornstarch; add to shrimp mixture. Bring to a boil; cook, stirring constantly, 1 minute or until thickened. Serve over rice.

SERVING SIZE 1 cup shrimp mixture and ½ cup rice CALORIES 268; FAT 4.8g (sat 0.5g, mono 1.6g, poly 1.7g); PROTEIN 17.9g; CARB 35.3g; FIBER 1.3g; CHOL 143mg; IRON 0.6mg; SODIUM 334mg; CALC 79mg

Chicken BLT Salad

This tempting chicken salad is a play on the classic BLT. Choose center-cut bacon, which is lower in fat and has 20 percent fewer calories.

MAKES 4 servings   HANDS-ON 15 min.   TOTAL 15 min.

½ **cup buttery garlic-and-herb spreadable cheese**

3 **cups chopped cooked chicken (about 6 breast halves)**

½ **cup grape tomatoes, halved**

⅓ **cup chopped green onion tops**

2 **bacon slices, cooked and crumbled**

1/16 **tsp. table salt**

⅛ **tsp. freshly ground black pepper**

Assorted mixed greens (optional)

1. Microwave cheese in a small microwave-safe bowl at HIGH 20 seconds. Stir in next 4 ingredients, tossing well. Add salt and pepper. Serve on assorted greens, if desired.

Note: We tested with Alouette Garlic & Herbs Spreadable Cheese.

SERVING SIZE 1 cup CALORIES 279; FAT 12.5g (sat 6.3g, mono 1.3g, poly 0.8g); PROTEIN 35.8g; CARB 3.2g; FIBER 0.4g; CHOL 117mg; IRON 1.2mg; SODIUM 350mg; CALC 42mg

SAVOR THE SOUTH
LINGER LONGER
INDULGE A LITTLE
MAKE IT HAPPEN

Mayo in Moderation

Swirled into macaroni salad, chicken salad, and pimiento cheese or slathered on bread to make a simple tomato sandwich, mayonnaise finds its way into many Southern recipes.

Made mostly of eggs and oil, regular mayonnaise is high in fat, containing about 90 calories and 10 grams of fat per tablespoon. The good news is that a little goes a long way. If you use a teaspoon instead of a tablespoon on your next sandwich, you'll cut the calories and fat by two-thirds. And if you choose mayonnaise made with heart-healthy oils like canola, peanut, or olive oil, that's even better.

In coleslaw, deviled eggs, and other mayo-based recipes, replacing some or all of the regular mayo with nonfat or low-fat Greek yogurt is another way to cut the fat; it ups the protein content, too. You also can use mayonnaise that's designed to be lighter. A tablespoon of "light" mayo has just 40 calories and 4 grams of fat; a tablespoon of "low-fat" mayo packs 15 calories and 1 gram of fat per tablespoon.

Chicken Blueberry Salad

A nutrition superstar, blueberries are packed with powerful antioxidants. And they're not just limited to muffins or fruit salad. Paired here with chicken, they add a sweet accent to your midday meal.

MAKES 4 servings   **HANDS-ON** 20 min.   **TOTAL** 1 hour, 32 min.

3   **Tbsp. olive oil**
½   **cup rice wine vinegar**
2   **tsp. minced fresh ginger**
1   **garlic clove, minced**
¼   **tsp. table salt**
½   **tsp. black pepper**
3   **skinned and boned chicken breast halves**
1   **celery rib, chopped**
½   **cup sweet onion, diced**
½   **cup red bell pepper, chopped**
1   **cup shredded carrot**
4   **cups torn mixed salad greens**
1   **cup fresh blueberries**

1. Whisk together first 6 ingredients. Reserve half of mixture, and chill.

2. Place chicken in a shallow dish or zip-top plastic freezer bag; pour remaining mixture over chicken. Cover or seal, and chill at least 1 hour.

3. Preheat grill to 350° to 400° (medium-high) heat. Remove chicken from marinade; discard marinade. Grill chicken, covered with grill lid, 6 minutes on each side or until done. Cut into thin slices.

4. Combine celery and next 3 ingredients; add reserved dressing, tossing to coat.

5. Place 1 cup greens on each of 4 plates. Top each with 3 ounces chicken, ¾ cup celery mixture, and ¼ cup blueberries.

SERVING SIZE 1 salad CALORIES 201; FAT 11.6g (sat 1.7g, mono 7.8g, poly 1.4g); PROTEIN 11.2g; CARB 14.6g; FIBER 4g; CHOL 28mg; IRON 1.1mg; SODIUM 248mg; CALC 26mg

Enjoy the Lighter Side of Southern Cuisine

The misperception that all Southern food is unhealthy keeps brothers Matt and Ted Lee busy explaining the lighter aspects of the region's cooking. "You get push-back from people who don't know Southern foods," says Ted. The brothers grew up in Charleston, authored *The Lee Bros. Charleston Kitchen* and other cookbooks, and have long championed authentic Southern ingredients.

Matt says making Southern menus as healthy as possible ironically means going back to the way Southerners cooked long ago: "If you look in old cookbooks from the 19th century, vegetables were not seasoned with a lot of butter or pork fat."

The brothers celebrate the seafood-centric cuisine of the coastal South and the healthy balance that comes from enjoying buttermilk pie one day and shrimp or crabs right off the boat the next. They note that Southerners use a variety of techniques, not just frying, to boost flavor. "Pickling adds so much satisfaction to vegetables," says Ted. "And char-grilling okra [gives it] a smoky, caramelized flavor."

Their secret to delicious Southern meals is adding little local touches—seasoning a dish with sea salt harvested off the coast of South Carolina or brightening up recipes with lemons, limes, and oranges grown in Charleston's walled gardens.

Just as hot and humid summers dictate lighter fashions in clothes, the Lees note,

Matt and Ted Lee, Charleston cookbook authors

Southern foods lighten up in summer with cold soups, chilled salads, grilled dishes, and liquid refreshments. "Southerners love and appreciate the value of a cold beverage," Ted says. "Just like a dish, cocktails have to have a balance of flavors, so we add a tiny pinch of salt to balance sweetness." A balanced cocktail can be as hydrating as a sports drink on sultry days, one reason folks down South often appear to "glow" rather than sweat.

"In old cookbooks from the 19th century, vegetables were not seasoned with a lot of butter or pork fat."

Avocado Salad-Hummus Pita

Avocado is a rich source of healthy monounsaturated fats. Enjoy these pitas as a light lunch, or with some fruit and yogurt as a side.

MAKES 8 servings   HANDS-ON 10 min.   TOTAL 10 min.

2   **large ripe avocados, coarsely chopped**
4   **large radishes, chopped**
2   **celery ribs, chopped**
2   **green onions, chopped**
2   **Tbsp. fresh lemon juice**
2   **Tbsp. olive oil**
½   **tsp. table salt**
¼   **to ½ tsp. freshly ground black pepper**
Hummus
4   **pita bread rounds, halved**
16 **lettuce leaves, torn in half**
2   **tomatoes, cut into 8 slices each**
1   **cup alfalfa sprouts (optional)**

1. Combine avocados and next 7 ingredients.

2. Spread ¼ cup of Hummus inside each pita half. Spoon about ⅓ cup avocado mixture into each half. Place 2 lettuce leaves, 2 tomato slices, and sprouts, if desired, into each pita half. Serve immediately.

SERVING SIZE: 1 filled pita half CALORIES 303; FAT 17g (sat 2.4g, mono 9.5g, poly 4g); PROTEIN 8.1g; CARB 33g; FIBER 7.7g; CHOL 0mg; IRON 2.5mg; SODIUM 628mg; CALC 78mg

Hummus

MAKES 8 servings   HANDS-ON 5 min.   TOTAL 5 min.

Process **1 (15-oz.) can drained and rinsed chickpeas** in a food processor until smooth, stopping to scrape down sides. Add **3 minced garlic cloves, ⅓ cup tahini, ¼ cup fresh lemon juice, ¼ cup water,** and **½ tsp. table salt;** pulse until blended.

SERVING SIZE ¼ cup CALORIES 91; FAT 5.8g (sat 0.8g, mono 2.1g, poly 2.5g); PROTEIN 3.2g; CARB 7.8g; FIBER 1.6g; CHOL 0mg; IRON 0.8mg; SODIUM 230mg; CALC 22mg

Go for the Greens

MY STAY-SLIM SECRET
Nina Hemphill Reeder, 29, health and fitness writer

If your favorite food also happens to be good for you and your waistline, go with it. For Nina Hemphill Reeder, the win-win ingredient is greens. "I love greens, including kale, collards, and mustard greens," says Reeder. As health and fitness editor of Atlanta's *Upscale* magazine, Reeder feels she should practice what she preaches. She cooks greens, a mineral-rich superfood, simply and incorporates them often into her meals. "I cook greens with chicken stock, onions, hot sauce, and vinegar," she says. "Sometimes, I'll have a big bowl of them with my meal or throw them into pasta."

Chopped Chicken Sandwich

Serve up a quick lunch using precooked chicken breasts. They pair nicely with the Sweet-and-Spicy Dressing and crunchy toasted pecan slaw.

MAKES 4 servings   HANDS-ON 15 min.   TOTAL 30 min.

4   **hoagie rolls**
½   **cup grated Swiss cheese, divided**
2   **cups chopped cooked chicken**
¼   **cup Sweet-and-Spicy Dressing**
Vegetable cooking spray
2½ **cups Crunchy Pecan Slaw**

1. Light 1 side of grill, heating to 350° to 400° (medium-high) heat; leave other side unlit.

2. Split rolls in half horizontally, and hollow out soft bread from tops and bottoms, leaving a ¼-inch-thick shell. Reserve soft bread for another use, if desired. Sprinkle bottom half of each roll with 1 Tbsp. Swiss cheese.

3. Stir together chicken and Sweet-and-Spicy Dressing in a small bowl. Divide chicken mixture evenly among bottom halves of rolls, and top each with 1 Tbsp. cheese. Cover with top halves of rolls. Lightly coat each sandwich with cooking spray, and wrap with aluminum foil.

4. Place sandwiches over unlit side of grill, and grill, covered with grill lid, 10 to 12 minutes. Unwrap sandwiches, place over unlit side of grill, and grill 5 minutes or until crust is crisp and cheese is melted. Remove from grill, and cut in half.

5. Remove top halves of rolls from sandwiches. Arrange about ½ cup Crunchy Pecan Slaw over chicken and cheese. Cover with top halves of rolls. Serve immediately.

SERVING SIZE 1 sandwich CALORIES 486; FAT 19.9g (sat 5.3g, mono 8.6g, poly 5.1g); PROTEIN 33.2g; CARB 45.2g; FIBER 2.9g; CHOL 72mg; IRON 2.5mg; SODIUM 620mg; CALC 206mg

Sweet-and-Spicy Dressing

MAKES 12 servings   HANDS-ON 5 min.   TOTAL 5 min.

¼   **cup lemon juice**
¼   **cup honey**
2   **Tbsp. hot sauce**
2   **Tbsp. canola oil**
1   **tsp. celery salt**
¼   **tsp. black pepper**

1. Whisk together all ingredients in a small bowl. Store in refrigerator in an airtight container up to 3 days.

SERVING SIZE 1 Tbsp. CALORIES 43; FAT 2.4g (sat 0.2g, mono 1.5g, poly 0.7g); PROTEIN 0.1g; CARB 6.1g; FIBER 0g; CHOL 0mg; IRON 0mg; SODIUM 146mg; CALC 1mg

Crunchy Pecan Slaw

You'll have slaw left over; keep it covered in the fridge, and serve it within a day or two.

MAKES 10 servings   HANDS-ON 20 min.   TOTAL 28 min.

1   **head napa cabbage, cut into thin strips**
1   **Braeburn apple, cut into thin strips**
½   **cup sliced radishes**
½   **cup Sweet-and-Spicy Dressing**
3   **green onions, sliced**
1   **cup chopped toasted pecans**

1. Toss together cabbage and remaining ingredients in a large bowl until blended.

SERVING SIZE 1 cup CALORIES 141; FAT 9.9g (sat 0.9g, mono 5.7g, poly 2.9g); PROTEIN 2.3g; CARB 13.7g; FIBER 3.7g; CHOL 0mg; IRON 0.8mg; SODIUM 136mg; CALC 49mg

Peanut Chicken Pitas

A traditional Southern ingredient, peanuts often star in Asian-inspired recipes such as this one, adding both flavor and extra protein.

MAKES 4 servings   HANDS-ON 15 min.   TOTAL 15 min.

1   **romaine lettuce heart, chopped**
1¼   **cups chopped cooked chicken breast**
¾   **cup frozen snow peas, thawed and trimmed**
¼   **cup shredded carrot**
¼   **cup chopped roasted lightly salted peanuts**
½   **cup light sesame-ginger dressing**
8   **(1-oz.) miniature whole wheat pita rounds, halved**

1. Combine chopped lettuce and next 4 ingredients in a large bowl. Drizzle with sesame-ginger dressing; toss to combine. Fill each pita half evenly with mixture.

Note: We tested with Newman's Own Low Fat Sesame Ginger Dressing and Toufayan Bakeries Hearth Baked Whole Wheat Pitettes Pita Bread.

SERVING SIZE 4 filled mini pita halves CALORIES 326; FAT 9.3g (sat 1.4g, mono 3.9g, poly 2.4g); PROTEIN 22.3g; CARB 40g; FIBER 5.5g; CHOL 37mg; IRON 2.5mg; SODIUM 701mg; CALC 32mg

Chapter Four

GOOD GRAZING

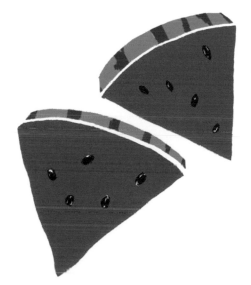

Your stomach is rumbling. It's way past lunch but not quite dinnertime. Before you give in to that bag of chips or box of cookies, take a minute to think about what you really want to eat. Something sweet? Something savory? A little bit of both? Snacking doesn't have to mean diving into a package of pork rinds or MoonPies, hitting up the vending machine, or raiding the office candy bowl. It can be a healthy, nutritious way to satisfy your hunger and give your body all the nutrition it needs.

Your blood sugar (or glucose) naturally dips about three to five hours after you eat a meal. That means **if you wait too long to refuel, you end up feeling ravenous and reach for anything you can get your hands on.** And, usually, the first available is not the healthiest choice. A planned snack can prevent this plunge in blood sugar and keep your metabolism revved up all day long. A recent review of a dozen studies about snacking found it actually can help keep your appetite in check so you don't overeat later.

"Snacking gives you sustained energy, so you can stay alert throughout the day," explains registered dietitian Constance Brown-Riggs, a spokesperson for the Academy of Nutrition and Dietetics in New York who spent childhood summers in North Carolina. "Your brain is the first thing to suffer from a lack of glucose. You can't think straight, you become short-tempered, and you find yourself screaming at colleagues or your kids, all because you're overly hungry."

Eat Up

The smartest snacks are those that **combine some protein** (like yogurt, cheese, meat, nuts) **with some carbs** (whole grains, fruits, vegetables) **and a bit of healthy fats.** Ideally, snacks should have some fiber (at least 2.5 grams) and not a lot of added sugar (less than 5 grams) or sodium (less than 260 milligrams). Having this balance helps fill you up while providing some important nutrients.

Snacking, in fact, can be a key way to help your body get some of these essential nutrients. "For some people, having a snack is really the only way to get in all the important nutrients from foods like fruits and vegetables," adds Brown-Riggs. Research based on data of nearly 16,000 adults in the U.S. found snackers were more likely to meet their daily needs of folic acid, calcium, magnesium, iron, fiber, and other vital nutrients. **Snacking is actually good for the whole family:** Studies have shown that youngsters and teens are far more likely to get more fruit and important nutrients if they snack between meals.

Having some healthy snacks can even help keep your jeans from getting too tight. Snacks can add some structure to your day, especially when you know you're not going to have time for a long, leisurely meal. Research has shown people who skipped meals but snacked—as well

A planned snack can prevent a plunge in blood sugar and keep your metabolism revved up all day long.

as those who ate their meals but still had snacks—were significantly less likely to be overweight or obese compared to those who did not snack between meals.

Planning out your snacks ahead of time is key to helping you make some figure-friendly choices. Preparing recipes like the Hoppin' John Parfaits (page 114) or Peanut Butter Dip (page 111) ahead of time means you have a smart, healthy choice to reach for when that midday hunger strikes. Studies show that afternoon snacks give you the most satisfaction for the fewest amount of calories. Snacking in the afternoon keeps your appetite in check before dinner while still giving you the nutrition and energy boost you need to power through the end of the day. And having a little appetizer while you're making dinner can help you slow down enough to enjoy preparing and eating the main event, rather than rushing through and overindulging.

Size Matters

Of course, eating between meals can have its limitations, especially if your snack turns into a full-size meal, complete with the calories to go with it. As part of an all-around healthy diet, **snacks by definition need to be on the small size (a handful of nuts, not a can full!).** Ideally, your snack should come in at about 200 calories or less. That's still enough to help you feel satisfied, especially if you're choosing from fruits, vegetables, nuts, low-fat dairy, and whole grains. You'll find all these and more in the recipes in this chapter.

The snacks and appetizers in this chapter are designed to be more like mini meals, not just nutritionally, but also in enjoyment. If you're craving a buttermilk chicken-and-waffle dinner or some barbecue pork served up with peaches, you can find their reduced-size (and lower-calorie) versions here.

It may take a few extra minutes to prepare these treats, but many can be made ahead of time and refrigerated or frozen so you always have a healthy snack on hand.

BBQ Peach Summer Rolls

A variety of flavors—sweet, spicy, tart, crisp—comes together in these colorful treats. Make them ahead so you have them on hand to grab and go when you feel like a satisfying snack.

MAKES 16 servings   **HANDS-ON** 35 min.   **TOTAL** 45 min.

Hot water

16 **(8- to 9-inch) round rice paper sheets**

2 **small peaches, peeled and thinly sliced**

16 **Bibb lettuce leaves**

1 **English cucumber, cut into thin strips**

1 **large ripe avocado, thinly sliced**

1 **lb. shredded barbecued pork (without sauce), warm**

1 **Granny Smith apple, peeled and cut into thin strips**

1½ **cups torn fresh mint, cilantro, and basil**

Sweet Pepper-Peanut Sauce

1. Pour hot water to depth of 1 inch into a large shallow dish. Dip 1 rice paper sheet in hot water briefly to soften (about 15 to 20 seconds). Pat dry with paper towels.

2. Place softened rice paper on a flat surface. Place 1 or 2 peach slices in center of rice paper; top with 1 lettuce leaf, 2 cucumber strips, 1 avocado slice, about 3 Tbsp. pork, 3 or 4 apple strips, and 1½ to 2 Tbsp. herbs. Fold sides over filling, and roll up, burrito style. Place roll, seam side down, on a serving platter. Cover with damp paper towels to keep from drying out.

3. Repeat procedure with remaining rice paper and filling ingredients. Serve with Sweet Pepper-Peanut Sauce.

SERVING SIZE 1 roll **CALORIES** 126; **FAT** 6.6g (sat 1.5g, mono 3.5g, poly 1.0g); **PROTEIN** 9.7g; **CARB** 7.9g; **FIBER** 1.7g; **CHOL** 24mg; **IRON** 0.8mg; **SODIUM** 88mg; **CALC** 19mg

Sweet Pepper-Peanut Sauce

MAKES 16 servings   **HANDS-ON** 10 min.   **TOTAL** 10 min.

Stir together ½ **cup sweet pepper relish, ¼ cup salted cocktail peanuts, 1½ Tbsp. fresh lime juice, 2 tsp. lite soy sauce, 2 tsp. toasted sesame oil, 1½ tsp. grated fresh ginger, 1 finely chopped green onion, 1 garlic clove, minced,** and **1 tsp. Asian hot chili sauce (such as Sriracha).** Cover and chill until ready to serve.

SERVING SIZE: about 1 Tbsp. **CALORIES** 30, **FAT** 1.7g (sat 0.2g, mono 1g, poly 0.5g); **PROTEIN** 0.7g; **CARB** 3.4g; **FIBER** 0.1g; **CHOL** 0mg; **IRON** 0mg; **SODIUM** 71mg; **CALC** 3mg

Corncakes
with Tomato-Lima Bean Relish

Top an easy-to-make corncake with a mix of lima beans and tomatoes—you get a little dose of protein and complex carbs for under 100 calories.

MAKES about 2 dozen   **HANDS-ON** 36 min.   **TOTAL** 1 hour, 19 min., including relish

1⅔ cups fresh corn kernels (3 large ears)
½ cup low-fat buttermilk
2   Tbsp. butter, melted
2   large eggs
2   garlic cloves
½ cup all-purpose flour
½ cup plain yellow cornmeal
1   tsp. freshly ground black pepper
¾ tsp. table salt
3   oz. reduced-fat jalapeño-Cheddar cheese, shredded (about ¾ cup)
Tomato-Lima Bean Relish

1. Pulse first 5 ingredients in a food processor 4 to 5 times or just until corn is coarsely chopped.

2. Stir together flour and next 4 ingredients in a large bowl; add corn mixture, stirring just until dry ingredients are moistened.

3. Pour ⅛ cup batter for each corncake onto a hot, lightly greased griddle or large nonstick skillet to form 2-inch cakes (do not spread or flatten cakes). Cook corncakes over medium heat 2 to 3 minutes, until edges start to brown. Turn and cook other side 2 to 3 minutes or until golden brown and edges look dry.

4. Spoon Tomato-Lima Bean Relish onto corncakes.

SERVING SIZE 1 corncake and about 1 Tbsp. relish **CALORIES** 82; **FAT** 3.1g (sat 1.5g, mono 1g, poly 0.3g); **PROTEIN** 3.6g; **CARB** 10.3g; **FIBER** 1g; **CHOL** 23mg; **IRON** 0.6mg; **SODIUM** 213mg; **CALC** 45.3mg

---

Tame Temptation

MY STAY-SLIM SECRET
Betsy LeRoy, age 53, restaurant owner

When you run a restaurant, delicious foods entice at every turn. "I feel tempted all day long," says Betsy LeRoy, owner of Pizza by Elizabeths in Greenville, Delaware, which offers 60 gourmet pizza toppings, including country sausage with rosemary onion sauté. LeRoy typically answers temptation by filling up first on organic field greens. "I try to stick with salads topped with either shrimp or chicken. But sometimes," she admits, "the best way to deal with temptation is to give in." She works off her occasional slices of indulgence at kickboxing or Pilates classes five days a week.

Tomato-Lima Bean Relish

MAKES 1½ cups   **HANDS-ON** 6 min.   **TOTAL** 43 min.

Place **1 cup frozen baby lima beans** and 1 cup water in a medium-size microwave-safe bowl. Cover bowl tightly with heavy-duty plastic wrap; fold back a small edge to allow steam to escape. Microwave at HIGH 15 to 18 minutes or just until beans are tender. Drain; return beans to bowl. Add ½ **cup sliced grape tomatoes, 3 Tbsp. chopped red onion, 1 Tbsp. extra virgin olive oil, 2 tsp. red wine vinegar, 1 tsp. minced fresh garlic, ½ tsp. table salt,** and ¼ **tsp. freshly ground black pepper** to bowl; toss gently. Add **2 Tbsp. chopped fresh dill;** toss gently. Chill until ready to serve.

SERVING SIZE 1 Tbsp. (makes about 1½ cups) **CALORIES** 16; **FAT** 0.6g
(sat 0.1g, mono 0.5g, poly 0.1g); **PROTEIN** 0.6g; **CARB** 2g; **FIBER** 0.5g;
CHOL 0mg; **IRON** 0.2mg; **SODIUM** 70mg; **CALC** 4mg

Fried Green Tomato Sliders

Fresh, firm tomatoes, battered and deep-fried, are another classic Southern comfort food. They get a healthier makeover when coated with panko (Japanese breadcrumbs) and cooked in olive oil.

MAKES 12 servings   **HANDS-ON** 50 min.   **TOTAL** 1 hour, 10 min.

1½ cups shredded red cabbage
1½ cups shredded napa cabbage
1 cup matchstick carrots
⅓ cup thinly sliced red onion
2 Tbsp. olive oil
2 Tbsp. fresh lime juice
½ cup chopped fresh cilantro, divided
½ tsp. table salt
¼ tsp. black pepper
¼ cup canola mayonnaise
2 to 3 tsp. Asian hot chili sauce (such as Sriracha)
12 slider buns or dinner rolls, warmed and split
12 Fried Green Tomatoes

1. Stir together first 6 ingredients and ¼ cup cilantro in a medium bowl. Season with salt and pepper. Let stand 10 minutes.

2. Stir together mayonnaise, hot chili sauce, and remaining ¼ cup cilantro. Spread buns with mayonnaise mixture. Divide tomato and cabbage mixture evenly among bottom halves of buns. Cover with top halves of buns, mayonnaise mixture sides down.

SERVING SIZE 1 slider **CALORIES** 202; **FAT** 7g (sat 0.5g, mono 3.5g, poly 1.9g); **PROTEIN** 6g; **CARB** 30g; **FIBER** 2.2g; **CHOL** 0mg; **IRON** 1.2mg; **SODIUM** 389mg; **CALC** 58mg

Fried Green Tomatoes

MAKES about 20 slices   **HANDS-ON** 30 min.   **TOTAL** 40 min.

Cut **4 medium-size green tomatoes (about 1⅓ lb.)** into ½-inch-thick slices; sprinkle with ½ **tsp. table salt** and ½ **tsp. black pepper**. Let stand 10 minutes. Combine **1 cup self-rising white cornmeal mix** and ½ **cup panko (Japanese breadcrumbs)** in a shallow dish or pie plate. Place ½ **cup all-purpose flour** in a second shallow dish. Whisk **4 large egg whites** in a medium bowl until foamy. Dredge tomato slices in flour, shaking off excess. Dip in egg whites, and dredge in cornmeal mixture. Cook half of tomato slices in **3 Tbsp. olive oil** in a nonstick skillet over medium heat 4 to 5 minutes on each side or until golden brown. Season with salt to taste. Place on a wire rack in a jelly-roll pan, and keep warm in a 225° oven. Repeat procedure with remaining tomato slices and oil.

SERVING SIZE 1 slice **CALORIES** 56; **FAT** 1.4g (sat 0.2g, mono 1.0g, poly 0.2g); **PROTEIN** 1.8g; **CARB** 8.7g; **FIBER** 0.5g; **CHOL** 0mg; **IRON** 0.4mg; **SODIUM** 75mg; **CALC** 4mg

Fruit Salsa with Cinnamon Crisps

Salsa can take many forms, from piquant south-of-the-border dips to nouveau styles featuring exotic spices. This salsa is a delicious take on a fruit salad served with crispy cinnamon-sprinkled pita.

MAKES 5 servings   HANDS-ON 14 min.   TOTAL 20 min.

1   pt. fresh strawberries, chopped
1   large banana, chopped
1   Red Delicious apple, chopped
1   kiwifruit, peeled and chopped
¼   cup fresh lemon juice
¼   cup sugar
¼   tsp. ground nutmeg
1¼   tsp. ground cinnamon, divided
2   pitas, split
Vegetable cooking spray
1   Tbsp. sugar

1. Combine first 4 ingredients. Stir together lemon juice, ¼ cup sugar, nutmeg, and ½ tsp. cinnamon; toss with fruit. Chill.

2. Preheat oven to 350°. Cut each pita half into eighths. Arrange pieces on baking sheets. Lightly coat with cooking spray. Combine remaining ¾ tsp.cinnamon and 1 Tbsp. sugar. Sprinkle over pita chips.

3. Bake at 350° for 6 to 8 minutes or until lightly browned. Serve with fruit salsa.

SERVING SIZE about 6 crisps and about 1 cup salsa CALORIES 165; FAT 0.9g (sat 0.2g, mono 0.2g, poly 0.3g); PROTEIN 3.2g; CARB 38.3g; FIBER 3.8g; CHOL 0mg; IRON 1.1mg; SODIUM 130mg; CALC 46mg

SAVOR THE SOUTH
LINGER LONGER
INDULGE A LITTLE
MAKE IT HAPPEN

Peanuts

Peanuts are used in many ways across the South. But peanuts aren't really nuts. Also called groundnuts or goober peas, peanuts grow underground and are classified as legumes. There are four major peanut varieties: runner, Virginia, Spanish, and Valencia.

Peanut butter is made from roasted peanuts, but the boiled peanuts popular in pockets of the South start with green or raw peanuts. Cooked in their shell in salted water, boiled peanuts are a good snack for a few reasons. Not only are they delicious and nutritious, the time it takes to peel off the shells prevents you from gobbling too many goobers too quickly.

A handful of peanuts (1 ounce or 30 dry roasted) weighs in at 170 calories and packs a fistful of nutrition: vitamin E, niacin, fiber, magnesium, and a whopping 7 grams of protein. (This is why they are offered as a tide-you-over snack on airplanes.)

NO–COOK SOUTHERN SNACKS THAT SATISFY

Want a snack with staying power? Don't just have a piece of fruit. Opt instead for a tasty trio of protein, whole grains, and produce. What you're after is a mix of protein (found in meats, dairy, and nuts) and fiber (from whole grains, fruits, and vegetables).

These two combine to help slow the release of sugar into the bloodstream and keep you feeling satisfied longer. The fats in nuts, avocado, cereals, crackers, cheese, and lean meats such as turkey or roast beef add flavor—and satisfaction, too. Just be careful not to overdo them. (Each gram of fat has 9 calories, more than twice the number of calories per gram of protein and carbohydrate.) For example, choose low-fat cheeses, or limit the serving size to keep your snack under 200 calories total.

So, enjoy orange sections with a handful of granola with nuts. Make a mini cheese plate with grapes, low-fat cheese, and a few whole grain crackers. Dip fresh apple slices into peanut butter, or wash down a crunchy granola bar with a glass of ice-cold fat-free milk.

Need more ideas? Try these Southern-inspired snacks to power you between meals.

BANANAS FOSTER YOGURT PARFAIT
In a glass, layer ½ cup plain fat-free Greek yogurt, ¼ cup banana slices, 1 Tbsp. chopped pecans, and 1 ½ tsp. sorghum syrup or honey — **170 calories**

BREAKFAST ANYTIME
⅓ cup low-fat granola cereal with raisins with ½ cup fat-free milk — **167 calories**

BUTTERMILK & BERRY SMOOTHIE
Blend 1 cup low-fat buttermilk with ½ cup frozen blueberries and ½ cup frozen sliced strawberries — **166 calories**

GOAT CHEESE & ROASTED RED BELL PEPPER QUESADILLA
Spread 1½ oz. goat cheese over 1 (6-inch) corn tortilla, and top with 1 oz. roasted red peppers — **164 calories**

HAM & GREEN TOMATO PITA
Fill 1 (4-inch) whole grain pita with 2 oz. sliced Virginia ham, 2 Tbsp. green tomato chutney, and ½ cup shredded lettuce — **164 calories**

MINI-CORNBREAD PANZANELLA
Make a mini-salad with 2 chopped tomatoes, ½ slice crumbled leftover cornbread, ¼ tsp. black pepper, and 2 Tbsp. low-fat buttermilk drizzled on top — **161 calories**

OPEN-FACED TURKEY & PEPPER JELLY SANDWICH
Top 1 (1-oz.) slice whole grain bread with 1 Tbsp. red pepper jelly, 2 oz. lower sodium turkey breast, and ⅓ cup cucumber slices — **154 calories**

PEANUT BUTTER DIP
Stir together 1 cup plain nonfat yogurt, ½ cup powdered sugar, and ¼ cup creamy reduced-fat peanut butter. Serve with 1 cup apple slices — **195 calories**

PIMIENTO CHEESE & PICKLES
Spread 3 Tbsp. pimiento cheese spread on 1 multigrain rice cake, and top with 3 pickled okra — **154 calories**

PROSCIUTTO & FIG CROSTINI
Place 1 oz. prosciutto and 1 Tbsp. fig preserves on 1 oz. pretzel bread. Top or serve with ¼ cup sliced cantaloupe — **185 calories**

SWEET & SALTY POPCORN MIX
Mix 1½ cups air-popped popcorn with 2 Tbsp. salted peanuts and 1 Tbsp. raisins — **183 calories**

SWEET PEACHES & CORNBREAD
Top ½ slice cornbread with ⅓ cup sliced peaches and 2 Tbsp. crumbled goat cheese — **175 calories**

Veggie-Hummus Rollups

For a throw-together appetizer or snack, prepare the vegetable mixture and keep it on hand in the fridge; then the rollups can be assembled as desired.

MAKES 9 servings   **HANDS-ON** 16 min.   **TOTAL** 26 min.

1   **red bell pepper, cut into thin strips**
1   **zucchini, cut into thin (2-inch) strips**
1   **portobello mushroom cap, cleaned and sliced**
2   **garlic cloves, chopped**
1   **tsp. canola oil**
¼   **tsp. black pepper**
    Vegetable cooking spray
2   **Tbsp. chopped basil**
1   **Tbsp. balsamic vinegar**
3   **Tbsp. refrigerated roasted red pepper hummus**
3   **(6-inch) flour tortillas**
4   **tsp. crumbled feta cheese with basil and sun-dried tomatoes**

1. Toss together first 6 ingredients in a large bowl. Heat a cast-iron grill pan over medium-high heat. Coat pan with cooking spray. Add vegetables to pan; cook 2 minutes on each side or until crisp-tender. Remove vegetables from pan, and return to bowl; sprinkle with basil, and drizzle with vinegar, tossing to coat. Cool 10 minutes.

2. Spread 1 Tbsp. hummus over each tortilla; sprinkle tortillas evenly with cheese. Spoon about ¾ cup vegetables over each tortilla. Roll up, and secure with wooden picks. Cut each rollup crosswise into 6 pinwheels. Serve warm or at room temperature.

SERVING SIZE 2 pinwheels CALORIES 65; FAT 2.2g (sat 0.4g, mono 1g, poly 0.6g); PROTEIN 2.1g; CARB 9.3g; FIBER 1.3g; CHOL 0.9mg; IRON 0.7mg; SODIUM 114mg; CALC 25mg

SAVOR THE SOUTH
LINGER LONGER
INDULGE A LITTLE
MAKE IT HAPPEN

Snack with Purpose

Do you ever hit the bottom of a box, bowl, or bag and wonder, "Did I really eat all of those?" It's easy to snack while answering e-mails, updating Facebook, watching TV, or doing other tasks. But, if you're not careful, your multitasking can make you oblivious to how much you're really packing away.

The first question to ask is: Do I really need a snack? If you're just bored and reaching for something to munch, get yourself some ice water or a glass of tea, and go back to the task at hand. If you truly didn't have enough at your last meal, measure out your snack and take a few dedicated minutes to enjoy it.

Keeping treats out of sight can also help minimize mindless snacking: Studies show that if a bowl of goodies is within arm's reach, you're more likely to mindlessly grab and gobble.

Hoppin' John Parfaits

Southerners traditionally eat Hoppin' John on New Year's Day to bring a year filled with good luck, or anytime they want a hearty meal. This miniature version can be made ahead and stored in the fridge for a quick snack.

MAKES 12 servings   HANDS-ON 30 min.   TOTAL 30 min.

1 **cup uncooked basmati rice**
3 **bacon slices**
1 **cup chopped sweet onion**
1 **jalapeño pepper, seeded and minced**
2 **(15.8-oz.) cans black-eyed peas, drained and rinsed**
1 **large tomato, finely chopped**
2 **green onions, thinly sliced**
1 **celery rib, finely chopped**
¼ **cup chopped parsley**
¼ **cup olive oil**
2 **Tbsp. apple cider vinegar**
½ **cup (2 oz.) shredded pepper Jack cheese**

1. Prepare rice according to package directions.

2. Meanwhile, cook bacon in a medium skillet over medium-high heat 10 to 12 minutes or until crisp. Remove bacon, and drain on paper towels, reserving 1 Tbsp. drippings in skillet. Crumble bacon.

3. Sauté onion and jalapeño pepper in hot drippings 3 to 5 minutes or until lightly browned; stir in black-eyed peas and 1 cup water. Reduce heat to medium, and simmer, stirring occasionally, 5 to 7 minutes or until liquid has almost completely evaporated.

4. Stir together tomato and next 5 ingredients in a small bowl. Evenly layer black-eyed pea mixture, hot cooked rice, and tomato mixture in 12 (7-oz.) glasses. Top with cheese and crumbled bacon.

SERVING SIZE 1 parfait CALORIES 170; FAT 6.4g (sat 1.6g, mono 4g, poly 0.6g); PROTEIN 4.6g; CARB 24.5g; FIBER 2.5g; CHOL 6.3mg; IRON 1.2mg; SODIUM 206mg; CALC 42mg

SAVOR THE SOUTH
LINGER LONGER
INDULGE A LITTLE
MAKE IT HAPPEN

Field Peas

If you grew up pushing peas to the side of your plate and looking for the family dog, it's time to discover new love for the little legumes.

Though green peas or English peas are enjoyed in the South, field peas such as black-eyed peas (often dried) are prized, year-round staples. Because they are an excellent source of protein, fiber, and nutrients, such as folate and potassium, field peas count as both proteins and vegetables.

"I love all kinds of peas," says E.J. Hodgkinson, executive chef at JCT Kitchen & Bar in Atlanta. "Lady peas are my favorite, as well as pink-eyed peas and Sea Island red peas."

Sweet Pea Crostini

Sweet baby peas offer up all the flavor and goodness of spring, but luckily their delightful taste can be found year-round in the freezer aisle. This colorful snack is a tasty nibble after lunch or before supper, or at a cocktail party.

MAKES 20 servings   **HANDS-ON** 15 min.   **TOTAL** 2 hours, 15 min.

2 **(9-oz.) packages frozen sweet peas, thawed**
3 **garlic cloves, chopped**
3 **Tbsp. extra virgin olive oil**
2 **Tbsp. fresh lemon juice**
⅟₁₆ **tsp. table salt**
40 **French bread baguette slices (15 ounces), toasted**
½ **cup (2 oz.) crumbled blue cheese or goat cheese**

1. Place peas and garlic in a food processor; with processor running, pour oil through food chute in a slow, steady stream, processing until smooth. Stir in lemon juice and salt; season with freshly ground black pepper to taste. Cover and chill 2 hours.

2. Spoon pea mixture onto toasted baguette slices; sprinkle with cheese.

SERVING SIZE: 2 crostini CALORIES 107; FAT 2.9g (sat 0.8g, mono 1.8g, poly 0.2g); PROTEIN 3.7g; CARB 16.6g; FIBER 1.6g; CHOL 2mg; IRON 1mg; SODIUM 214mg; CALC 16mg

Make Simple, Healthy Swaps

How'd you like to grow up with New Orleans celebrity chef Emeril Lagasse cooking your family meals? Sisters Jilly Lagasse and Jessie Lagasse Swanson learned a lot about great food from their father. "He taught us so much," says Jessie. "Especially that you have to know about the science and the feel for cooking. You need to have both."

Jessie, a certified public accountant in New Orleans and mother of two, and Jilly, a pastry chef and professional makeup artist who divides her time between New Orleans and London, came together on a culinary project after they were both diagnosed with gluten intolerance.

Their cookbook, *The Gluten-Free Table*, shares delicious gluten-free recipes with an eye toward weight control. "These days, some gluten-free products like boxed cookies can be really high in fat and calories," says Jessie. "I trade out bacon fat for olive oil, and cream for chicken or veggie stock, and I bake foods instead of frying."

Jessie says a lot of traditional New Orleans dishes cooked with tomatoes and the "trinity" of green pepper, celery, and onion fit in just fine with their dietary restrictions and are also figure-friendly. "I like jambalaya with chicken, shrimp, some sausage, and it's full of vegetables. I use very little oil and flavor it with chicken broth."

Jessie was amused to learn that her dad, who famously proclaimed that "pork fat

Jilly Lagasse and Jessie Lagasse Swanson, New Orleans cookbook authors

rules!" on TV, also led cooking classes on "Creole light" cuisine back in the 1980s.

She said her own cooking lesson is that eating more healthfully gets easier the more you do it.

"It takes persistence and perseverance, but after a while it becomes second nature to you."

> ## "I trade out bacon fat for olive oil, and cream for chicken or veggie stock, and I bake foods instead of frying."

Shrimp Boil Skewers

Get the flavor of a shrimp boil without the mess—or the calories! These skewers are perfect for a backyard party and already portioned for you.

MAKES 24 servings   **HANDS-ON** 30 min.   **TOTAL** 1 hour

- **24 (6-inch) wooden skewers**
- **2 Tbsp. butter**
- **¾ cup finely chopped red bell pepper**
- **½ cup finely chopped sweet onion**
- **1 garlic clove, minced**
- **2 cups fresh corn kernels (about 4 medium ears)**
- **½ to ¾ tsp. Creole seasoning**
- **¼ cup chopped fresh flat-leaf parsley**
- **1 Tbsp. red wine vinegar**
- **¼ cup Old Bay seasoning**
- **24 baby red potatoes (about 1 lb.)**
- **½ lb. smoked sausage, cut into 24 slices**
- **24 peeled and deveined, extra-large raw shrimp (about 1¼ lb.)**

1. Soak skewers in water 30 minutes. Melt butter in a medium skillet over medium heat; add bell pepper and next 2 ingredients, and sauté 4 minutes. Stir in corn and Creole seasoning, and sauté 3 minutes. Remove from heat, and stir in parsley and vinegar.

2. Bring Old Bay seasoning and 5 qt. water to a boil, covered, in a large stockpot. Add potatoes, and cook, uncovered, 10 minutes. Add sausage, and cook 3 minutes. Add shrimp; cook 3 minutes or just until shrimp turn pink and potatoes are tender. Drain.

3. Thread 1 potato, 1 shrimp, and 1 sausage piece onto each skewer. Arrange on serving plates or a long shallow platter. Spoon corn mixture over skewers.

SERVING SIZE 1 skewer **CALORIES** 78; **FAT** 3.7g (sat 1.6g, mono 1.5g, poly 0.3g); **PROTEIN** 5.3g; **CARB** 6.3g; **FIBER** 0.7g; **CHOL** 38mg; **IRON** 0.4mg; **SODIUM** 165mg; **CALC** 19mg

---

Rewrite the Recipe

MY STAY-SLIM SECRET
Dana Braun, great-niece of Julia Child

When you're looking for slim alternatives, you can't let a recipe rule you. So says Dana Braun, a pediatric occupational therapist in Atlanta, who has a take-charge, can-do spirit in her very DNA thanks in part to her great-aunt, the culinary icon Julia Child. "One thing handed down in my family was to enjoy good food, savor and respect it," says Braun. But that doesn't mean blind allegiance to a recipe.

Braun uses her creativity to keep flavors she craves while making recipes healthier—cooking green beans with turkey bacon and sautéed onions, for example, and mixing mashed potatoes with mashed cauliflower.

Chicken and Mini Waffles
with Spiced Honey

Chicken and waffles can be an indulgent dinner. This quick-and-easy version uses chicken tenders and a buttermilk batter for a snack-size treat that won't have you loosening your belt.

MAKES 24 servings **HANDS-ON** 10 min. **TOTAL** 1 hour, 3 min.

12 **chicken breast tenders, each cut in half crosswise (1 lb., 10 oz.)**
¾ **cup nonfat buttermilk**
1½ **cups panko (Japanese breadcrumbs)**
½ **tsp. garlic powder**
¼ **tsp. smoked paprika**
¼ **tsp. freshly ground black pepper**
¼ **tsp. table salt**
Vegetable cooking spray
24 **whole grain mini waffles, toasted**
¾ **cup honey**
¾ **tsp. ground cinnamon**
½ **tsp. grated fresh ginger**
½ **tsp. hot sauce**

1. Stir together chicken and buttermilk in a medium bowl. Chill 30 minutes. Place a large baking sheet in oven, and preheat oven to 450°.

2. Place panko in a shallow bowl. Stir together garlic powder and next 3 ingredients. Remove chicken from buttermilk, and pat dry; discard buttermilk.

3. Sprinkle chicken evenly with spice mixture; dredge in panko. Remove baking sheet from oven; coat with cooking spray. Immediately place chicken on hot baking sheet; coat chicken with cooking spray.

4. Bake at 450° for 20 to 25 minutes or until chicken is crisp and lightly browned.

5. Arrange waffles on a wire rack in a jelly-roll pan. Bake at 450° for 3 minutes on each side or until toasted.

6. Meanwhile, stir together honey and next 3 ingredients in a small microwave-safe bowl. Microwave at HIGH 30 seconds or until warm.

7. Place waffles on a serving platter; top waffles with chicken, and drizzle with honey mixture. Serve immediately.

SERVING SIZE 1 waffle, 1 chicken piece, and 1½ tsp. honey mixture **CALORIES** 101; **FAT** 1.5g (sat 0.4g, mono 0.4g, poly 0.3g); **PROTEIN** 7.6g; **CARB** 14.6g; **FIBER** 0.3g; **CHOL** 22mg; **IRON** 0.6mg; **SODIUM** 121mg; **CALC** 15mg

Grilled Watermelon
with Blue Cheese and Prosciutto

Adding a bit of savory blue cheese and salty prosciutto to sweet watermelon makes for a wonderful combination. Brush the watermelon wedges with a bit of oil to keep them from sticking to the grill.

MAKES 12 servings   **HANDS-ON** 20 min.   **TOTAL** 20 min.

3 (½-inch-thick) watermelon rounds, quartered
1 Tbsp. olive oil
⅛ tsp. kosher salt
½ tsp. freshly ground black pepper
2 oz. thinly sliced prosciutto
2 oz. blue cheese, crumbled
Fresh basil leaves
2 tsp. bottled balsamic glaze

1. Preheat grill to 350° to 400° (medium-high) heat. Brush both sides of each watermelon quarter with olive oil, and season with desired amount of salt and pepper. Cut prosciutto into thin strips.

2. Grill watermelon quarters, without grill lid, 1 minute on each side or until grill marks appear.

3. Transfer watermelon to a serving plate; top with blue cheese, prosciutto strips, and fresh basil. Drizzle watermelon with balsamic glaze. Serve immediately.

SERVING SIZE 1 wedge **CALORIES** 44; **FAT** 3g (sat 1.2g, mono 1.2g, poly 0.2g); **PROTEIN** 7g; **CARB** 2g; **FIBER** 0.1g; **CHOL** 7mg; **IRON** 0.2mg; **SODIUM** 213mg; **CALC** 28mg

Do a Mini Makeover

MY STAY-SLIM SECRET
Ty Pennington, 49, design guru

If anyone knows the power of a makeover, it's Atlanta native Ty Pennington, the Los Angeles-based home-design guru and charismatic host of the TV series *Extreme Makeover: Home Edition*.

He says that, just as new ideas can freshen up living spaces, a lighter approach in the kitchen can refresh old recipes. When he's got a hankering for Southern fried oysters or po'boys, he opts instead for a miniature

version: an oyster slider. And to drink? "They drink green tea in LA, but I miss Southern sweet tea," he says. "Today I'd give it a makeover with half sweet and half unsweetened and a fresh sprig of mint."

Pepper Jelly &
Goat Cheese Cakes

In the South, pepper jelly is often served with cream cheese and crackers as a savory snack. This upscale version adds toasted pecans and a touch of hot sauce. Grind pecans in your food processor for the best texture.

MAKES 24 servings   **HANDS-ON** 14 min.   **TOTAL** 2 hours, 44 min.

Miniature paper baking cups

Vegetable cooking spray

¼ **cup Italian-seasoned breadcrumbs**

¼ **cup ground toasted pecans**

2 **Tbsp. grated Parmesan cheese**

2 **Tbsp. butter, melted**

6 **oz. ⅓-less-fat cream cheese, softened**

1 **(3-oz.) goat cheese log, softened**

2 **Tbsp. milk**

1 **Tbsp. Asian hot chili sauce (such as Sriracha)**

1 **large egg**

¼ **cup green pepper jelly**

¼ **cup red pepper jelly**

1. Preheat oven to 350°. Place paper baking cups in 2 (12-cup) miniature muffin pans, and coat with cooking spray. Stir together breadcrumbs and next 3 ingredients in a small bowl; firmly press about 1 tsp. mixture in bottom of each baking cup.

2. Beat cream cheese and goat cheese at medium speed with an electric mixer until light and fluffy. Add milk and next 2 ingredients, beating just until blended. Spoon cheese mixture into baking cups, filling three-fourths full.

3. Bake at 350° for 10 minutes or until set. Remove from oven to a wire rack, and cool completely (about 20 minutes). Remove from pans; place on a serving platter. Cover and chill 2 to 12 hours.

4. Microwave green pepper jelly in a small microwave-safe bowl at HIGH 20 to 25 seconds or until melted. Repeat procedure with red pepper jelly in another small microwave-safe bowl. Spoon 1 tsp. melted green pepper jelly over each of 12 cheesecakes, and 1 tsp. melted red pepper jelly over each of 12 remaining cheesecakes just before serving.

SERVING SIZE 1 cheesecake **CALORIES** 75; **FAT** 4.5g (sat 2.4g, mono 1.0g, poly 0.4g); **PROTEIN** 1.9g; **CARB** 6.6g; **FIBER** 0.2g; **CHOL** 17mg; **IRON** 0.2mg; **SODIUM** 101mg; **CALC** 20mg

Tomato & Feta Cheese Crostini

Just right for a party, you can also reheat leftover crostini in a toaster oven for an afternoon snack.

MAKES 10 servings   **HANDS-ON** 19 min.   **TOTAL** 19 min.

2   **large tomatoes, seeded and diced**
⅛   **tsp. table salt**
1   **tsp. olive oil**
6   **oz. herb-flavored feta cheese, crumbled**
2   **Tbsp. chopped fresh basil**
¼   **tsp. black pepper**
1   **(12-oz.) French bread baguette**
2   **Tbsp. olive oil**
2   **garlic cloves, halved**
Garnish: mixed fresh herb sprigs (such as basil, oregano, and parsley)

1. Preheat grill to 300° to 350° (medium) heat. Stir together tomatoes, salt, and 1 tsp. oil in a bowl. Stir together cheese, basil, and pepper in another bowl.

2. Cut bread diagonally into 20 (½-inch-thick) slices. Brush both sides of bread with 2 Tbsp. olive oil. Grill bread, without grill lid, 2 minutes on each side or until golden. Remove from grill.

3. Rub cut sides of garlic over bread slices. Top bread slices with tomato mixture, and sprinkle with feta mixture.

SERVING SIZE 2 crostini **CALORIES** 174; **FAT** 7.5g (sat 3.2g, mono 3.3g, poly 0.5g); **PROTEIN** 6.4g; **CARB** 22g; **FIBER** 1.1g; **CHOL** 12mg; **IRON** 1.2mg; **SODIUM** 459mg; **CALC** 55mg

---

Always Take the Stairs

MY STAY-SLIM SECRET
Mimi Bean, 50, cookbook author

When you test recipes for a living, it's hard to control the calories "in," so you better increase the calories "out." Mimi Bean, author of *Cooking for Mr. Right,* takes advantage of her Atlanta home's energy-burning layout. "Try living in a four-story townhouse," she says. "I call my place 'the StairMaster house.'" Even outside her home, Bean ignores elevators and escalators in favor of climbing the stairs. Walking up or down the stairs burns about 7 calories a minute, which might not sound like much. But taking the stairs for five minutes a day five days a week can add up to 2.5 pounds of weight loss in a year.

Marinated Shrimp & Artichokes

Southern shrimp shine in this Mediterranean-inspired dish, which is as enjoyable as a filling, make-ahead snack as it is a cocktail party appetizer.

MAKES 16 servings   HANDS-ON 11 min.   TOTAL 11 min., plus 1 day for marinating

¼ **cup white balsamic vinegar**

2 **Tbsp. finely chopped fresh parsley**

2 **Tbsp. finely chopped green onions**

3 **Tbsp. olive oil**

1 **(0.75-oz.) envelope garlic-and-herb dressing mix**

1 **lb. peeled and deveined, large cooked shrimp**

1 **(14-oz.) can quartered artichoke hearts, drained**

2 **oz. feta cheese, cut into ½-inch cubes**

1 **cup large pitted black olives**

1 **cup halved grape tomatoes**

2 **Tbsp. chopped fresh basil**

1. Whisk together first 5 ingredients in a large bowl. Add shrimp and next 4 ingredients; toss gently to coat. Cover and chill 8 to 24 hours, stirring occasionally.

2. Stir in basil just before serving. Serve with a slotted spoon.

Note: We tested with Good Seasons Garlic & Herb Salad Dressing & Recipe Mix.

SERVING SIZE: ¾ cup CALORIES 61; FAT 3.4g (sat 0.7g, mono 2g, poly 0.5g); PROTEIN 4.8g; CARB 2.6g; FIBER 0.1g; CHOL 39mg; IRON 0.4mg; SODIUM 218mg; CALC 35mg

Chapter Five

DINNER BELL

Dinner is the most anticipated meal of the day. It may begin with cocktails and crudités on the veranda or iced tea and conversation in the kitchen long before the sun dips below the horizon. It's a time when families gather at the table, friends catch up over drinks and appetizers, and there's time to sit a spell and relax. On busy nights, it might be a one-pot dish, a reheated casserole, or a quick-fix meal served up in a hurry. But **dinner in the South is often a more languid and leisurely affair,** a social occasion that starts in the kitchen as guests pitch in to help husk the corn, shell the peas, or sample what's simmering on the stove.

When the meal is served, whether it's on paper plates on the patio or fine china in the dining room, it may include juicy tomatoes from the garden drizzled with olive oil, or perhaps a spicy dip made with farm-fresh corn, served up with Cornbread Crab Cakes (page 159) or Honey-Grilled Pork Tenderloins (page 183).

No matter how much time you have or what you're in the mood for, casual or formal, dinner is an opportunity to bring out the very best of your cooking, your crockery—and, of course, your table manners.

The Meat-and-Three Principle

Though the Southern foods typically celebrated beyond the South are meaty—fried chicken, pulled pork, barbecued shrimp, chicken-fried steak—vegetable side dishes take the starring role in a true Southern supper.

Walk into a luncheonette in Nashville, Tennessee, or Jackson, Mississippi, and you're sure to find a "meat-and-three" option on the menu. There are even entire restaurants devoted to the meat-and-three idea, offering a small portion of a meaty main and your choice of three vegetables or starchy sides from a long list or buffet of options. This Southern tradition, popular at both lunch and dinner, dates back to the early 20th century, when impoverished Southerners served up the vegetables they raised (think turnips, field peas, sweet potatoes, and collard greens) along with the "three Ms": meat, meal, and molasses. "The meat was usually a little bit of pork or fatback; the meal was cornmeal, and the molasses was for a little sweetness," notes Marcie Cohen Ferris, Ph.D., an associate professor of American Studies at the University of North Carolina in Chapel Hill.

In a Southern meat-and-three meal, the focus wasn't—and still isn't—on a big slab of meat in the center of the dish. Rather, the meat is an accompaniment to a mostly vegetable-and-grains meal. It's an idea that fits right in with the United States Department of Agriculture (USDA) MyPlate recommendations to fill your plate mostly with fruits, vegetables, and grains, with just a small amount of protein.

Dinner is an opportunity to bring out the very best of your cooking, your crockery—and, of course, your table manners.

Of course, some of the most popular Southern side dishes are also sometimes fried or laden with cream, cheese, and butter. So, what's the best advice for picking those non-meaty sides? "Choose a variety of colors and textures and cooking methods—not all boiled, not all fried, not all raw," suggests registered dietitian Sarah-Jane Bedwell of Nashville.

Many traditional Southern ingredients are very healthy in their simplest forms: beta-carotene-rich sweet potatoes, heart-healthy pecans, antioxidant-rich greens and tomatoes.

When you use herbs more than salt for flavor, and roast, grill, or sauté instead of fry, Bedwell notes, you start to see the healthiest side of Southern food.

Homegrown Goodness

Warm days, rich soil, and a long growing season means there's lots of fresh produce almost all year long throughout the South. Many Southerners keep at least a small garden in their yard from which they can harvest a rich assortment of fruits and vegetables.

"People down in the South have an almost cult-like devotion to fresh tomatoes," notes Southern food historian Sheri Castle. "They don't require a lot of space, and they are one of the easiest things to grow. You can get perfection in just a single pot."

Even in bigger cities like Atlanta or Orlando, many Southerners keep at least a small window box of herbs growing in a sunny spot. In more rural areas you'll often find proud rows of summer squash, cucumbers, snap beans, and zucchini right next to the azaleas. This is a great reminder to eat what's growing, cook something fresh, and cut some flowers for the table.

The Whole (Grain) Story

There's a whole lot being said about whole grains. If you've picked up a health magazine or browsed the Internet lately, you've likely heard that most of us should be eating more whole grains. These are foods that contain the essential parts of the entire grain seed—including the bran, germ, and endosperm. In white flour or white rice, these nutrient-rich ingredients are removed in milling.

Whole grains are important for many reasons, from lowering the risk of chronic diseases like diabetes and heart disease to helping keep your weight at a healthy level and preventing strokes. The Dietary Guidelines for Americans (DGA) recommends we consume three or more servings of whole grains each day.

> In addition to corn, you'll find plenty of other nutritious whole grains on Southern menus, from barley and buckwheat to quinoa and wild rice.

Happily, many delicious Southern dishes are chock-full of whole grains. Take corn: Fresh off the cob; dried and popped on the stove-top; or turned into corncakes, cornmeal, or tortillas, corn is one of the most antioxidant-rich vegetables out there. To make sure you're getting the whole grain variety, look for the term "whole corn" or "whole grain corn" on the label of cornmeal, grits, or polenta. If it says "degermed corn," the most nutritious part (the germ) has been stripped away.

In addition to corn, you'll also find plenty of other nutritious whole grains on Southern menus, from barley and buckwheat to quinoa and wild rice. Brown rice is considered a whole grain, along with black or red rice. Though long-grain white rice is popular in the South, it's generally considered less nutritious than its brown cousin because the bran and germ of the rice have been removed. A Harvard School of Public Health study estimates that replacing about two servings a week of white rice with brown rice can lower your risk of diabetes by 16 percent.

Spicing It Up

At many Southern restaurants, including "farm-to-table" eateries, you'll find a range of tasty condiments already waiting for you at the table: a jar of green tomato or cabbage chowchow, a crock of homemade pickles, a bottle of hot sauce, or hot peppers packed in vinegar.

In South Florida, fruit salsas made with mango and jalapeño enliven meats, poultry, and fish. "We like to doctor up our own plates and add our own finishing touches," says Southern food expert Castle. "Everyone likes their dish done a little differently."

You don't need to add a lot of sodium to get the job done. Southern cooking often gets spiced up with vinegar, ground red pepper, or even a squeeze of lemon to add flavor without salt. "Adding a little acidity to a dish, whether that's through vinegar or a little bit of citrus, boosts flavor without calories or sodium," adds Castle. "It gives a dish that seems flat a whole new taste."

The dishes in this chapter come preloaded with plenty of flavor. From slaw to salad, sides to main courses, beans to barbecue, now's your chance to dig into the many tastes and textures that can be found in a healthy Southern supper. It's dinnertime!

Let Local Seafood and Vegetables Shine

From heirloom tomatoes and Bayou Le Batre shrimp to field peas with a touch of smoked bacon, foods from local farmers, fishermen, and foragers figure prominently on the menu at Chris Hastings's Hot and Hot Fish Club in Birmingham, Alabama.

Winner of the James Beard Foundation Award for Best Chef in the South, and conqueror of chef Bobby Flay on the Food Network's *Iron Chef* competition, Hastings believes the secret to healthy and contemporary Southern cooking is keeping it grounded in fresh, local ingredients.

"As a 20-year advocate for local sourcing," he says, "I can tell you there's never been a better time to access the best ingredients."

Acknowledging the nationwide farm-to-table culinary trend, Hastings applauds the popularity of farmers' markets and groceries that bring more locally sourced meats, cheese, vegetables, and seafood.

"Your ability to access healthier options are numerous," says Hastings. "The support of this movement and its evolution will guarantee better and more affordable choices for all of our communities over time, which will lead to healthier communities for everyone."

Giving vegetables star billing is a Southern food trend Hastings enthusiastically supports with mouthwatering items on the menu at Hot and Hot: grilled Vidalia onions with basil lime

Chris Hastings, Birmingham chef

vinaigrette, black lentil tabbouleh, and freshly dug potatoes with buttermilk gravy. "There's a renewed excitement for vegetables, grains, and healthy cooking techniques that tip the balance back to our beloved vegetables and a healthier relationship to meat generally," he says.

Treating those ingredients right and celebrating their inherent deliciousness is the first step to better eating in the South: "Forgive my Southern speak but, if it ain't delicious, it ain't going to fly, period."

"I can tell you there's never been a better time to access the best ingredients."

Broccoli Slaw with Candied Pecans

Broccoli and cabbage are what I like to call "humble heroes"—they contain powerful compounds associated with heart health and cancer prevention. You can substitute toasted pecan pieces for the glazed, since pecans are naturally slightly sweet.

MAKES 10 servings   **HANDS-ON** 15 min.   **TOTAL** 1 hour, 15 min.

⅓ **cup thinly sliced green onions**

⅓ **cup canola mayonnaise**

⅓ **cup plain fat-free yogurt**

¼ **cup sugar**

¼ **cup red wine vinegar**

1 **tsp. lemon zest**

¼ **tsp. table salt**

⅛ **tsp. ground red pepper**

1 **(12-oz.) package fresh broccoli florets, coarsely chopped**

4 **cups thinly sliced napa cabbage (Chinese cabbage)**

¼ **cup golden raisins**

2 **tsp. chopped praline pecans**

1. Whisk together first 8 ingredients in a large bowl. Add broccoli, cabbage, and raisins; toss to coat. Cover and chill 1 hour. Sprinkle with 2 tsp. pecans.

Note: We tested with Hoody's Deep South Praline Pecans.

SERVING SIZE ¾ cup slaw and about 2 tsp. pecans CALORIES 157; FAT 10.8g (sat 0.6g, mono 6.1g, poly 3.1g); PROTEIN 2.9g; CARB 14.5g; FIBER 2.7g; CHOL 2.8mg; IRON 0.4mg; SODIUM 150mg; CALC 48mg

Butternut Squash Soup
with a Kick

Liven up an American classic with favorite Southern flavors: Ginger and jalapeño add a pleasant punch of heat.

MAKES 8 servings   HANDS-ON 25 min.   TOTAL 1 hour, 20 min.

1   leek
1¼ cups chopped celery
⅔   cups chopped carrot
1   Tbsp. chopped fresh
     ginger
1   Tbsp. seeded and
     chopped jalapeño
     pepper
2   tsp. olive oil
1   (1¾-lb.) butternut
     squash, peeled and cut
     into 1-inch cubes
4   cups reduced-sodium
     fat-free chicken broth
1   cup fat-free
     half-and-half
¼   tsp. table salt
¼   tsp. freshly ground
     black pepper

1. Remove root, tough outer leaves, and tops from leek, leaving 1 inch of dark leaves. Rinse thoroughly under cold running water to remove grit and sand. Chop leek to measure 1½ cups.

2. Sauté leek, celery, and next 3 ingredients in hot oil in a Dutch oven over medium heat 10 to 15 minutes or until tender.

3. Add butternut squash and chicken broth; bring to a boil. Cover, reduce heat, and simmer 30 minutes or until squash is tender. Remove from heat; let cool 10 minutes.

4. Process squash mixture, in batches, in a blender or food processor until smooth, stopping to scrape down sides as needed. Return to Dutch oven; stir in half-and-half, salt, and pepper.

5. Cook mixture over medium heat, stirring often, 5 minutes or until thoroughly heated.

SERVING SIZE 1 cup CALORIES 109; FAT 2.0g (sat 0.4g, mono 1.2g, poly 0.4g); PROTEIN 3.8g; CARB 19.3g; FIBER 2.8g; CHOL 0mg; IRON 1.3mg; SODIUM 166mg; CALC 89mg

Grilled Green Tomato Caprese

Southerners know green tomatoes don't have to be fried. We also pickle them or use them in jams and chutneys. This play on Caprese salad uses grilled green tomatoes instead of ripe red ones.

MAKES 12 servings   HANDS-ON 17 min.   TOTAL 1 hour, 17 min.

¼ **cup olive oil**
¼ **cup white balsamic vinegar**
1 **Tbsp. brown sugar**
⅛ **tsp. salt**
2 **garlic cloves, minced**
7 **medium-size green tomatoes, cut into ¼-inch-thick slices (about 2⅓ lb.)**
6 **oz. fresh mozzarella cheese pearls**
¼ **tsp. kosher salt**
¼ **tsp. freshly ground black pepper**
⅓ **cup thinly sliced fresh basil**

1. Combine first 5 ingredients in a large zip-top plastic bag; add tomatoes, seal, and shake gently to coat. Chill 1 hour.

2. Preheat grill to 350° to 400° (medium-high) heat. Remove tomatoes from marinade, reserving marinade. Grill tomatoes, covered with grill lid, 3 to 4 minutes on each side or until tender and grill marks appear.

3. Arrange slices of warm grilled tomatoes on a large, shallow platter, and top with mozzarella cheese pearls. Drizzle with reserved marinade; sprinkle with salt and pepper. Sprinkle with basil.

SERVING SIZE 3 tomato slices, ½ oz. cheese, and 2 tsp. dressing
CALORIES 106; FAT 8.0g (sat 2.6g, mono 4.2g, poly 0.7g); PROTEIN 3.3g; CARB 5.9g; FIBER 0.8g; CHOL 12mg; IRON 0.5mg; SODIUM 84mg; CALC 15mg

Balance Fried with Fresh

MY STAY-SLIM SECRET
Tony Conway, age 57, caterer

How would you like to be invited to 2,000 parties a year? That's the life for Tony Conway, owner of A Legendary Event catering company in Atlanta. His menus range from black-tie fancy to garden-party fresh, and Conway's never far from his Texas-boy roots.

"My favorite food is fried chicken," he says. To keep the indulgences in check, he always balances a splurge with something slim, like a fresh salad or a healthy dose of collard greens with that fried chicken. Another healthy lesson Conway shares: To avoid leftovers and waste, cook only what you need for the meal at hand.

Grilled Okra and Tomatoes

A classic pair, okra and tomatoes are often seen stewed together. Here, put both on the grill to develop a charred flavor.

MAKES 4 servings   **HANDS-ON** 10 min.   **TOTAL** 10 min.

1   lb. fresh okra, trimmed
1   pt. cherry tomatoes
2   Tbsp. olive oil
¼   tsp. table salt
½   tsp. black pepper
Vegetable cooking spray
2   Tbsp. chopped fresh
      basil

1. Combine first 5 ingredients in a large bowl.

2. Coat cold cooking grate of grill with cooking spray, and place on grill. Preheat grill to 350° to 400° (medium-high) heat. Place okra and tomatoes on cooking grate, and grill tomatoes, covered with grill lid, 3 minutes or just until they begin to pop. At the same time, grill okra, covered with grill lid, 2 to 3 more minutes or until tender.

3. Transfer okra and tomatoes to a serving dish, and sprinkle with basil. Serve immediately.

SERVING SIZE about 1 cup **CALORIES** 110; **FAT** 7g (sat 1g, mono 5g, poly 0.8g); **PROTEIN** 3g; **CARB** 11g; **FIBER** 5g; **CHOL** 0mg; **IRON** 1.2mg; **SODIUM** 161mg; **CALC** 103mg

SAVOR THE SOUTH
LINGER LONGER
INDULGE A LITTLE
MAKE IT HAPPEN

Okra

Ask about okra and you'll get mixed reactions. Some love it; others loathe it. The biggest objection: the slime. The edible green pods of the okra plant contain sugars and proteins that mix when heated to form mucilage, a substance that even sounds gooey. But this slimy compound is full of good stuff. It's a soluble fiber (like the kind in oatmeal) that helps lower blood cholesterol and improve digestive health. Okra's also a good source of fiber, vitamin C, vitamin K, and folate, and weighs in at just 25 calories per cup.

Large okra can be woody and aren't as tasty, so choose little pods (no longer than 4 inches). Quick frying, long cooking, and pickling all reduce the slime factor.

In the South, okra is often battered in cornmeal and fried, stewed with tomatoes, added to soups and gumbos as a thickener, or pickled for a cold, crunchy treat.

"Grilled okra makes believers of us all," adds Atlanta-based food stylist Gena Berry. She spritzes okra with olive oil and gives it a quick char on a hot grill just until grill marks appear. "Follow with a sprinkle of salt," she says, "and there's no slime."

Herbed Tomato-Zucchini Tart

This simple vegetable tart uses wonderful summer produce from the farmers' market or your garden. Beneath the veggies is a decadent layer of cheese. Serve with sliced grilled chicken to round out your meal.

MAKES 8 servings   HANDS-ON 12 min.   TOTAL 1 hour, 7 min.

- ½ **(14.1-oz.) package refrigerated piecrusts**
- 1 **large zucchini, cut into ¼-inch-thick slices**
- 2 **plum tomatoes, cut into ¼-inch-thick slices**
- **Vegetable cooking spray**
- ¼ **tsp. garlic powder**
- ⅓ **cup light garlic-and-herbs spreadable cheese, softened**
- 4 **ounces goat cheese (about ½ cup), softened**
- 8 **pitted kalamata olives, chopped**
- 1 **Tbsp. extra virgin olive oil**
- ¼ **tsp. freshly ground black pepper**
- 2 **Tbsp. small fresh basil leaves**

1. Preheat oven to 400°. Fit piecrust into a 9-inch tart pan with removable bottom; press into fluted edges. Fold any excess dough over outside of pan, and pinch to secure to pan. Line pastry with aluminum foil, and fill with pie weights or dried beans. Bake at 400° for 20 minutes or until edges are lightly browned. Remove from oven to a wire rack; remove weights and foil. Cool completely on a wire rack (about 20 minutes).

2. Arrange zucchini and tomato slices in a single layer on a baking sheet coated with cooking spray; lightly coat vegetables with cooking spray. Sprinkle vegetables with garlic powder. Bake at 400° for 15 minutes or until tender.

3. Stir together spreadable cheese and goat cheese in a small bowl; spread over bottom of piecrust. Arrange cooked zucchini and tomato slices, alternately, in concentric circles over cheese mixture; sprinkle with olives. Drizzle with olive oil; sprinkle with pepper and basil leaves.

Note: We tested with Rondelé light garlic-and-herb spreadable cheese.

SERVING SIZE ⅛ tart CALORIES 193; FAT 13.4g (sat 6.1g, mono 6.0g, poly 0.8g); PROTEIN 4.9g; CARB 13.9g; FIBER 0.6g; CHOL 14mg; IRON 0.5mg; SODIUM 299mg; CALC 44mg

Lemon-Herb Cornmeal Madeleines

These savory madeleines are a perfect partner for grilled fish, chicken, and salads—and their small size keeps portions in check. If you bake them in batches, be sure to keep the batter in the fridge while the first batch is in the oven.

MAKES 2 dozen   HANDS-ON 6 min.   TOTAL 58 min.

1   **cup self-rising white cornmeal mix**
¼   **cup all-purpose flour**
3   **Tbsp. sugar**
1   **tsp. lemon zest**
1   **tsp. fresh lemon juice**
1½ **tsp. finely chopped fresh thyme**
1   **cup nonfat buttermilk**
¼   **cup butter, melted**
2   **large egg whites**

1. Preheat oven to 400°. Whisk together first 6 ingredients in a large bowl. Whisk together buttermilk, melted butter, and egg whites; add to dry mixture, stirring just until moistened.

2. Spoon batter into lightly greased and floured shiny madeleine pans, filling three-fourths full.

3. Bake at 400°, in batches, 12 minutes or until golden brown. Remove from pans immediately. Serve warm, or cool completely on wire racks (20 minutes).

SERVING SIZE 1 madeleine CALORIES 58; FAT 1.9g (sat 1.2g, mono 0.5g, poly 0.1g); PROTEIN 1.3g; CARB 8.5g; FIBER 0.2g; CHOL 5mg; IRON 0.2mg; SODIUM 32mg; CALC 14mg

SAVOR THE SOUTH
LINGER LONGER
INDULGE A LITTLE
MAKE IT HAPPEN

License to Dine

Lots of us have trouble navigating restaurant menus to find healthy options. But all you really need is a little diners' education.

Start by mapping out your choices. Use online menus to help plan a safe route, especially if it's your first visit. Read the menu, and listen carefully when servers list the specials. (Seafood, vegetables, and grilled dishes are usually good places to start.)

Next, use your mirrors. Get a visual on portions by looking at the plates on other tables. Way too large? See if you can get a half portion, box up half to take home, or split a plate with your tablemate.

Ask questions: If the "chicken with spring greens" comes with only a wisp of lettuce, you might want the shrimp-topped salad instead.

Signal your intentions: Be specific about what you want or don't want. For example, "Can you lightly brush the fish with oil?" or "Please ask the chef not to salt my food."

Turnip Greens Stew

Greens and beans are traditional Southern recipe partners for a delicious and nutritious meal. And yes, ham is considered a lean protein.

MAKES 6 servings   HANDS-ON 5 min.   TOTAL 30 min.

2   **cups chopped cooked ham**
1   **Tbsp. vegetable oil**
3   **cups chicken broth**
2   **(16-oz.) packages frozen chopped turnip greens**
1   **(10-oz.) package frozen diced onion, red and green bell peppers, and celery**
1   **tsp. sugar**
1   **tsp. seasoned pepper**

1. Sauté ham in hot oil in a Dutch oven over medium-high heat 5 minutes or until lightly browned. Add broth and remaining ingredients; bring to a boil. Cover, reduce heat to low, and simmer, stirring occasionally, 25 minutes.

Note: We tested with McKenzie's Seasoning Blend for frozen diced onion, red and green bell peppers, and celery. You may substitute 1 chopped onion, 1 chopped red bell pepper, 1 chopped green bell pepper, and 1 chopped celery rib.

SERVING SIZE 1⅓ cups CALORIES 149; FAT 4.7g (sat 1.2g, mono 1.9g, poly 1.3g); PROTEIN 10.6g; CARB 11.9g; FIBER 3.4g; CHOL 19mg; IRON 1.5mg; SODIUM 642mg; CALC 159mg

SAVOR THE SOUTH
LINGER LONGER
INDULGE A LITTLE
MAKE IT HAPPEN

Greens

On New Year's Day, Southerners traditionally eat greens (along with cornbread and black-eyed peas) for good luck and good fortune in the coming year. Greens—which include collard greens, turnip greens, mustard greens, and kale—don't just symbolize money. They are valuable for good health, too.

These slightly bitter vegetables are members of the Brassica family (think cabbage, broccoli, and Brussels sprouts). Their dark green leaves serve up a garden of nutrients including vitamin A, calcium, B vitamins, and sulfur-containing phytonutrients and antioxidants associated with fighting cancer.

Greens are a calorie bargain (40 calories per cup raw), and an excellent source of vitamin C when eaten raw or consumed with their cooking liquid. Known as "pot likker," and traditionally sopped up with cornbread, this liquid is a good source of water-soluble nutrients that leach out of the leaves.

Peach-Ginger Slaw

This is sweet, spicy, and savory all in one crunchy dish! Peanuts, pepper jelly, peaches, and fresh ginger offer a truly Southern blend of flavors.

MAKES 10 servings   HANDS-ON 10 min.   TOTAL 10 min.

3   **Tbsp. pepper jelly**
¼   **cup rice wine vinegar**
1   **Tbsp. dark sesame oil**
1   **tsp. grated fresh ginger**
¼   **cup canola oil**
¼   **tsp. table salt**
1   **(16-oz.) package shredded coleslaw mix**
2   **peaches, unpeeled and coarsely chopped (about 1⅓ cups)**
¼   **cup chopped unsalted, dry-roasted peanuts**

1. Microwave jelly in a large microwave-safe bowl at HIGH 15 seconds or until melted. Whisk in vinegar and next 2 ingredients. Gradually add canola oil in a slow, steady stream, whisking constantly until smooth. Stir in salt.

2. Add coleslaw mix and peaches, tossing gently to coat. Sprinkle with peanuts. Serve immediately, or cover and chill up to 8 hours, sprinkling with peanuts just before serving.

SERVING SIZE ½ cup CALORIES 127; FAT 8.9g (sat 0.9g, mono 5g, poly 2.7g); PROTEIN 1.7g; CARB 10.7g; FIBER 1.9g; CHOL 0mg; IRON 0.2mg; SODIUM 73mg; CALC 25mg

Okra-and-Corn Maque Choux

Head for southern Louisiana and you're likely to find maque choux (say it "mock-shoe") on the menu. Use fresh corn and okra for best results. Not into spicy food? You can easily trade the hot sausage for a milder version.

MAKES 8 servings   HANDS-ON 28 min.   TOTAL 28 min.

Sauté ¼ **lb. spicy smoked sausage, diced,** in a large skillet over medium-high heat 3 minutes or until browned. Add ½ **cup chopped sweet onion,** ½ **cup chopped green bell pepper,** and **2 minced garlic cloves,** and sauté 5 minutes or until tender. Add **3 cups fresh corn kernels, 1 cup sliced fresh okra,** and **1 cup peeled, seeded, and diced tomato (½ lb.);** cook, stirring often, 10 minutes. Season with ¼ **tsp. table salt** and ¼ **tsp. freshly ground black pepper.**

Note: We tested with Conecuh Original Spicy and Hot Smoked Sausage.

SERVING SIZE ½ cup CALORIES 110; FAT 5g (sat 1.7g, mono 2.1g, poly 0.8g); PROTEIN 5g; CARB 14g; FIBER 2g; CHOL 10mg; IRON 0.6mg; SODIUM 186mg; CALC 23mg

Greens-and-Beans Risotto

Collards are usually cooked all by their lonesome, maybe with a bit of bacon, but this recipe turns them into a main dish, as an elegant brown rice risotto with beans and greens.

MAKES 8 servings   HANDS-ON 5 min.   TOTAL 37 min.

1   **Tbsp. table salt**
1   **(16-oz.) package chopped fresh collard greens**
1   **cup chopped onion (about 1 large)**
3   **large garlic cloves, minced**
1   **Tbsp. olive oil**
3   **cups chicken broth**
2   **Tbsp. all-purpose flour**
1   **(15.5-oz.) can cannellini beans, drained and rinsed**
½   **tsp. table salt**
¼   **tsp. freshly ground black pepper**
1   **(3.5-oz.) bag brown rice**
½   **tsp. dried crushed red pepper**
¾   **cup grated Parmesan cheese, divided**
Garnish: ¼ cup chopped fresh parsley

1. Bring 4 qt. water to a boil in a large Dutch oven. Add 1 Tbsp. salt, and stir until dissolved. Add collard greens to Dutch oven, and cook 2 minutes or until wilted. Drain greens in colander; rinse with cold water. Drain and pat dry with paper towels. Set aside.

2. Sauté onion and garlic in hot oil in Dutch oven over medium heat 3 to 4 minutes or until tender.

3. Whisk together chicken broth and flour; add to Dutch oven, and bring to a boil, whisking frequently. Add cannellini beans, ½ tsp. salt, pepper, and reserved collard greens. Simmer, uncovered, 5 minutes. Reduce heat to low, and stir in rice and red pepper. Simmer, stirring frequently, 10 minutes or until greens and rice are tender. Remove from heat, and stir in ½ cup Parmesan cheese.

4. Sprinkle each serving with remaining ¼ cup cheese. Serve immediately.

SERVING SIZE ¾ cup CALORIES 171; FAT 5g (sat 1.6g, mono 1.3g, poly 1.2g); PROTEIN 10g; CARB 23g; FIBER 5g; CHOL 8mg; IRON 1mg; SODIUM 385mg; CALC 189mg

Roasted Red Bliss Potato Salad

Potato salad gets gussied up with a French accent, thanks to Dijon mustard, crème fraîche (a cultured cream with a high content of butterfat), and Champagne vinegar (you can substitute white wine vinegar).

MAKES 9 servings   HANDS-ON 9 min.   TOTAL 39 min.

2　lb. small Red Bliss potatoes, quartered
2　Tbsp. olive oil
⅓　cup crème fraîche
3　Tbsp. Champagne vinegar or white wine vinegar
2　Tbsp. minced shallots
1　tsp. fresh lemon juice
1　tsp. Dijon mustard
½　tsp. table salt
¼　tsp. freshly ground black pepper
2　Tbsp. chopped fresh chives
1　Tbsp. chopped fresh parsley

1. Preheat oven to 400°. Toss together potatoes and oil; place in a single layer on a jelly-roll pan. Bake at 400° for 30 to 35 minutes or until lightly browned.

2. Meanwhile, whisk together crème fraîche and next 6 ingredients in a large bowl. Remove potatoes from oven, and add to crème fraîche mixture. Add chives and parsley, tossing gently to coat.

SERVING SIZE ½ cup CALORIES 130; FAT 6.2g (sat 2.4g, mono 2.8g, poly 0.5g); PROTEIN 2.3g; CARB 16.6g; FIBER 1.8g; CHOL 8.3mg; IRON 0.8mg; SODIUM 157mg; CALC 12mg

Personalize Your Plate

MY STAY-SLIM SECRET
Lanier Dabruzzi, age 29, registered dietitian

If you don't like beets and can't live without bacon, design a healthy eating plan that suits you. "We personalize everything here in the South, from monogrammed towels to initials on our back car windows," says Lanier Dabruzzi. "So why wouldn't we personalize our diets?" The Atlanta-based registered dietitian puts the "My" into the USDA's MyPlate diet advice by choosing Southern options for lean meat, grains, fruits, vegetables, and low-fat dairy. "I could have Cajun-seasoned South Carolina shrimp, sweet corn on the cob, and a strawberry and spinach salad—with a low-fat banana pudding (made with milk) for dessert."

Buy Whole Ingredients, Use Every Last Bit

Boneless, skinless chicken breasts may be quick and easy to cook, but Hugh Acheson isn't looking for easy. The award-winning Georgia chef and cookbook author with restaurants in Athens and Atlanta wants maximum taste and value for food cost, so he encourages folks to buy and cook the whole bird.

"You'll get deeper flavors (from cooking on the bone)," he says. "And if I butcher the whole chicken, I get breasts, wings, thighs, oysters, giblets, and three quarts of stock all for close to the cost of buying chicken stock made by someone else."

The idea behind nose-to-tail cooking, a term coined to describe using all parts of the pig, is extending to other foods. Even vegetable scraps such as carrot tops and onion trimmings are used to season broths. Acheson says Southern cooking has a long history of this kind of frugality. "It was a very economically minded cuisine," he says, "where nothing was wasted."

Acheson also encourages taking time to cook: "Understand the beauty of slow roasting a pork shoulder," he says. "It takes longer than pork chops but you retain moisture cooking on the bone, and it's fun to cook that way." Acheson, author of *A New Turn in the South*, is recognized as a leader in the farm-to-table restaurant movement.

At his Five & Ten eatery in Athens, you're just as likely to see a farmer enjoying dinner

Hugh Acheson,
Georgia chef and cookbook author

as a University of Georgia professor or a member of the band R.E.M.

Whether Acheson's pickling tomatoes or grilling pasture-raised poultry, he seeks out foods raised carefully by local farmers. He says that quality ingredients might cost a bit more up front, but they often taste better and stretch further. When the ingredient is this delicious, you're less likely to let any part of it go to waste.

"A pork shoulder takes longer than pork chops, but you retain moisture cooking on the bone."

Slow-Cooker Veggie Chili

Corn, beans, and squash are known as the Three Sisters in Native American agriculture because they can be grown at the same time in the same soil. This tasty, easy recipe makes enough to feed you and up to 15 sisters.

MAKES 16 servings   HANDS-ON 20 min.   TOTAL 8 hours, 20 min.

4   **medium carrots, diced (1 cup)**
2   **celery ribs, diced (½ cup)**
1   **medium-size sweet onion, diced (1¼ cups)**
Vegetable cooking spray
2   **(8-oz.) packages cremini mushrooms, quartered**
1   **large zucchini, chopped (2 cups)**
1   **yellow squash, chopped (1 cup)**
2   **Tbsp. chili powder**
1   **Tbsp. ground cumin**
1   **tsp. seasoned pepper**
¼   **tsp. salt**
1   **(16-oz.) can pinto beans, drained and rinsed**
1   **(16-oz.) can kidney beans, drained and rinsed**
1   **(15.5-oz.) can cannellini beans, drained and rinsed**
1   **(15-oz.) can black beans, drained and rinsed**
3   **(14.5-oz.) cans diced tomatoes, undrained**
1   **(8-oz.) can tomato sauce**
1   **cup frozen whole kernel corn, thawed**
2   **cups fully cooked, shelled fresh edamame (green soybeans)**
1   **cup (4 oz.) shredded sharp Cheddar cheese**

1. Sauté first 3 ingredients in a large nonstick skillet coated with cooking spray over medium-high heat 10 minutes or until onions are tender. Transfer to a 6-qt. slow cooker.

2. Add mushrooms, zucchini, and squash to skillet; sauté over medium-high 3 minutes. Add chili powder and next 3 ingredients; sauté 5 more minutes. Transfer to slow cooker.

3. Add pinto beans and next 7 ingredients to slow cooker; stir well. Cover and cook on LOW 8 hours.

4. Ladle chili into bowls; top each serving with cheese.

Note: Cool leftovers, and freeze in plastic freezer containers or zip-top plastic freezer bags for up to two months.

SERVING SIZE 1 cup chili and 1 Tbsp. cheese CALORIES 161; FAT 3.5g (sat 1.6g, mono 0.8g, poly 0.6g); PROTEIN 9.8g; CARB 22.8g; FIBER 6.1g; CHOL 6mg; IRON 2.2mg; SODIUM 495mg; CALC 115mg

Texas Caviar Rice and Beans

This Lone Star State favorite can be prepared ahead easily. Serve it with rice as a hearty main vegetarian dish, or use it as a dip for tailgating and other informal get-togethers.

MAKES 6 servings   HANDS-ON 20 min.   TOTAL 43 min.

1 **(15.8-oz.) can black-eyed peas, drained and rinsed**

1 **(15-oz.) can no-salt-added black beans, drained and rinsed**

⅓ **cup finely chopped roasted red bell peppers**

¼ **cup seeded and finely chopped poblano pepper**

Texas Vinaigrette

2 **(8.8-oz.) pouches fully cooked basmati rice**

⅔ **cup thinly sliced celery**

¾ **cup (3 oz.) shredded pepper Jack cheese**

1¼ **cups chopped tomatoes**

¾ **cup loosely packed fresh cilantro leaves**

⅓ **cup thinly sliced green onions**

6 **oz. tortilla chips**

Garnish: sliced pickled jalapeño peppers

1. Stir together first 5 ingredients in a medium-size microwave-safe glass bowl; let stand 20 minutes, stirring occasionally. Microwave at HIGH 2 minutes or until thoroughly heated, stirring at 30-second intervals.

2. Heat rice according to package directions; fluff with a fork. Layer rice, bean mixture, celery, cheese, tomato, cilantro, and green onions in 2-qt. trifle bowl or straight-sided bowl. Serve with tortilla chips.

Note: We tested with Tasty Bite Basmati Rice.

SERVING SIZE about 1 cup rice-bean mixture and 1 oz. tortilla chips CALORIES 451; FAT 18.9g (sat 4.3g, mono 8.2g, poly 4.4g); PROTEIN 12.8g; CARB 58.8g; FIBER 8.3g; CHOL 15mg; IRON 3.9mg; SODIUM 371mg; CALC 182mg

Texas Vinaigrette

You'll need only half of this dressing for the Texas Caviar Rice and Beans. Store the remainder in an airtight container in the refrigerator for up to one week.

MAKES 7 Tbsp.   HANDS-ON 3 min.   TOTAL 3 min.

Whisk together **3 Tbsp. olive oil, 2 Tbsp. fresh lime juice, 1½ Tbsp. chopped fresh cilantro, 1½ Tbsp. hot sauce, 1 minced garlic clove, ¼ tsp. chili powder,** and **¼ tsp. ground cumin** in a small bowl.

SERVING SIZE about 1 Tbsp. CALORIES 53; FAT 5.9g (sat 0.8g, mono 4.2g, poly 0.6g); PROTEIN 0.1g; CARB 0.6g; FIBER 0.1g; CHOL 0mg; IRON 0.1mg; SODIUM 30mg; CALC 2mg

Bloody Mary Tomato Salad
with Quick Pickled Shrimp

Brunch is so good you could have it all day. You don't even have to add the alcohol to enjoy this dish! Chilled shrimp and tangy Bloody Mary mix make a perfect pairing with hearty fresh tomatoes.

MAKES 6 servings   HANDS-ON 16 min.   TOTAL 3 hours, 16 min.

Quick Pickled Shrimp
Bloody Mary Vinaigrette
3 **lb. assorted tomatoes, sliced**
⅓ **cup diagonally sliced celery**
½ **cup firmly packed celery leaves**
Garnishes: chilled pickled dilly green beans, lemon slices, fresh flat-leaf parsley

1. Prepare Quick Pickled Shrimp and Bloody Mary Vinaigrette.

2. Arrange tomatoes and sliced celery on a large chilled platter; drizzle with Bloody Mary Vinaigrette. Spoon Quick Pickled Shrimp over tomato mixture; top with celery leaves. Serve immediately.

SERVING SIZE about 1 cup tomato mixture, ⅓ cup shrimp, and 4 tsp. vinaigrette CALORIES 181; FAT 10g (sat 1.4g, mono 6.7g, poly 1.2g); PROTEIN 12g; CARB 11g; FIBER 3g; CHOL 95mg; IRON 1mg; SODIUM 327mg; CALC 74mg

Quick Pickled Shrimp

MAKES 6 servings   HANDS-ON 5 min.   TOTAL 3 hours, 5 min.

Stir together **⅓ cup thinly sliced red onion, ¼ cup olive oil, 2 Tbsp. chopped fresh dill, 2 Tbsp. chopped fresh flat-leaf parsley, 3 Tbsp. red wine vinegar, 1¼ tsp. Creole seasoning, 1 thinly sliced lemon,** and **1 minced garlic clove** in a large shallow dish or zip-top plastic freezer bag; add **1 lb. peeled, medium-size cooked shrimp,** turning to coat. Cover or seal, and chill 3 to 6 hours, turning once. Remove shrimp from marinade, discarding marinade.

SERVING SIZE about ⅓ cup CALORIES 99; FAT 5g (sat 0.7g, mono 3.4g, poly 0.6g); PROTEIN 10g; CARB 2g; FIBER 0.3g; CHOL 95mg; IRON 0.3mg; SODIUM 188mg; CALC 46mg

Bloody Mary Vinaigrette

MAKES ½ cup   HANDS-ON 2 min.   TOTAL 2 min.

Whisk together **¼ cup spicy Bloody Mary mix, 2 Tbsp. olive oil, 1 Tbsp. lemon juice, 1½ tsp. prepared horseradish, ½ tsp. freshly ground black pepper, ½ tsp. hot sauce, ¼ tsp. celery salt,** and **¼ tsp. Worcestershire sauce** in a small bowl.

Note: We tested with Zing Zang Bloody Mary Mix.

SERVING SIZE 4 tsp. CALORIES 44; FAT 5g (sat 0.6g, mono 3.3g, poly 0.5g); PROTEIN 0g; CARB 1g; FIBER 0g; CHOL 0mg; IRON 0.1mg; SODIUM 105mg; CALC 4mg

Cornbread Crab Cakes

Crumbled cornbread adds even more Southern flair to crab cakes. Lemon zest, Old Bay seasoning, garlic, hot sauce, and jalapeños up the flavor with minimal calories.

MAKES 16 cakes   HANDS-ON 45 min.   TOTAL 2 hours, 30 min.

1   **(8-oz.) container reduced-fat sour cream**
2   **Tbsp. chopped pickled jalapeño pepper slices**
2   **Tbsp. chopped fresh cilantro**
⅔   **cup finely diced red bell pepper**
½   **cup sliced green onions**
2   **tsp. olive oil**
1   **garlic clove, minced**
⅓   **cup reduced-fat mayonnaise**
¼   **cup chopped fresh parsley**
2   **large eggs, lightly beaten**
1   **tsp. hot sauce**
1   **tsp. Old Bay seasoning**
1   **tsp. lemon zest**
2   **cups Light Cornbread crumbs**
1   **lb. fresh lump crabmeat**
Vegetable cooking spray

1. Stir together first 3 ingredients. Cover and chill up to 3 days.

2. Sauté bell pepper and onions in hot oil in a small nonstick skillet over medium-high heat 1 minute; add garlic, and sauté 1 minute. Remove from heat; cool 15 minutes.

3. Combine bell pepper mixture, mayonnaise, and next 5 ingredients in a large bowl. Fold in cornbread and crabmeat. Shape mixture into 16 (2½-inch) cakes (about ¼ cup each); place on a lightly greased baking sheet. Cover loosely with plastic wrap, and chill 1 hour.

4. Lightly coat cakes with cooking spray. Cook crab cakes, in batches, in a large nonstick skillet or griddle over medium heat 3 to 4 minutes on each side or until lightly browned. Serve immediately with cilantro-jalapeño sour cream.

SERVING SIZE 2 crab cakes and 2 Tbsp. sour cream mixture CALORIES 193; FAT 9.9g (sat 3.4g, mono 3.6g, poly 2.2g); PROTEIN 14.1g; CARB 11.4g; FIBER 1.1g; CHOL 100mg; IRON 1.1mg; SODIUM 440mg; CALC 126mg

Light Cornbread

MAKES 10 servings   HANDS-ON 10 min.   TOTAL 30 min.

Preheat oven to 425°. Add **2 tsp. vegetable oil** to a 10-inch cast-iron skillet; heat in oven 5 minutes. Stir together **2 cups self-rising white cornmeal mix** and **2 Tbsp. sugar** in a large bowl. Add **2 cups nonfat buttermilk, 1 large egg, lightly beaten,** and **¼ cup vegetable oil,** stirring just until blended. Pour batter into hot skillet. Bake 20 to 22 minutes or until golden and cornbread pulls away from sides.

SERVING SIZE ⅒ of cornbread CALORIES 172; FAT 7.8g (sat 1.0g, mono 3.2g, poly 3.3g); PROTEIN 4.5g; CARB 22.3g; FIBER 1.6g; CHOL 19mg; IRON 1.5mg; SODIUM 361mg; CALC 151mg

Shrimp Risotto

This smart recipe for dreamy shrimp risotto with sugar snap peas cuts the fat and calories by using fat-free chicken broth. Arborio rice, when cooked with the patient stirring required, yields a creamy, satisfying consistency.

MAKES 5 servings   HANDS-ON 57 min.   TOTAL 57 min.

- ¾ **lb. unpeeled, medium-size raw shrimp**
- 1 **small onion, diced**
- 1 **garlic clove, minced**
- 1 **Tbsp. olive oil**
- 1½ **cups uncooked Arborio rice**
- ⅔ **cup dry white wine**
- 4 **cups reduced-sodium fat-free chicken broth**
- 1 **(8-oz.) package sliced fresh mushrooms**
- ⅔ **cup fresh sugar snap peas**
- ¼ **tsp. table salt**
- ½ **tsp. freshly ground black pepper**
- ½ **cup shredded Parmesan cheese**

1. Peel shrimp, and devein, if desired. Sauté onion and garlic in hot olive oil over medium-high heat in a medium saucepan 10 minutes or until tender. Add rice, and sauté 2 minutes. Reduce heat to medium.

2. Add wine and 1 cup broth. Cook, stirring constantly, until liquid is absorbed. Repeat procedure with remaining broth, ½ cup at a time. (Total cooking time is 30 to 45 minutes.) When adding the last ½ cup broth, stir in mushrooms and sugar snap peas.

3. Cook, stirring constantly, 10 minutes. Add shrimp, and cook, stirring constantly, 5 minutes or just until shrimp turn pink. Remove from heat, and stir in salt and pepper. Sprinkle with cheese.

SERVING SIZE 1 cup CALORIES 379; FAT 6.8g (sat 2.3g, mono 2.7g, poly 0.5g); PROTEIN 22.3g; CARB 52.4g; FIBER 3.6g; CHOL 52mg; IRON 1.2mg; SODIUM 471mg; CALC 154mg

Lime-Orange Catfish

Catfish doesn't always have to be fried and served with fried potatoes. It can be prepared most any way you'd enjoy other lean white-fleshed fish. This recipe is inspired by the citrus fruits of Florida, which help create a light and lovely sauce for the grilled fish.

MAKES 6 servings   **HANDS-ON** 15 min.   **TOTAL** 30 min.

¼ **cup fresh lime juice**

⅓ **cup orange juice**

2 **tsp. sugar**

1 **garlic clove, pressed**

¼ **tsp. table salt**

½ **tsp. dry mustard**

½ **tsp. paprika**

¼ **tsp. black pepper**

2 **Tbsp. olive oil**

6 **(6-oz.) catfish fillets**

Vegetable cooking spray

Garnishes: lime slices and orange slices, fresh parsley sprigs

1. Whisk together first 8 ingredients; gradually whisk in olive oil until well blended. Reserve half of juice mixture, and set aside.

2. Place catfish in a shallow dish or zip-top plastic bag; pour remaining marinade over catfish. Cover or seal bag, and chill 15 minutes, turning catfish once.

3. Remove catfish from marinade, discarding marinade.

4. Coat cold cooking grate of grill with cooking spray; place on grill. Preheat grill to 350° to 400° (medium-high) heat. Place catfish on cooking grate, and grill 5 minutes on each side or until done. Remove to a serving platter; drizzle with reserved marinade.

SERVING SIZE 1 fillet and ⅙ sauce CALORIES 260; FAT 14.9g (sat 2.9g, mono 7.8g, poly 2.4g); PROTEIN 26.2g; CARB 4.1g; FIBER 0.2g; CHOL 94mg; IRON 0.5mg; SODIUM 266mg; CALC 19mg

Brighten Up to Lighten Up

MY STAY-SLIM SECRET
Capi Peck, age 60, chef

Southern chefs prove daily that you can stay true to food traditions while battling the bulge. "The secret is to lighten things up with bright flavors," says Capi Peck, chef at Trio's Restaurant in Little Rock, Arkansas. "Instead of butter, I'll use a citrus sauce on fish. For shrimp, I make a vibrant cucumber salsa or use roasted red peppers to wake up the taste buds without all the calories." She improves the nutritional profile of fried green tomatoes by frying in heart-healthy canola oil and serving them with a rémoulade sauce made with light mayonnaise, fresh herbs, capers, and lemon.

Glazed Salmon
with Stir-fried Vegetables

Salmon is loaded with heart-healthy omega-3 fats that may also keep your brain sharp and your skin looking younger—and who doesn't want that? Try it here with a sweet-and-sour glaze and stir-fried vegetables.

MAKES 4 servings   **HANDS-ON** 29 min.   **TOTAL** 29 min.

¼ **cup apple jelly**

3 **Tbsp. rice vinegar**

1 **Tbsp. lite soy sauce**

1 **tsp. cornstarch**

4 **(6-oz.) skinless salmon fillets**

¼ **tsp. table salt**

2 **carrots, cut into thin strips (1 cup)**

1 **parsnip, cut into thin strips (½ cup)**

2 **tsp. vegetable oil**

8 **green onions, cut into thin strips (2 cups)**

1 **small red bell pepper, cut into thin strips (1 cup)**

1. Whisk together apple jelly, vinegar, 2 Tbsp. water, soy sauce, and cornstarch in a small bowl.

2. Preheat broiler with oven rack 5½ inches from heat. Sprinkle salmon fillets evenly with salt; place on a lightly greased rack in an aluminum foil-lined broiler pan.

3. Broil 10 minutes or just until fish flakes with a fork.

4. Meanwhile, stir-fry carrots and parsnip in hot oil in a large skillet over medium-high heat 2 minutes. Add green onions and bell pepper; stir-fry 2 to 3 minutes or until crisp-tender. Remove vegetables from skillet, and keep warm.

5. Add jelly mixture to skillet, and cook, stirring constantly, 1 minute or until thickened.

6. Spoon about ⅔ cup vegetables onto each of 4 plates; drizzle each serving with 1 Tbsp. sauce. Top vegetables with salmon fillets, and drizzle 1 Tbsp. sauce over each fillet.

SERVING SIZE about ⅔ cup vegetables, 1 salmon fillet, and 2 Tbsp. sauce **CALORIES** 404; **FAT** 15.8g (sat 3.4g, mono 6.7g, poly 4.3g); **PROTEIN** 37.7g; **CARB** 26.9g; **FIBER** 3.2g; **CHOL** 87mg; **IRON** 1.1mg; **SODIUM** 398mg; **CALC** 61mg

Salmon Croquettes

Croquettes can feature almost any fish, poultry, or meat, though salmon is a Southern favorite. Using fresh salmon instead of canned boosts flavor, gives a better texture, and keeps the sodium down.

MAKES 4 servings   HANDS-ON 18 min.   TOTAL 18 min.

1   Tbsp. chopped fresh parsley
1   tsp. finely chopped capers
¼   cup canola mayonnaise, divided
1   Tbsp. Dijon mustard, divided
4   tsp. fresh lemon juice, divided
⅜   tsp. table salt, divided
3   garlic cloves, minced and divided
¾   lb. skinless salmon fillet, cut into chunks
¼   cup finely chopped shallots
2   Tbsp. minced red bell pepper
⅛   tsp. ground red pepper
1   large egg, lightly beaten
1   cup panko (Japanese breadcrumbs)
1   Tbsp. canola oil

1. Stir together parsley, capers, 2 Tbsp. mayonnaise, 1½ tsp. mustard, 1 tsp. lemon juice, ⅛ tsp. salt, and 1 minced garlic clove in a small bowl. Chill.

2. Pulse salmon in a food processor 4 times or until coarsely chopped. Combine shallots, bell pepper, ground red pepper, egg, remaining 2 Tbsp. mayonnaise, remaining 1½ tsp. mustard, remaining 3 tsp. juice, remaining ¼ tsp. salt, and remaining 2 minced garlic cloves in a large bowl; add salmon, stirring just until combined. Stir in panko. Shape mixture into 8 (2½-inch) patties.

3. Cook patties in hot oil in a large skillet over medium heat 3 to 4 minutes on each side or until browned. Serve with mayonnaise mixture.

SERVING SIZE 2 croquettes and 1 Tbsp. mayonnaise mixture CALORIES 318; FAT 15.8g (sat 2.2g, mono 8g, poly 4.3g); PROTEIN 22.2g; CARB 19g; FIBER 1g; CHOL 90mg; IRON 0.8mg; SODIUM 520mg; CALC 27mg

Farmers' Market Pasta Salad

Hit the market when vegetables such as tomatoes, zucchini, peppers, and corn are at their freshest. Use precooked chicken to speed the prep time. You can also sub cheese-filled tortellini for a different take on pasta salad.

MAKES 8 servings   HANDS-ON 18 min.   TOTAL 33 min., including vinaigrette

- 2 **cups halved baby heirloom tomatoes**
- 2 **small zucchini, thinly sliced into half moons**
- 1 **small red bell pepper, cut into thin strips**
- 1 **cup fresh corn kernels**
- 1 **cup diced firm, ripe fresh peaches (about 2 medium)**
- ½ **cup thinly sliced green onions**

Parmesan Vinaigrette
- 1 **(8-oz.) package penne pasta**
- 2 **cups shredded smoked chicken (about 10 oz.)**
- ⅓ **cup torn fresh basil**
- ⅓ **cup torn fresh cilantro**

1. Toss together first 7 ingredients in a large bowl, and let stand 10 minutes.

2. Meanwhile, prepare pasta according to package directions. Add hot cooked pasta and chicken to tomato mixture; toss gently to coat. Season with salt and pepper to taste. Transfer to a serving platter, and top with basil and cilantro.

SERVING SIZE 1⅔ cups CALORIES 361; FAT 17.8g (sat 3.5g, mono 10.4g, poly 1.9g); PROTEIN 19.8g; CARB 31.9g; FIBER 3.1g; CHOL 35mg; IRON 2.1mg; SODIUM 313mg; CALC 139mg

Parmesan Vinaigrette

MAKES 1 cup   HANDS-ON 5 min.   TOTAL 5 min.

Process ½ **cup freshly grated Parmesan cheese,** ½ **cup olive oil, 2 tsp. lemon zest, 3 Tbsp. fresh lemon juice, 1 Tbsp. balsamic vinegar, 2 garlic cloves, 2 tsp. freshly ground black pepper,** and ½ **tsp. table salt** in a blender or food processor until smooth. Add ¼ **cup fresh basil** and ¼ **cup fresh cilantro;** pulse 5 or 6 times or until just blended.

SERVING SIZE 2 Tbsp. CALORIES 155; FAT 15.5g (sat 2.9g, mono 10.5g, poly 1.5g); PROTEIN 3.2g; CARB 1.3g; FIBER 0.2g; CHOL 5mg; IRON 0.2mg; SODIUM 274mg; CALC 107mg

Country Chicken & Buttermilk Soup

This comforting chicken soup is filled with vegetables and uses nonfat buttermilk and fat-free chicken broth instead of a heavier cream base. It's as satisfying as chicken and dumplings, with none of the guilt.

MAKES 6 servings   HANDS-ON 35 min.   TOTAL 1 hour, 5 min.

2   **skinned and boned chicken breast halves (about 1½ lb.)**
5   **cups reduced-sodium fat-free chicken broth**
1   **Tbsp. butter**
2   **medium-size red potatoes, cut into wedges**
1   **celery rib, chopped**
¼   **large white onion, coarsely chopped**
½   **carrot, peeled and chopped**
½   **cup fresh or frozen green peas**
½   **cup fresh or frozen corn kernels**
1   **Tbsp. chopped fresh parsley**
2   **cups nonfat buttermilk**
½   **cup all-purpose flour**
½   **tsp. table salt**
½   **to 1 tsp. dried crushed red pepper**
1   **tsp. Worcestershire sauce**

1. Bring chicken and broth to a boil in a large saucepan, and cook 5 to 7 minutes or until done. Drain, reserving 4 cups broth. Let chicken cool, and chop.

2. Melt butter in a Dutch oven; add potato wedges and next 3 ingredients, and sauté 3 to 4 minutes or until onion is tender. Add reserved broth, and simmer 30 minutes or until potato is tender. Add chicken, peas, corn, and parsley.

3. Stir together buttermilk and flour until smooth; add to potato mixture, and cook, stirring constantly, 5 minutes. Stir in salt, red pepper, and Worcestershire sauce. Serve immediately.

SERVING SIZE 1½ cups CALORIES 267; FAT 4.7g (sat 2.1g, mono 1.1g, poly 0.6g); PROTEIN 26.7g; CARB 30.1g; FIBER 2.8g; CHOL 56mg; IRON 1.7mg; SODIUM 543mg; CALC 124mg

Skillet Fried Chicken

Fried chicken isn't off limits for healthy eating. This lighter version uses pan-frying instead of deep-frying. Take the skin off the chicken to help cut calories and fat, too.

MAKES 4 servings   HANDS-ON 1 hour   TOTAL 3 hours

1   **cup all-purpose flour**
½   **cup whole wheat flour**
1   **tsp. ground ginger**
½   **tsp. hot paprika**
½   **tsp. fine sea salt**
2   **bone-in chicken breasts, skinned and halved**
2   **bone-in chicken thighs, skinned**
2   **chicken drumsticks, skinned**
¼   **cup peanut oil**

1. Sift together first 6 ingredients; place mixture in a large zip-top plastic bag. Sprinkle salt evenly over chicken. Add chicken, 1 piece at a time, to bag; seal. Shake bag to coat chicken. Remove chicken from bag, shaking off excess flour. Place chicken on a wire rack; place rack in a jelly-roll pan. Reserve remaining flour mixture. Loosely cover chicken; chill 1½ hours. Let chicken stand at room temperature 30 minutes. Return chicken, 1 piece at a time, to flour mixture, shaking bag to coat chicken. Discard excess flour mixture.

2. Heat peanut oil in a large skillet over medium-high heat. Add chicken to pan. Reduce heat to medium-low, and cook 25 minutes or until done, carefully turning every 5 minutes.

3. Line a clean wire rack with brown paper bags; arrange chicken in a single layer on bags. Let stand for 5 minutes.

SERVING SIZE 1 chicken breast half or 1 thigh and 1 drumstick
CALORIES 467; FAT 19.6g (sat 3.8g, mono 8.1g, poly 5.7g); PROTEIN 36.0g;
CARB 35.5g; FIBER 2.8g; CHOL 125mg; IRON 3.1mg; SODIUM 459mg;
CALC 27mg

Don't Fry This at Home

MY STAY-SLIM SECRET
Evelyn Crayton, age 60, professor of nutrition

Alabama native Evelyn Crayton has a simple rule: "I do not fry foods at home. It is too much temptation." A registered dietitian and professor of nutrition at Auburn University, Crayton prefers instead to have a fried treat—fried catfish, hush puppies, or fried chicken—once a week or so when dining out in Montgomery. She notes that limiting fried food to once weekly is a healthy Southern tradition.

"Folks used to gather for a meal of fried chicken with all of the side dishes on a Sunday afternoon," she says. "Through the week we dined on a pot of vegetables with hot cornbread."

Summer Salad
with Grilled Chicken and Peaches

Grilling peaches brings out their natural sweetness, which balances the peppery arugula in this salad. For best results, grill peach halves cut sides down first. Silicone basting brushes work well to distribute small amounts of oil.

MAKES 4 servings   HANDS-ON 20 min.   TOTAL 41 min.

2   **medium-size ripe peaches, unpeeled and halved**
2   **Tbsp. extra virgin olive oil, divided**
2   **(6-oz.) skinned and boned chicken breasts**
½   **tsp. table salt, divided**
¼   **tsp. freshly ground black pepper**
4   **cups firmly packed arugula**
½   **cup toasted pecan halves (28 halves)**
2   **Tbsp. honey**
2   **Tbsp. balsamic vinegar**
2   **oz. crumbled goat cheese**
2   **Tbsp. finely chopped fresh chives**

1. Preheat grill to 350° to 400° (medium-high) heat. Brush peach halves with 1½ tsp. olive oil; brush chicken breasts with 1½ tsp. oil. Sprinkle peaches with ⅛ tsp. salt and ⅛ tsp. pepper; sprinkle chicken with ¼ tsp. salt and ⅛ tsp. pepper.

2. Grill chicken, covered with grill lid, 7 to 8 minutes on each side or until done. At the same time, grill peaches, covered with grill lid, 4 minutes on each side or until tender. Remove from grill; let the peaches stand 5 minutes. Cut chicken breasts into thin slices.

3. Divide arugula among 4 plates; top each salad with a peach half, one-fourth of sliced chicken, and 2 Tbsp. pecans.

4. Whisk together honey, balsamic vinegar, remaining 1 Tbsp. oil, and remaining ⅛ tsp. salt; drizzle each salad with 2 Tbsp. dressing. Sprinkle one-fourth of cheese and 1½ tsp. chives over each salad.

SERVING SIZE 1 salad CALORIES 340; FAT 22.7g (sat 5.6g, mono 12.1g, poly 3.8g); PROTEIN 18.3g; CARB 17.5g; FIBER 2.3g; CHOL 50mg; IRON 1.3mg; SODIUM 416mg; CALC 178mg

Apple-a-Day Pork Chops

Apples, rosemary, and pork find themselves together in a lot of recipes, but golden raisins give an extra touch of sweetness to the pork loin here. When you see "loin" in a cut of pork or beef, it's a clue that you're choosing one of the leanest cuts.

MAKES 6 servings **HANDS-ON** 22 min. **TOTAL** 22 min.

6 (4-oz.) boneless pork
    loin chops
½ tsp. table salt
½ tsp. freshly ground
    black pepper
Vegetable cooking spray
2 tsp. olive oil
1 medium-size red
    cooking apple, peeled
    and chopped (1⅓ cups)
¾ cup golden raisins
¾ cup Marsala or apple
    cider
1½ tsp. chopped fresh
    rosemary

1. Sprinkle pork chops with salt and pepper, and coat with cooking spray. Cook chops in a large nonstick skillet over medium-high heat 3 minutes on each side or until browned. Remove chops from skillet; keep warm. Add oil to skillet; reduce heat to medium.

2. Add apple and raisins; cook, stirring often, 3 minutes. Add Marsala and rosemary; cook, stirring constantly, 2 minutes or until most of liquid evaporates. Serve apple mixture over chops.

SERVING SIZE 1 pork chop and ¼ cup apple mixture **CALORIES** 238; **FAT** 7.6g (sat 2g, mono 3.3g, poly 0.8g); **PROTEIN** 21.9g; **CARB** 18.3g; **FIBER** 2g; **CHOL** 66g; **IRON** 1.2mg; **SODIUM** 244mg; **CALC** 40mg

SAVOR THE SOUTH
LINGER LONGER
INDULGE A LITTLE
MAKE IT HAPPEN

Salt Strategies

Though most of us consume too much of it, salt is that miracle seasoning that enhances the true flavor of most everything. Here are simple ways to use it sparingly but wisely.

Swap your shaker for a grinder. You can add a more precise amount of salt to your plate with a grinder, which crushes big salt crystals into finer granules.

Buy the sea. Sea salt is often livelier in flavor than table salt, so you can use less of it by weight to season. Sea salts come in many colors (gray from France, red from Hawaii, pink from the Himalayas) with slightly different flavors, depending on where they are harvested.

Keep kosher. Amy Myrdal, registered dietitian with the Culinary Institute of America's campus in Napa Valley, notes that flakier kosher salts contain less sodium by volume than table salt. "Kosher salt, which is very soft and fluffy, has granules that melt quickly on the tongue, and 1 teaspoon contains only 1,120 milligrams of sodium (compared to regular table salt with 2,360 milligrams)."

BBQ in a Jar

Serve this twist on a traditional barbecue dinner at your next family picnic with slices of cornbread on the side. Smoked pulled chicken or rotisserie chicken can be substituted for the pork.

MAKES 6 servings   HANDS-ON 17 min.   TOTAL 27 min.

½ **cup sugar**

½ **cup apple cider vinegar**

⅓ **cup vegetable oil**

½ **tsp. mustard seeds**

¼ **tsp. table salt**

¼ **tsp. celery seeds**

¼ **tsp. freshly ground black pepper**

1 **(16-oz.) package shredded coleslaw mix**

1 **(22-oz.) can baked beans in a sweet and smoky sauce**

2 **cups shredded barbecued pork without sauce (10 oz.)**

9 **Tbsp. bottled barbecue sauce**

1. Combine first 7 ingredients in a small saucepan. Bring to a boil; reduce heat, and simmer 3 minutes or until sugar is dissolved.

2. Place coleslaw in a medium bowl; pour hot sugar mixture over slaw, tossing to coat. Let stand 10 minutes.

3. Microwave beans in a small microwave-safe bowl at HIGH 2 minutes or until thoroughly heated, stirring after 1 minute. Microwave pork in another small microwave-safe bowl at HIGH 1 to 2 minutes or until thoroughly heated, stirring once.

4. Layer about 6 Tbsp. beans, ⅓ cup pork, 1½ Tbsp. barbecue sauce, and ⅔ cup coleslaw into each of 6 (1-pint) canning jars.

Note: We tested with Bush's Grillin' Beans Smokehouse Tradition.

SERVING SIZE 1 filled jar CALORIES 468; FAT 20g (sat 3.8g, mono 8.4g, poly 6g); PROTEIN 18g; CARB 57g; FIBER 5.9g; CHOL 40mg; IRON 1.7g; SODIUM 817mg; CALC 102mg

Baked Smokin' Mac & Cheese

Creamy, cheesy, a crunchy topping, and plenty of carbs: No wonder mac and cheese is the ultimate comfort food. It's even made appearances as a side on Southern meat-and-three plates. Not only is this version lighter, it's got a little ham, too. Use elbow pasta if you can't find cellentani.

MAKES 8 servings   HANDS-ON 30 min.   TOTAL 1 hour

1   **lb. uncooked cellentani (corkscrew) pasta**
2   **Tbsp. butter**
¼   **cup all-purpose flour**
3   **cups fat-free milk**
1   **(12-oz.) can fat-free evaporated milk**
1   **cup (4 oz.) shredded smoked Gouda cheese**
½   **cup (2 oz.) shredded 1.5% reduced-fat sharp Cheddar cheese**
3   **oz. fat-free cream cheese, softened**
½   **tsp. salt**
¼   **tsp. ground red pepper, divided**
1   **(8-oz.) package chopped smoked ham**
Vegetable cooking spray
1¼ **cups cornflakes cereal, crushed**
1   **Tbsp. butter, melted**

1. Preheat oven to 350°. Prepare cellentani pasta according to package directions.

2. Meanwhile, melt 2 Tbsp. butter in a Dutch oven over medium heat. Gradually whisk in flour; cook, whisking constantly, 1 minute. Gradually whisk in milk and evaporated milk until smooth; cook, whisking constantly, 8 to 10 minutes or until slightly thickened. Whisk in Gouda cheese, next 3 ingredients, and ⅛ tsp. ground red pepper until smooth. Remove from heat, and stir in ham and pasta.

3. Pour pasta mixture into a 13- x 9-inch baking dish coated with cooking spray. Stir together crushed cereal, 1 Tbsp. melted butter, and remaining ⅛ tsp. ground red pepper; sprinkle over pasta mixture.

4. Bake at 350° for 30 minutes or until golden and bubbly. Let stand 5 minutes before serving.

Note: We tested with Barilla Cellentani pasta and Cabot 1.5% Reduced Fat Sharp Cheddar Cheese.

CALORIES 453; FAT 12.1g (sat 6.8g, mono 2.3g, poly 0.3g); PROTEIN 26.8g; CARB 59.9g; FIBER 2.1g; CHOL 48mg; IRON 3mg; SODIUM 846mg; CALC 398mg

Honey-Grilled Pork Tenderloins

Tenderloins are one of the leanest cuts of pork with 120 calories per 3-ounce serving—about the same as a skinless chicken breast.

MAKES 8 servings   HANDS-ON 21 min.   TOTAL 3 hours, 21 min.

2 **(1-lb.) pork tenderloins**
¼ **cup lite soy sauce**
½ **tsp. ground ginger**
5 **garlic cloves, minced**
2 **Tbsp. brown sugar**
3 **Tbsp. honey**
2 **tsp. dark sesame oil**
Garnish: fresh cilantro

1. Remove silver skin from tenderloins, leaving a thin layer of fat. Butterfly pork tenderloins by making a lengthwise cut down center of each tenderloin, cutting to within ¼ inch of other side. (Do not cut all the way through tenderloins.) Lay flat.

2. Combine soy sauce, ginger, and garlic in a shallow dish or zip-top plastic freezer bag; add pork, turning to coat. Cover or seal, and chill 3 hours, turning occasionally.

3. Preheat grill to 350° to 400° (medium-high) heat. Stir together brown sugar, honey, and sesame oil in a small bowl.

4. Grill tenderloins, covered with grill lid, 15 minutes or until a meat thermometer inserted into thickest portion registers 145°, turning occasionally and basting with honey mixture.

SERVING SIZE 3 ounces CALORIES 181; FAT 3.6g (sat 1g, mono 1.4g, poly 0.9g); PROTEIN 24.5g; CARB 11.5g; FIBER 0.1g; CHOL 74mg; IRON 1.2mg; SODIUM 337mg; CALC 12mg

SAVOR THE SOUTH
LINGER LONGER
INDULGE A LITTLE
MAKE IT HAPPEN

Mind Your Manners

Sit up straight, place your napkin on your lap, sip slowly, and eat at a leisurely pace. Not just good manners learned in Southern charm schools, these table traditions are good for your health.

Rather than rushing through your meal, take a break between bites and rest your fork and knife on the plate. This pause gives you leave to talk to your tablemates, aids digestion, and gives your body time to appreciate how hungry or full you feel.

Etiquette experts advise cutting one small bite at a time and never taking a utensil to your mouth with more food on it than you can fit in your mouth.

It's neater in polite society, but it also slows you down and keeps the meal at a leisurely pace.

Pork Chops with Grilled Pineapple Salsa

There's a Caribbean flair to this recipe, and the pineapple salsa is a great accompaniment to pork chops. Fruit salsas add bold flavors and a serving of fruit to the meal.

MAKES 8 servings   HANDS-ON 13 min.   TOTAL 23 min.

8   (4-oz.) boneless pork loin chops (about ½ inch thick)
4   tsp. Cajun seasoning
Vegetable cooking spray
1   fresh pineapple, peeled, cored, and sliced
⅓   cup chopped fresh cilantro
⅓   cup finely chopped shallots
¼   cup seeded and minced jalapeño pepper
2   Tbsp. fresh lime juice
1½ tsp. grated fresh ginger
¼   tsp. freshly ground black pepper

1. Preheat grill to 350° to 400° (medium-high) heat. Rub chops evenly with Cajun seasoning; coat with cooking spray. Coat pineapple slices with cooking spray.

2. Grill chops and pineapple slices, covered with grill lid, 3 to 4 minutes on each side or until a meat thermometer inserted in thickest portion of pork registers 145° and pineapple is golden. Let pork stand 10 minutes.

3. Meanwhile, chop pineapple. Stir together pineapple, cilantro, and next 5 ingredients. Serve salsa over pork chops.

SERVING SIZE 1 pork chop and about ½ cup salsa CALORIES 207; FAT 6g (sat 1.7g, mono 2.2g, poly 0.7g); PROTEIN 22.1g; CARB 16.7g; FIBER 1.7g; CHOL 66mg; IRON 1.1mg; SODIUM 316mg; CALC 34mg

Pulled Pork Tacos
with Avocado-Peach Salsa

Use whole wheat flour tortillas to add a serving of whole grains.

MAKES 10 servings   HANDS-ON 27 min.   TOTAL 8 hours, 39 min., including salsa

2 Tbsp. ground cumin
2 Tbsp. ground coriander
2 tsp. garlic powder
¾ tsp. table salt
½ tsp. freshly ground black pepper
¼ tsp. ground red pepper
3 lb. boneless pork shoulder roast (Boston butt)
1 Tbsp. vegetable oil
1 large sweet onion, vertically sliced
1 cup reduced-sodium fat-free chicken broth
¼ cup apple cider vinegar
3 Tbsp. brown sugar
20 (6-inch) fajita-size 96% fat-free flour tortillas
Avocado-Peach Salsa

1. Combine first 6 ingredients; remove 1 Tbsp. spice mixture for onions. Sprinkle remaining spice mixture over pork. Cook pork in hot oil in a large skillet over medium-high heat 2 to 3 minutes on all sides or until browned. Remove pork from skillet; place in a 5-qt. slow cooker. Add onions to skillet; sprinkle with reserved 1 Tbsp. spice mixture, and sauté 5 minutes or until golden brown. Add chicken broth, vinegar, and brown sugar. Remove from heat; pour over pork in slow cooker.

2. Cover and cook on LOW 8 hours or until pork is fork-tender. Transfer pork to a cutting board, reserving 1 cup cooking liquid; let stand 10 minutes. Shred pork with 2 forks. Toss pork with reserved 1 cup cooking liquid.

3. Warm tortillas according to package directions. Serve pork with tortillas and Avocado-Peach Salsa.

SERVING SIZE ½ cup pork, 2 tortillas, and about ¼ cup Avocado-Peach Salsa CALORIES 494; FAT 20.6g (sat 5.6g, mono 10.1g, poly 2.7g); PROTEIN 28.5g; CARB 46.6g; FIBER 4.8g; CHOL 81mg; IRON 5mg; SODIUM 792mg; CALC 207mg

Avocado-Peach Salsa

MAKES 11 servings   HANDS-ON 8 min.   TOTAL 8 min.

Toss together **2 peeled and diced peaches, 2 seeded and diced plum tomatoes, 1 diced avocado, ¼ cup peeled and diced jicama, 1 Tbsp. minced red onion, 3 Tbsp. lime juice, 1 tsp. olive oil, ¼ tsp. table salt,** and **¼ tsp. ground red pepper** in a large bowl. Cover and chill until ready to serve.

SERVING SIZE about ¼ cup CALORIES 50; FAT 3.2g (sat 0.5g, mono 2.1g, poly 0.4g); PROTEIN 0.8g; CARB 5.8g; FIBER 2g; CHOL 0mg; IRON 0.2mg; SODIUM 56mg; CALC 6mg

Molasses Glazed Flank Steak Soft Tacos

Flank steak is one of the leanest cuts of beef, with only 6 grams of fat per 3-ounce serving. The molasses-and-mustard marinade adds big flavor to the steak, which is grilled and sliced very thin.

MAKES 6 servings   HANDS-ON 22 min.   TOTAL 2 hours, 32 min.

½ **cup light molasses**
¼ **cup coarse-grained Dijon mustard**
1 **Tbsp. olive oil**
1 **(1½-lb.) flank steak**
6 **(8-inch) soft taco-size flour tortillas, warmed**
1⅓ **cups chopped tomato**
1 **cup shredded lettuce**
¾ **cup (3 oz.) shredded 1.5% reduced-fat sharp Cheddar cheese**
½ **cup light sour cream**

1. Whisk together first 3 ingredients in a small bowl; reserve ¼ cup for basting. Pour remaining molasses mixture into a large shallow dish or zip-top plastic freezer bag; add steak, turning to coat. Cover or seal, and chill 2 hours, turning occasionally. Remove meat from marinade, discarding marinade.

2. Preheat grill to 350° to 400° (medium-high) heat. Grill steak, covered with grill lid, 6 minutes on each side or to desired degree of doneness, brushing often with reserved ¼ cup marinade. Remove steak from grill; let stand 10 minutes. Cut diagonally across the grain into thin strips.

3. Fill each warm tortilla with 3 oz. steak, about 3 Tbsp. tomato, about 2½ Tbsp. lettuce, 2 Tbsp. cheese, and 1 Tbsp. sour cream.

SERVING SIZE 1 taco CALORIES 502; FAT 18g (sat 6.1g, mono 4.5g, poly 0.6g); PROTEIN 34g; CARB 50g; FIBER 1g; CHOL 88mg; IRON 4.2mg; SODIUM 668mg; CALC 252mg

Chapter Six

DESSERTS TO LIVE FOR

A whole chapter devoted to dessert in a healthy Southern cookbook? Yes, indeed! For many of us, life wouldn't be nearly as divine without dessert. From the banana cream pie served up nightly at Emeril's in New Orleans to the towering six-layer coconut cake at the Peninsula Grill in Charleston, sweet treats are celebrated in the South. Whether you prefer a classic fruit cobbler, a gooey mud pie, or a spiced molasses cookie, a sweet something is a happy end to a meal, no matter where you live.

There's really nothing wrong with the idea of dessert. The trouble often comes when we start thinking of it as a departure from healthy eating habits. Indulging a little is, after all, one of the core principles of this book. **"I simply don't believe in food guilt," says nutritionist Angela LeMond of Plano, Texas. "You can't live life with an all-or-nothing approach."**

LeMond advises her clients to designate foods not as good or bad but as "anytime" and "sometimes" items. "Anytime foods" include the undeniably good-for-you stuff, such as leafy greens, lean proteins, and whole grains. "Sometimes foods" include rich desserts, fried appetizers, cocktails, and other goodies we enjoy now and then. **If you eat "anytime foods" at least 80 to 90 percent of the time, and "sometimes foods" 10 to 20 percent of the time, you're following a healthy rule of thumb.**

Even the super-serious Dietary Guidelines for Americans, put together by the United States Department of Agriculture, give a nod to the need for the occasional sweet. The guidelines say desserts and other SoFAS (short for "solid fats and added sugars") can be included in a healthy diet, provided you get enough of the good stuff from the other food groups and you don't go overboard overall on calories.

Numerous nutrition studies support the occasional indulgence as one factor in long-term weight control. Researchers have found that people who allow themselves treats every now and then experience significantly more weight loss over all, and better weight maintenance in the long run, than those who are much more strict in their eating habits.

"If you are very rigid in your approach to food, you're much more likely to eventually go off track," explains J. Graham Thomas, Ph.D., an assistant professor at the Weight Control and Diabetes Research Center in Providence, Rhode Island, which coordinates the National Weight Control Registry, an ongoing study involving people who have lost at least 30 pounds and kept it off for more than a year. "Ultimately, when you have a more flexible approach, you maintain better weight control over the years."

Sweet on Fruit

Now, of course, a good dessert doesn't rely only on butter and sugar. **A smart Southern dessert can help provide your daily fruit fix.**

There's really nothing wrong with the idea of dessert. The trouble often comes when we start thinking of it as a departure from healthy eating habits.

From blueberries to rhubarb, fruit provides vitamins, minerals, and a dose of fiber. Plus, most fruit is naturally low in calories, so you have some room to play with if you're keeping an eye on your waistline.

Fruit contains sugar, of course. To reduce the need for added sugar in a fruit dessert, just add some heat. Roasting plums in the oven or peaches on the grill concentrates and caramelizes the natural sugars within to unleash an avalanche of taste. A pinch of sugar or spice on top might be all you need to finish the dish. Blackberry-Lemon Buttermilk Sorbet (page 201) or Peach-and-Blueberry Parfaits (page 222) are delicious Southern ways to help achieve your healthy five-a-day! That's Southern living, done quite right.

As an added bonus, the phytonutrients that give blackberries their deep purple color, peach skin its blush, and rhubarb its tang have been shown to support our immune system, cognitive function, and eye and skin health while reducing the risk of cancer, heart disease, and other chronic ailments. You're not just eating dessert; you're boosting brain and body power!

Dainty and Divine

Of course, some of the richest desserts earn their "to-die-for" status because they're loaded with more than their fair share of fat, sugar, and other calorie heavies. Here's where a savvy Southerner makes a distinction. When dessert involves a simple citrus fruit compote or slices of sweet, juicy watermelon, we dig in and eat up. But we take a smaller share when it comes to cakes, pies, ice cream, and other rich indulgences.

A simple way to do this for yourself and your guests is to **serve your most indulgent desserts in dainty dishes.** A sliver of pecan pie served on a pretty bread plate or a perfect dollop of cold, creamy ice cream presented in a demitasse cup makes a sensible serving seem oh-so-special.

Another approach, employed by considerate Southern hosts, is to downsize a big dessert into bite-sized or miniature portions. Recipes like Mini Berry Cobblers (page 217) and Fig Hand Pies (page 210) are designed with portion control in mind. When you bake dessert in individual servings, it's easy for you and your guests to enjoy every single bite without worrying that you've dished up too much. And hungry athletes home from the tennis court or football field can always have two servings because they've earned it!

Southern cooks also use smart substitutions to lighten up the foods we crave. But, of course, they still have to pass the lip-smacking test. In some cases, we've adopted new favorite recipes where low-fat or reduced-fat milk stand in for whole milk. We sometimes find occasion

Sometimes there's just no substitute for the real thing. Keep an eye on your serving size when butter and other calorie-dense ingredients join the party.

to slip in a few more egg whites and a few less whole eggs. And we often use light sour cream, reduced-fat cream cheese, or fat-free Greek yogurt in place of all or some of the full-fat variety. Fat-free sweetened condensed milk, nonfat or low-fat buttermilk, and reduced-fat graham crackers and whipped toppings also offer easy ways to cut calories without sacrificing our sense of indulgence. **Pretty garnishes, like fresh mint or lemon zest, help heighten and brighten the flavor of desserts without adding calories.**

Of course, sometimes there's just no substitute for the real thing. Many traditional Southern cooks still rely on leaf lard, the highest grade of rendered pork fat used for cooking and the one with the most neutral flavor, to create moist, flaky piecrusts worthy of blue ribbons. While lard and other animal-based fats are viewed more favorably by nutritionists today, they're still high in calories. So use lard, butter, and calorie-dense ingredients like packed brown sugar in the recipes that follow only as specified, and keep an eye on your serving size when they join the party.

When it comes to cravings for chocolate, well, North and South can probably agree that nothing else will do. Dark chocolate dishes up more antioxidants, but all chocolate delivers a healthy dose of happiness. Humorist and illustrator Sandra Boynton has said of carob, an oft-used "healthy" stand-in for chocolate: "Carob works on the principle that, when mixed with the right combination of fats and sugar, it can duplicate chocolate in color and texture. Of course, the same can be said of dirt." Ha!

There's no dirt or carob in these recipes—not even in the Mocha-Pecan Mud Pie (page 218). This chapter serves up a sideboard of Southern beauties designed to satisfy your sweet tooth and keep you looking your best. Whether it's a slice of lighter-than-air Angel Food Cake (page 197) or a few comforting Flourless Peanut Butter-Chocolate Chip Cookies (page 213), every delicious dessert here weighs in at 330 calories or less per serving. **Now that's sweet!**

Blackberry-Lemon Buttermilk Sorbet, page 201

Angel Food Cake with Lemon Glaze

Because of its low fat content, light and airy angel food cake wears its own health halo. The lemon glaze adds a touch of creamy sweetness. Serve with fresh strawberries, if you like.

MAKES 16 servings   HANDS-ON 15 min.   TOTAL 2 hours, 35 min.

2½ cups granulated sugar
1½ cups all-purpose flour
¼ tsp. table salt
18 large egg whites
    (2½ cups)
1 tsp. cream of tartar
1 tsp. fresh lemon juice
1 tsp. vanilla extract
1 cup powdered sugar
2 Tbsp. fresh lemon juice

1. Preheat oven to 375°. Sift together first 3 ingredients.

2. Beat egg whites and cream of tartar at high speed with a heavy-duty electric stand mixer, using whisk attachment, until stiff peaks form. Gradually fold in granulated sugar mixture, one-third cup at a time, folding just until blended after each addition. Fold in 1 tsp. lemon juice and vanilla. Spoon batter into a 10- x 4-inch tube pan.

3. Bake at 375° on an oven rack one-third up from bottom of oven 50 to 55 minutes or until cake springs back when lightly touched. Invert pan on a wire rack, and let stand 1 hour and 30 minutes or until cake is completely cool. Run a knife around cake to loosen edges; remove from pan. Place cake on a serving platter.

4. Stir together powdered sugar and 2 Tbsp. lemon juice; drizzle evenly over top of cake.

SERVING SIZE $\frac{1}{16}$ of cake CALORIES 221; FAT 0.2g (sat 0g, mono 0g, poly 0.1g); PROTEIN 5.3g; CARB 50.3g; FIBER 0.3g; CHOL 0mg; IRON 0.6mg; SODIUM 99mg; CALC 5mg

Dish Up Praise

MY STAY-SLIM SECRET
Sarah-Jane Bedwell, age 31, nutrition blogger

Need a delicate way to deal with a heavy dose of Southern hospitality? Nashville nutrition blogger and registered dietitian Sarah-Jane Bedwell, a self-professed "Southern Belle who likes to eat well," advises: "If your well-intentioned host has a hard time hearing 'no, thank you' to seconds or thirds, use flattery to help stick to your guns. You might say, 'Aunt Nora, that was just so delicious and I am so stuffed now that I just couldn't do another slice justice! But you know I will be looking forward to having it again next time.'"

Almond Biscotti

Biscotti are twice-baked cookies with a dry, crunchy texture—perfect for dipping in a cup of tea or strong coffee.

MAKES 2 dozen   HANDS-ON 10 min.   TOTAL 2 hours, 20 min.

4 **large eggs**
1 **cup sugar**
2 **Tbsp. vegetable oil**
1 **tsp. vanilla extract**
1 **tsp. almond extract**
3⅓ **cups all-purpose flour**
2 **tsp. baking powder**
1 **cup chopped almonds**

1. Beat eggs and sugar at high speed with an electric mixer 5 minutes or until foamy. Add oil and extracts, beating until blended.

2. Combine flour and baking powder; add to sugar mixture, beating well. Gently fold almonds into dough. Cover and freeze 30 minutes or until firm.

3. Preheat oven to 325°. Divide dough in half; lightly flour hands, and shape each portion into an 8- x 5-inch slightly flattened log on a lightly greased baking sheet.

4. Bake at 325° for 30 minutes or until firm. Cool on pan 5 minutes; transfer to a wire rack, and cool at least 15 minutes.

5. Cut each log diagonally into ½-inch-thick slices with a serrated knife, using a gentle sawing motion; place slices on lightly greased baking sheets.

6. Bake at 325° for 15 minutes; turn cookies over, and bake 15 more minutes. Remove to wire racks, and cool 20 minutes.

SERVING SIZE 1 biscotti CALORIES 121; FAT 3.5g (sat 0.5g, mono 1.7g, poly 0.7g); PROTEIN 3.1g; CARB 19.3g; FIBER 0.8g; CHOL 27mg; IRON 1mg; SODIUM 39mg; CALC 32mg

Blackberry-Lemon Buttermilk Sorbet

Sweet and tart come together in this refreshingly delicious, low-fat treat.
Enjoy on a warm night or whenever you want a taste of summer.

MAKES 8 servings   HANDS-ON 15 min.   TOTAL 9 hours, 5 min.

5   **cups fresh blackberries**
1   **cup sugar**
½   **tsp. lemon zest**
2   **Tbsp. fresh lemon juice**
2   **cups low-fat buttermilk**

1. Bring first 4 ingredients to a boil in a medium saucepan, stirring constantly. Reduce heat, and simmer 15 minutes. Remove from heat; cool 5 minutes.

2. Process blackberry mixture in a blender or food processor until smooth, stopping to scrape sides as needed.

3. Press blackberry puree through a fine wire-mesh strainer into a bowl, using back of a spoon to squeeze out juice. Discard pulp and seeds. Stir buttermilk into blackberry juice.

4. Pour mixture into freezer container of a 1½-qt. electric ice-cream maker, and freeze according to manufacturer's instructions. (Instructions and times may vary.) Transfer sorbet to a freezer-safe container; cover and freeze 8 hours or until firm.

5. Let stand at room temperature 30 minutes before serving.

SERVING SIZE ½ cup CALORIES 162; FAT 1g (sat 0.4g, mono 0.2g, poly 0.3g); PROTEIN 3.3g; CARB 37.1g; FIBER 4.5g; CHOL 3mg; IRON 0.6mg; SODIUM 66mg; CALC 98mg

Bourbon Balls

An adult-friendly favorite throughout the South, these confections typically combine crushed cookies, corn syrup, chopped nuts, and bourbon, formed into balls. The powdered sugar coating helps keep the alcohol from evaporating.

MAKES 4 dozen   **HANDS-ON** 28 min.   **TOTAL** 28 min.

1 **(12-oz.) package vanilla wafers, finely crushed**
1 **cup chopped pecans or walnuts**
¾ **cup powdered sugar**
2 **Tbsp. unsweetened cocoa**
2½ **Tbsp. light corn syrup**
½ **cup bourbon**
Powdered sugar

1. Combine vanilla wafers, pecans, powdered sugar, and cocoa in a large bowl; stir well.

2. Combine corn syrup and bourbon, stirring well. Pour bourbon mixture over wafer mixture; stir until blended. Shape into 1-inch balls; roll in additional powdered sugar. Store in an airtight container up to 2 weeks.

SERVING SIZE 1 bourbon ball **CALORIES** 67; **FAT** 3.1g (sat 0.4g, mono 1.3g, poly 0.5g); **PROTEIN** 0.5g; **CARB** 8.6g; **FIBER** 0.5g; **CHOL** 1mg; **IRON** 0.3mg; **SODIUM** 28mg; **CALC** 7mg

SAVOR THE SOUTH
LINGER LONGER
INDULGE A LITTLE
MAKE IT HAPPEN

Pecans

Drive through South Georgia, the state that produces the most pecans, and you're bound to see farms lined with pretty pecan trees. The nuts are harvested in late fall with a method that's literally "shake, rattle, and roll." Farm machines grab hold of the tree trunks and shake the nuts until they rattle loose and fall to the ground.

Whether you call them pah-CAHNS or PEE-cans, these marvelous nuts are pretty darn good for you. According to the USDA, pecans have the most antioxidants of any tree nut. The American Heart Association includes pecans as a certified heart-healthy food. Pecans are a good source of protein, heart-healthy fats, and 19 vitamins and minerals including vitamin A, vitamin E, and potassium.

Because of their rich and slightly sweet taste, they play a versatile role in desserts, baked goods, salads, and entrées. And they're ideal as snacks. One ounce of pecans (a handful or 19 halves) contains 195 calories and 3 grams of fiber.

Cinnamon Swirl Cake

The heavenly aroma of cinnamon and the nutty crunch of pecans may have you thinking this cake is a splurge, but the fat-free buttermilk and egg substitute keep the calories and fat low, so you can indulge and still feel virtuous.

MAKES 16 servings   HANDS-ON 15 min.   TOTAL 2 hours, 10 min.

½ **cup firmly packed light brown sugar**
½ **cup chopped pecans, toasted**
2 **tsp. ground cinnamon**
1 **(18.25-oz.) package white cake mix**
1⅓ **cups fat-free buttermilk**
¾ **cup egg substitute**
⅓ **cup sugar**
1 **tsp. vanilla extract**

1. Preheat oven to 325°. Combine first 3 ingredients; set aside.

2. Beat cake mix and next 4 ingredients at medium speed with an electric mixer 2 minutes or until blended. Pour one-third of cake batter into a greased and floured 12-cup Bundt pan. Sprinkle with half of brown sugar mixture. Repeat layers twice, ending with batter.

3. Bake at 325° for 45 minutes or until a wooden pick inserted in center comes out clean. Cool in pan on a wire rack 10 minutes. Remove from pan, and cool completely on wire rack.

SERVING SIZE ¹⁄₁₆ of cake CALORIES 218; FAT 5.9g (sat 0.7g, mono 2.9g, poly 2.1g); PROTEIN 3.7g; CARB 38.2g; FIBER 0.7g; CHOL 0mg; IRON 0.8mg; SODIUM 260mg; CALC 106mg

Walk It Out

MY STAY-SLIM SECRET
Patty Callahan Henry, age 49, novelist

Many of us have jobs that require long hours at a desk working our brains and our keyboards instead of our muscles. Instead of heading to the gym, novelist Patti Callahan Henry prefers the stress-busting solitude of walking to energize her body and mind. "I walk for miles and miles to untangle plot lines," says the Birmingham author of *And Then I Found You* and nine other novels set in the South. She says long walks through her hilly neighborhood are as important to her creative process as to her health.

Classic Strawberry Shortcake

The name shortcake comes from adding butter, or shortening, to dough, which makes it even more tender and biscuit-like. Served with fresh, sweet strawberries, it's the perfect way to end a meal.

MAKES 15 servings   HANDS-ON 25 min.   TOTAL 2 hours, 39 min.

4   cups sliced fresh
    strawberries
½   cup sugar, divided
2¾ cups all-purpose flour
4   tsp. baking powder
6   Tbsp. cold butter,
    cut up
1½ cups low-fat
    buttermilk
1   tsp. vanilla extract
½   cup whipping cream,
    whipped

1. Toss together strawberries and ¼ cup sugar in a medium bowl. Cover and let stand at room temperature 2 hours.

2. Preheat oven to 450°. Combine flour, baking powder, and remaining ¼ cup sugar in a large bowl; cut butter into flour mixture with a pastry blender or fork until crumbly. Add buttermilk and vanilla, stirring just until dry ingredients are moistened.

3. Drop dough by heaping tablespoonfuls 2 inches apart onto a lightly greased baking sheet.

4. Bake at 450° for 14 minutes or until golden.

5. Split shortcakes in half horizontally. Spoon strawberries with syrup onto each shortcake bottom; cover with tops of shortcakes. Top each shortcake with whipped cream.

SERVING SIZE 1 biscuit, ¼ cup berries, and 1 Tbsp. whipped cream
CALORIES 200; FAT 7.8g (sat 4.7g, mono 2g, poly 0.4g); PROTEIN 3.5g;
CARB 29g; FIBER 1.4g; CHOL 24mg; IRON 1.3mg; SODIUM 174mg;
CALC 104mg

Easy Tropical Banana Sundaes

This speedy dessert brings out the taste of the tropics any time of year, with a blend of orange juice, pineapple juice, and ripe bananas. It's served with creamy low-fat vanilla frozen yogurt.

MAKES 4 servings   HANDS-ON 25 min.   TOTAL 25 min.

1   **cup orange juice**
1   **cup pineapple juice**
2   **Tbsp. reduced-calorie butter**
2   **Tbsp. dark brown sugar**
3   **bananas, each cut into 8 pieces**
½   **tsp. vanilla extract**
¼   **tsp. ground cinnamon**
1   **cup vanilla low-fat frozen yogurt**
¼   **cup chopped macadamia nuts (optional)**

1. Cook juices in a medium-size nonstick skillet over medium heat, stirring occasionally, 14 to 16 minutes or until mixture is reduced to ¾ cup. Remove from skillet.

2. Melt butter in skillet over medium-high heat; add brown sugar, and cook, stirring often, 2 minutes. Add bananas; cook, stirring occasionally, 2 minutes. Stir in vanilla and cinnamon. Add juice mixture, and cook, stirring occasionally, 1 minute.

3. Place ¼ cup frozen yogurt into each of 4 sundae dishes. Divide banana mixture evenly among dishes, spooning banana mixture over yogurt. Top each sundae with 1 Tbsp. chopped nuts, if desired.

SERVING SIZE 1 sundae CALORIES 322; FAT 14.6g (sat 6.0g, mono 7.2g, poly 0.5g); PROTEIN 6.3g; CARB 44.4g; FIBER 2.8g; CHOL 48mg; IRON 0.6mg; SODIUM 81mg; CALC 148mg

---

Dress in Columns

MY STAY-SLIM SECRET
Betsy Crawford, age 65, wardrobe consultant

Betsy Crawford won't hesitate to tell you, "Take that off; it's not for you." As a wardrobe consultant for the Worth Collection in Atlanta, she works to find the right look for customers of all shapes and sizes. Crawford says a great belt is a tall, slim girl's best friend. But, if your goal is to look more like that tall gal, she advises "interior and exterior column dressing." Start by making the interior column of your outfit a single color (an espresso brown sweater over espresso brown suede pants, for example). "Then," she says, "you can add an exterior column in a contrasting color (such as a below-the-hip-length red jacket)."

Fig Hand Pies

Figs trees can be found in many a backyard throughout the South. Marzipan gives the crust a hint of almond flavor.

MAKES 8 servings   HANDS-ON 25 min.   TOTAL 3 hours, 40 min.

¼ **cup butter, cut up**
2 **Tbsp. marzipan (almond paste)**
1¼ **cups all-purpose flour**
½ **tsp. table salt**
4 to 5 **Tbsp. ice water**
4 **oz. dried Mission figs, quartered (¾ cup)**
Vegetable cooking spray
1½ **Tbsp. honey**
1 **tsp. balsamic vinegar**
1 **Tbsp. fig preserves**
1 **tsp. butter**
½ **tsp. vanilla extract**
Parchment paper
1 **large egg**
1 **Tbsp. sugar**

1. Combine butter and marzipan in a small bowl; chill 15 minutes. Stir together flour and salt in a large bowl; cut butter and almond paste into flour mixture with a pastry blender until it resembles small peas. Sprinkle ice water, 1 Tbsp. at a time, over surface of mixture in bowl; stir with a fork until dry ingredients are moistened.

2. Divide dough into 8 equal portions. Roll 1 portion of dough at a time into a 4-inch circle on a lightly floured surface. Stack circles between sheets of wax paper; cover stack with plastic wrap. Chill 2 to 24 hours.

3. Pour 2 cups boiling water over figs in a small heatproof bowl. Let stand 15 minutes; drain figs, discarding water.

4. Sauté figs in a medium skillet coated with cooking spray over medium-high heat 2 minutes. Add honey and vinegar; cook 1 minute or until liquid evaporates. Remove from heat; stir in preserves, butter, and vanilla. Cool completely (about 30 minutes).

5. Preheat oven to 425°. Working with 1 dough circle at a time, spoon 1½ Tbsp. fig mixture into center of circle; moisten edges with water. Fold pastry in half, pressing edges to seal using a fork dipped in flour. Place on a parchment paper-lined baking sheet. Repeat procedure with remaining dough circles and fig mixture.

6. Whisk together egg and 1 Tbsp. water. Brush pies with egg mixture. Cut 2 slits in top of each pie with a sharp paring knife; sprinkle with sugar.

7. Bake at 425° for 15 to 20 minutes or until golden. Remove from pan to a wire rack, and cool 15 minutes.

SERVING SIZE 1 pie CALORIES 213; FAT 8.2g (sat 4.3g, mono 2.6g, poly 0.7g); PROTEIN 3.7g; CARB 32g; FIBER 2.1g; CHOL 40mg; IRON 1.4mg; SODIUM 214mg; CALC 37mg

Flourless Peanut Butter-Chocolate Chip Cookies

This gluten-free cookie solves your need for something sweet, either as a midday treat or a simple finish for supper. The classic peanut butter-chocolate combo is a surefire winner.

MAKES 2 dozen   HANDS-ON 15 min.   TOTAL 47 min.

1   **cup creamy peanut butter**
¾   **cup sugar**
1   **large egg**
½   **tsp. baking soda**
¼   **tsp. table salt**
1   **cup semisweet chocolate morsels**
Parchment paper

1. Preheat oven to 350°. Stir together peanut butter and next 4 ingredients in a medium bowl until well blended. Stir in chocolate morsels.

2. Drop dough by rounded tablespoonfuls 2 inches apart onto parchment paper-lined baking sheets.

3. Bake at 350° for 12 to 14 minutes or until puffed and lightly browned. Cool on baking sheets on a wire rack 5 minutes. Transter to wire rack, and cool 15 minutes.

SERVING SIZE 1 cookie CALORIES 137; FAT 8.2g (sat 2.7g, mono 2.8g, poly 1.6g); PROTEIN 3.6g; CARB 14.7g; FIBER 1.2g; CHOL 7.8mg; IRON 0.3mg; SODIUM 104mg; CALC 1.2mg

Key Lime Pie

Legend has it that Key lime pie was created in the 1800s in Key West, Florida, using local limes along with sweetened condensed milk (which held up without refrigeration). This lighter version tastes just as rich. Freeze the pie for a few minutes to make it easier to transfer it to a pretty pie plate.

MAKES 8 servings   HANDS-ON 15 min.   TOTAL 4 hours, 15 min.

¾ **cup egg substitute**

2 **tsp. lime zest**

½ **cup fresh lime juice (about 3 limes)**

1 **(14-oz.) can fat-free sweetened condensed milk**

1 **(9-inch) ready-made graham cracker piecrust**

1 **(8-oz.) container fat-free frozen whipped topping, thawed**

Garnishes: lime twists

1. Preheat oven to 350°. Process first 4 ingredients in a blender until smooth, stopping to scrape down sides as needed. Pour mixture into piecrust.

2. Bake at 350° for 10 to 12 minutes or until set. Cool completely on a wire rack (about 1 hour). Spread whipped topping over pie; chill 3 to 4 hours.

SERVING SIZE ⅛ pie CALORIES 316; FAT 6.1g (sat 1.1g, mono 4.3g, poly 0.4g); PROTEIN 6.9g; CARB 55.4g; FIBER 0.1g; CHOL 6mg; IRON 1mg; SODIUM 199mg; CALC 146mg

SAVOR THE SOUTH
LINGER LONGER
INDULGE A LITTLE
MAKE IT HAPPEN

Live in the Moment

Taking a bite of pecan pie and slowly savoring the sweet filling, the crunchy pecans, and the flaky pastry does more than make your taste buds happy. Nutrition experts say that being present and fully aware of what you're eating can help with weight control.

Thoroughly enjoying the food you're having can help you feel fuller with less, so why not make the most of those delicious bites? Before you even dive in, stop to appreciate the look of the dish. Inhale the aroma. Listen to the crack of that crème brûlée. Notice the texture, the way it melts on your tongue, and the flavors you taste at beginning, middle, and end of the bite, and the way it makes you feel. Was that just one bite? You bet!

Living in the moment works the other way, too. If that tempting restaurant special actually turns out to be a fairly dismal dessert, being mindful as it goes in your mouth will prompt you to put the fork down before you've eaten the whole not-very-good thing. That way you can save the calories for something more worthwhile.

Mini Berry Cobblers

Pick your favorite mix—strawberries, blueberries, raspberries, blackberries—to star in this tasty dessert, served in individual mini-skillets for easy portion control. If you don't have mini-skillets, you can use oven-safe ramekins.

MAKES 12 servings   HANDS-ON 25 min.   TOTAL 1 hour

18 oz. mixed fresh berries (4 cups)
¼ cup sugar
1 Tbsp. butter, melted
1 Tbsp. cornstarch
1½ cups all-purpose flour
⅓ cup sugar
3 Tbsp. minced crystallized ginger
2 tsp. baking powder
½ tsp. table salt
½ cup cold butter, cubed
½ cup low-fat buttermilk
Garnish: fresh mint sprigs

1. Preheat oven to 400°. Toss together first 4 ingredients in a medium bowl.

2. Whisk together flour and next 4 ingredients in a large bowl. Cut cold butter into flour mixture with a pastry blender or fork until crumbly. Add buttermilk, stirring just until dry ingredients are moistened. Turn dough out onto a lightly floured surface, and knead 3 or 4 times. Pat into a 6- x 4-inch (1-inch-thick) rectangle. Cut rectangle into 6 squares; cut squares diagonally into 12 triangles.

3. Arrange 12 (3½-inch) lightly greased miniature cast-iron skillets on an aluminum foil-lined baking sheet. Divide berry mixture among skillets. Place 1 dough triangle over berry mixture in each skillet.

4. Bake at 400° for 20 to 24 minutes or until fruit bubbles and crust is golden brown. Cool 15 minutes before serving. Serve warm or at room temperature.

SERVING SIZE 1 cobbler CALORIES 210; FAT 9.1g (sat 5.6g, mono 2.3g, poly 0.5g); PROTEIN 2.5g; CARB 30.7g; FIBER 2.3g; CHOL 23mg; IRON 1.1mg; SODIUM 254mg; CALC 70mg

Mocha-Pecan Mud Pie

Here's a frozen version of mud pie that isn't quite the calorie bomb you might expect, thanks to light ice cream. Let the pie slices soften a little bit before serving, to better enjoy the chocolate and coffee flavors.

MAKES 9 servings   HANDS-ON 15 min.   TOTAL 8 hours, 33 min.

½ **cup chopped pecans**
Vegetable cooking spray
1 **tsp. sugar**
1 **pt. light coffee ice cream, softened**
1 **pt. light chocolate ice cream, softened**
1 **cup coarsely chopped reduced-fat cream-filled chocolate sandwich cookies, divided (about 10 cookies)**
1 **(6-oz.) ready-made chocolate crumb piecrust**
2 **Tbsp. light chocolate syrup**

1. Preheat oven to 350°. Place pecans in a single layer on a baking sheet coated with cooking spray; sprinkle evenly with sugar.

2. Bake at 350° for 8 to 10 minutes or until lightly toasted and fragrant, stirring halfway through. Cool.

3. Stir together ice cream, ¾ cup cookie chunks, and ⅓ cup pecans; spoon into piecrust. Freeze 10 minutes. Press remaining cookie chunks and pecans evenly on top. Cover with plastic wrap, and freeze 8 hours. Cut pie into 9 equal wedges; drizzle each slice with about ½ tsp. chocolate syrup.

Note: We tested with Keebler Chocolate Ready Crust, Häagen-Dazs Light Coffee Ice Cream, and Häagen-Dazs Light Dutch Chocolate Ice Cream.

SERVING SIZE ⅑ of pie and about ½ tsp. chocolate syrup CALORIES 285; FAT 13.3g (sat 4.3g, mono 6.3g, poly 2.1g); PROTEIN 4.5g; CARB 38.2g; FIBER 1.4g; CHOL 13mg; IRON 1.8mg; SODIUM 189mg; CALC 58mg

---

Share with the Group

MY STAY-SLIM SECRET
Melanie Young, age 54, public relations pro

Dining out is part of the job for Melanie Young, who handles public relations for hospitality, food, and beverage businesses. Her Chattanooga, Tennessee, upbringing helps her keep calories in check.

Her secret? "Be a polite Southern girl, and share your food!" When checking out the latest hot chef in New York or New Orleans, Young and her tablemates are enthusiastic samplers. "Take two bites and say, 'This dish is so amazing! You must taste it,'" she advises. "Then hand out lots of tastes until the dish is gone." The pass-the-plate, share-the-calories approach lets you sample a variety of dishes without going overboard.

Molasses-Spice Crinkles

Molasses, which is made from cooked-down cane sugar, has long been used as a sweetener in Southern recipes. Paired with ginger, cinnamon, and other spices, it helps give these cookies their signature sweet-spicy taste.

MAKES 52 cookies   HANDS-ON 20 min.   TOTAL 1 hour, 46 min.

¾ **cup butter, softened**
1 **cup granulated sugar**
¼ **cup light molasses**
1 **large egg**
2 **cups all-purpose flour**
1 **tsp. baking powder**
1 **tsp. baking soda**
1 **tsp. ground ginger**
1 **tsp. ground cinnamon**
½ **tsp. ground nutmeg**
¼ **tsp. table salt**
¼ **tsp. ground cloves**
¼ **tsp. ground allspice**
½ **cup sparkling sugar**

1. Beat butter at medium speed with an electric mixer until creamy. Gradually add granulated sugar, beating well. Add molasses and egg; beat well.

2. Stir together flour and next 8 ingredients; add one-fourth of flour mixture at a time to butter mixture. Beat at low speed just until blended after each addition, stopping to scrape bowl as needed. Cover and chill 1 hour.

3. Preheat oven to 375°. Shape dough into 1-inch balls, and roll in sparkling sugar. Place 2 inches apart on ungreased baking sheets.

4. Bake at 375° for 8 to 9 minutes. (Tops will crack.) Cool on baking sheets 3 minutes. Transfer to wire racks, and cool completely (about 15 minutes).

Note: Sparkling sugar is available at specialty food stores or baking supply stores.

SERVING SIZE 1 cookie CALORIES 70; FAT 2.8g (sat 1.7g, mono 0.7g, poly 0.1g); PROTEIN 0.7g; CARB 10.7g; FIBER 0.2g; CHOL 11mg; IRON 0.3mg; SODIUM 69mg; CALC 11mg

Peach-and-Blueberry Parfaits

Fresh summer peaches and blueberries are layered with custard and angel food cake for a refreshingly light dessert. Go upscale with footed parfait glasses, or give it a down-home feel by serving in small Mason jars.

MAKES 8 servings   HANDS-ON 30 min.   TOTAL 2 hours, 30 min.

2   **cups 1% low-fat milk**
1   **large egg**
⅓   **cup sugar**
1   **Tbsp. cornstarch**
1   **tsp. vanilla extract**
3   **lb. fresh peaches, peeled and chopped (about 7 cups)**
1   **pt. fresh blueberries**
½   **(14-oz.) angel food cake, cubed (about 6 cups)**
Garnish: fresh mint sprigs

1. Whisk together first 4 ingredients in a small nonaluminum saucepan over medium-low heat, and cook, stirring constantly, 15 minutes or until slightly thickened. (Mixture should lightly coat the back of a spoon.) Remove from heat; stir in vanilla.

2. Pour mixture into a small bowl, and place plastic wrap directly over surface of custard to prevent film from forming; chill 2 hours or until ready to serve.

3. Layer fruit and cake in 8 Mason jars or tall glasses. Drizzle each with ¼ cup custard.

SERVING SIZE 1 parfait CALORIES 210; FAT 1.8g (sat 0.7g, mono 0.5g, poly 0.4g); PROTEIN 5.8g; CARB 45g; FIBER 3.2g; CHOL 26.3mg; IRON 0.7mg; SODIUM 222mg; CALC 125mg

Healthy Weekdays Allow Weekend Splurges

Relaxed and polished with pops of color: That's one way to describe Tibi, the ultrachic fashion line created by Amy Smilovic. From breezy silks to laser-cut leather, her clothes are youthful and sophisticated. So is she.

Married with two young boys and a global fashion company to run, the St. Simons, Georgia, native designs busy days around healthy habits.

When commuting from her Connecticut home to Tibi's Soho office by train, she tracks her fitness on a high-tech pedometer: "On a day I've driven into the city (instead of taking the train), I can see that I've burned 3,000 fewer fuel points. It makes a difference climbing those stairs at Grand Central!"

Three times a week she blends shakes with spinach, Greek yogurt, coconut water, ginger, mint, and fresh fruit. Other go-to weekday lunches include green salads with fresh feta cheese and kalamata olives.

Smilovic says healthy eating during the week allows her to splurge with burgers and fries with the boys on weekends. "I never feel deprived," she says. "I look at food intake by the week, not by the day."

Smilovic, a graduate of the University of Georgia, says she wouldn't turn down a serving of her home state's peach cobbler. "I'm OK with that because I've eaten carefully for most days of the week," she says. "I'd eat up, but I wouldn't follow up with

Amy Smilovic, Georgia-born, New York-based fashion designer

bacon and biscuits the next morning."

Her personal cooking style, inspired by the Georgia coast, is as streamlined as the Tibi clothing and accessories she designs: "I like fresh shrimp, cherry tomatoes, fresh corn, and stir-fried okra, not deep-fat fried," she says. "And I'm famous for my strawberry shortcake."

"I never feel deprived. I look at food intake by the week, not by the day."

Roasted Plums with Sour Cream

This super-simple recipe (just five ingredients, plus water) showcases juicy baked plums served with reduced-fat sour cream. Dark purple plums hold up best to the heat of roasting.

MAKES 4 servings   **HANDS-ON** 10 min.   **TOTAL** 35 min.

4   **large purple plums, cut in half and pitted**
½   **tsp. vanilla extract**
¼   **cup firmly packed brown sugar**
¼   **cup reduced-fat sour cream**
2   **Tbsp. brown sugar**

1. Preheat oven to 450°. Place plum halves, cut sides down, in an 8-inch square baking dish. Stir together ⅓ cup water and vanilla; pour over fruit. Sprinkle ¼ cup brown sugar evenly over fruit.

2. Bake plums at 450° for 25 to 30 minutes or until skins just start to blister. Divide fruit and syrup evenly among 4 bowls. Top each with 1 Tbsp. reduced-fat sour cream and ½ Tbsp. brown sugar.

SERVING SIZE 1 plum, 1 Tbsp. sour cream, and ½ Tbsp. brown sugar **CALORIES** 131; **FAT** 2g (sat 1.1g, mono 0.6g, poly 0.1g); **PROTEIN** 0.9g; **CARB** 28.6g; **FIBER** 0.9g; **CHOL** 5.9mg; **IRON** 0.3mg; **SODIUM** 19mg; **CALC** 37mg

---

SAVOR THE SOUTH
LINGER LONGER
INDULGE A LITTLE
MAKE IT HAPPEN

Save Room for Dessert

If you live for dessert, that may just be the place to start when dining out.

Your waiter may think you're jumping the gun, but if you ask for the dessert menu first, you can see which sweets are worth waiting for and eat lighter earlier in the meal to save room for your sweet indulgence.

Have your heart set on the coconut cream pie? Choose a salad instead of a cream-based soup or fried calamari appetizer. Opt for green beans or brown rice instead of the mac-and-cheese side. And choose the grilled pork tenderloin instead of the batter-fried fish, and you'll have calories left for that pie.

Tipsy Red and Yellow Watermelon Salad

Raspberry liqueur and vodka give this colorful spiked fruit salad its lighthearted moniker. Serve at a backyard barbecue or block party (just keep the kids away!).

MAKES 6 servings   **HANDS-ON** 16 min.   **TOTAL** 1 hour, 16 min.

½ **(6-lb.) seedless red watermelon**

½ **(6-lb.) seedless yellow watermelon**

1 **cup fresh lemon juice (about 10 to 12 lemons)**

⅔ **cup sugar**

½ **cup vodka**

⅓ **cup black raspberry liqueur**

¹⁄₁₆ **tsp. fine sea salt**

1 **Tbsp. chopped fresh mint**

Garnish: fresh mint sprigs

1. Scoop watermelons into balls using various-size melon ballers, and place watermelon in a large bowl.

2. Whisk together lemon juice and next 4 ingredients in a medium bowl until sugar dissolves. Pour lemon juice mixture over watermelon balls; stir gently to coat. Cover and chill 1 to 2 hours.

3. Gently toss watermelon balls. Sprinkle with chopped fresh mint. Serve Immediately with a slotted spoon.

SERVING SIZE about 1 cup **CALORIES** 228; **FAT** 0.1g (sat 0g, mono 0g, poly 0g); **PROTEIN** 0.7g; **CARB** 41.5g; **FIBER** 0.7g; **CHOL** 0mg; **IRON** 0.5mg; **SODIUM** 25mg; **CALC** 14mg

SAVOR THE SOUTH
LINGER LONGER
INDULGE A LITTLE
MAKE IT HAPPEN

Sweeten the Package

A few delicious sips or just one bite, cleverly presented, might be all you need of something indulgently rich. When the dish is pleasing to the eye, a petite portion can be perfectly satisfying.

One-bite appetizers or desserts can be served on teaspoons or, if you've got them, long-handled silver iced tea spoons, laid across a small plate. A creamy soup served in dainty demitasse cups makes guests feel special without feeling stuffed.

Or, how about a three-martini lunch? (No, not that kind!) Serve a cold soup, a shrimp salad entrée, and then a dessert, each in its own martini glass. Martini glasses hold a modest 5 ounces, but they put the food on a pedestal and place the widest portion of it right before your eyes, making it feel more substantial and special.

Vanilla Bean Baby Pound Cakes with Whiskey Sauce

Real vanilla bean and warm whiskey sauce give these petite cakes their rich flavor. You can bake the cakes in mini-Bundt pans if you're feeling fancy—or in standard muffin pans.

MAKES 18 servings   HANDS-ON 10 min.   TOTAL 1 hour, 48 min., including sauce

1   vanilla bean, split lengthwise
⅔   cup unsalted butter, softened
1¾ cups sugar
3   large eggs
2¾ cups all-purpose flour
1½ tsp. baking powder
½   tsp. table salt
1   cup nonfat buttermilk
Whiskey Sauce

1. Preheat oven to 350°. Scrape seeds from vanilla bean into bowl of a heavy-duty electric stand mixer. Add butter, and beat at medium speed until creamy. Gradually add sugar, beating at medium speed until light and fluffy. Add eggs, 1 at a time, beating just until blended after each addition and stopping to scrape down sides of bowl as needed.

2. Combine flour, baking powder, and salt; add to butter mixture alternately with buttermilk, beginning and ending with flour mixture. Spoon batter into 18 lightly greased and floured muffin cups.

3. Bake at 350° for 23 to 26 minutes or until a wooden pick inserted in center comes out clean. Cool in pans on a wire rack 10 minutes; remove from pans to wire rack, and cool completely (about 1 hour).

SERVING SIZE 1 cake and 1 Tbsp. Whiskey Sauce CALORIES 289; FAT 9.5g (sat 5.7g, mono 2.5g, poly 0.6g); PROTEIN 3.8g; CARB 47g; FIBER 0.5g; CHOL 54mg; IRON 1.1mg; SODIUM 146mg; CALC 62mg

Whiskey Sauce

MAKES 1¾ cups   HANDS-ON 5 min.   TOTAL 5 min.

Bring **1½ cups firmly packed light brown sugar, ½ cup 1% low-fat milk,** and **¼ cup butter** to a boil in a small saucepan over medium heat, stirring constantly. Cook, stirring occasionally, 1 minute or until sugar dissolves and mixture is bubbly. Remove from heat; stir in ¼ **cup bourbon or whiskey.** Serve warm.

SERVING SIZE 1 Tbsp. CALORIES 103; FAT 2.6g (sat 1.7g, mono 0.7g, poly 0.1g); PROTEIN 0.3g; CARB 18.4g; FIBER 0g; CHOL 7mg; IRON 0.1mg; SODIUM 31mg; CALC 25mg

Toasted Pecan Caramel Sauce

Dessert sauces allow you to easily dress up a small scoop of sorbet or low-fat ice cream, creamy yogurt, or fresh fruit without adding a lot of fat or calories. Serve this pecan sauce warm to heighten its so-called decadence.

MAKES about 1 cup   HANDS-ON 8 min.   TOTAL 20 min.

¾ **cup sugar**
1 **tsp. light corn syrup**
½ **cup evaporated milk**
¼ **cup chopped toasted**
    pecans
1½ **tsp. butter**

1. Sprinkle sugar in a 2-qt. saucepan. Stir together ⅓ cup water and corn syrup, and pour over sugar in saucepan. Cook, without stirring, over medium-high heat 12 to 14 minutes or until sugar is dissolved and mixture is golden. Remove from heat. Gradually whisk in evaporated milk. (Mixture will bubble.) Stir in pecans and butter.

SERVING SIZE 1 Tbsp. CALORIES 63; FAT 2.1g (sat 0.7g, mono 0.9g, poly 0.4g); PROTEIN 0.7g; CARB 10.8g; FIBER 0.2g; CHOL 3mg; IRON 0.1mg; SODIUM 11mg; CALC 21mg

Strawberry Sauce

Just four ingredients go into this dessert topping, so use fruit at its peak for the best flavor.

MAKES 1⅔ cups   HANDS-ON 5 min.   TOTAL 5 min.

1 **(16-oz.) container fresh**
    strawberries, hulled
½ **tsp. lime zest**
1 **Tbsp. fresh lime juice**
2½ **Tbsp. honey**

1. Process all ingredients in a blender or food processor 1 minute or until smooth, stopping to scrape down sides as needed.

SERVING SIZE 1 Tbsp. CALORIES 12; FAT 0.1g (sat 0g, mono 0g, poly 0g); PROTEIN 0.1g; CARB 3.1g; FIBER 0.4g; CHOL 0mg; IRON 0.1mg; SODIUM 0.3mg; CALC 3mg

Chapter Seven

COMPANY'S COMING

Whether it's an over-the-top Derby Day bash complete with fabulous hats, fancy frocks, and frosty mint juleps, a Lowcountry boil with peel-and-eat shrimp and ice-cold beer, or a Sunday supper on a table set with sweet tea and fine china, Southerners know how to throw a party. "Entertaining has everything to do with the core of who Southerners really are," says Marcie Cohen Ferris, an American Studies professor at the University of North Carolina, Chapel Hill.

Much of the famed Southern hospitality also stems from the region's predominantly agrarian backbone. "Until the early 20th century, when people traveled here it was to mostly remote regions, and they leaned on this tradition of hospitality," notes Ferris. **"Food has always been our favorite way to express hospitality."**

From backyard barbecues to black-tie balls, Southern get-togethers typically share these traits: a welcoming atmosphere, friendly company, and an abundance of good food and drinks.

Setting the Scene

A good Southern host always indicates just how gussied up guests need to get. Southerners pay particular mind to dress code suggestions on invitations. **As the saying goes: You can never be overdressed, but you sure can be underdressed.**

Table settings help set the tone. Red plastic cups let you know to look for the keg. At a formal dinner party, Great-Grandma's china, crisp linens, and sterling silver flatware make you want to dress in your Sunday best. Somewhere in between, you'll find classic down-home comfort, lemonade served up in Mason jars with monogrammed paper napkins and cocktail stirrers destined to be dawdled over by twinkly-eyed gents in checkered shirts.

Fresh flowers fill tables, even at tailgates and outdoor concerts. Southern entertaining is all about making even everyday things just a little more special.

Raising Your Glass

It wouldn't be a party without a little libation. From cocktails mixed with barrel-aged bourbons to punches that pack a punch, drinks down South help prime the pump for conversation (and dancing). Even nonalcoholic beverages get star treatment with pretty glasses and garnishes of fresh lemon or mint.

Beverage choice is often based on location. A Louisiana pig roast just wouldn't be the same without bottles of Abita beer on ice, and the same can be said for Lone Star beer at a Texas barbecue or Sweetwater

A Southern party wouldn't be a party without a few libations.

beer at gatherings in Atlanta. And almost no Southern brunch would be complete without a Bloody Mary or a bubbly mimosa.

Making your drink a nonalcoholic one at least half the time cuts calories and also pays other dividends. "Alcohol decreases your inhibition, so you lose track of what you're eating," notes nutritionist Angela Lemond of Plano, Texas. "So alternate your cocktails with a glass of sparkling water to keep your drinking (and eating) in check."

You want to enjoy your cocktail, but not so much you can't remember the party!

Working the Room

How to avoid overdoing it? For starters, remember the *social* part of social gatherings. "I try to focus on the folks in the room," says interior designer Liz McDermott, a regular on the Atlanta party circuit, "and delve into spicy conversations—not the spicy chicken wings."

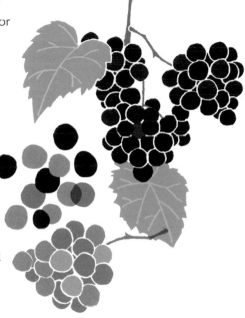

But don't say no to everything. "I tell my clients not to deprive themselves of those special foods they may only get a couple of times a year," says nutritionist Constance Brown-Riggs. If you get to have Aunt Tilda's caramel cake or your grandma's sweet potato pie only every now and then, take a small amount—and savor every bite. You won't regret it later or give in to cravings for something less enjoyable.

Slowing down is also an important party strategy. "Often we're so caught up in visiting with friends or family that we mindlessly eat everything in sight," notes Brown-Riggs. If you're at a sit-down affair, take a few minutes to concentrate on what you're being served, and chew your food well. You'll start to feel full after about 20 minutes.

Keeping your hands occupied can also help. Hold a drink in one hand and your party clutch in another and you won't have any fingers free for the finger foods. At Southern fetes, it's not uncommon to see a dieter's minefield: a groaning sideboard loaded with platters of delectable foods. **But there are ways to navigate the buffet without limiting yourself to crudités.** Researchers at Cornell University who studied 300 people who frequented all-you-can-eat buffets in six states found slimmer people are more likely to circle the buffet before digging in. **In other words, find out what you really want first and limit your choices to something you'll really savor.** Slimmer subjects in the study also were about seven times more likely than heavier ones to pick smaller-sized plates, sit farther away from the buffet, and chew their food longer than their heavier counterparts.

Sound familiar? Savor your food, linger longer, indulge a little, and make it happen: The SLIM principles work whatever the social setting. Now, who's ready to party?

Brunch Buffet

Brunch is a chance for our Southern hospitality to truly shine. It's often a cornucopia of Southern fare, from shrimp and grits in Savannah to oysters Rockefeller and crawfish étouffée in New Orleans. A Sunday brunch after church may find many in their weekly best, but whether it's in a club, restaurant, or your dining room, it's a chance to hobnob and catch up on the weekly goings-on. Casual or formal, brunch is always a welcome affair!

Menu for 6

Baked Pears with Toasted Oat Topping

Shrimp and Grits

Avocado Fruit Salad

Brown Sugared Turkey Bacon

Lime-Raspberry Bites

Add a green salad with the Oregano-Feta Dressing on page 70, and you're good to go!

Baked Pears with Toasted Oat Topping

MAKES 6 servings   HANDS-ON 25 min.   TOTAL 1 hour, 11 min., including topping

3   **Bosc pears**
2   **Tbsp. honey**
2   **Tbsp. fresh lemon juice**
⅓   **cup toasted slivered almonds**
⅓   **cup sweetened dried cranberries**
½   **cup orange juice**
6   **Tbsp. vanilla bean 2% reduced-fat Greek yogurt**
Toasted Oat Topping

1. Preheat oven to 375°. Peel pears, and cut in half, cutting through stem and bottom ends. Scoop out core and some pulp to form an oval hole in center of each pear half. Place pears, cut sides up, in an 8-inch square or 11- x 7-inch baking dish.

2. Combine honey and lemon juice in a bowl. Stir in almonds and cranberries.

3. Spoon honey mixture into center of pear halves. Pour orange juice into baking dish.

4. Bake, covered, at 375° for 15 minutes; uncover and bake 12 more minutes or until pears are tender and thoroughly heated.

5. Place pear halves on individual plates; drizzle orange juice mixture evenly over pear halves. Spoon 1 Tbsp. yogurt onto each pear half, and sprinkle each pear with about 2½ tsp. Toasted Oat Topping. Serve immediately.

Note: We tested with Craisins.

SERVING SIZE 1 pear half with 2½ tsp. topping CALORIES 196; FAT 4.5g (sat 0.9g, mono 2.2g, poly 1.0g); PROTEIN 3.6g; CARB 39.5g; FIBER 5.2g; CHOL 3mg; IRON 0.8mg; SODIUM 14mg; CALC 53mg

Toasted Oat Topping

MAKES ⅓ cup   HANDS-ON 5 min.   TOTAL 15 min.

Preheat oven to 350°. Stir together **⅓ cup uncooked regular oats** and **2 tsp. light brown sugar** in a small bowl; add **1 tsp. butter, melted**, tossing to coat. Spread mixture evenly on a baking sheet. Bake at 350° for 14 to 16 minutes or until lightly toasted, stirring after 7 minutes.

SERVING SIZE about 2½ tsp. CALORIES 24; FAT 0.8g (sat 0.4g, mono 0.2g, poly 0.1g); PROTEIN 0.5g; CARB 3.9g; FIBER 0.4g; CHOL 1.5mg; IRON 0.2mg; SODIUM 5mg; CALC 1mg

Shrimp and Grits

MAKES 6 servings   HANDS-ON 25 min.   TOTAL 30 min.

Parmesan Grits:

- ½ **tsp. table salt**
- 1 **cup uncooked quick-cooking grits**
- ½ **cup freshly grated Parmesan cheese**
- ½ **tsp. freshly ground pepper**

Creamy Shrimp Sauce:

- 1 **lb. unpeeled, medium-size raw shrimp**
- ¼ **tsp. freshly ground black pepper**
- ⅛ **tsp. table salt**
- **Vegetable cooking spray**
- 1 **Tbsp. olive oil**
- 1 **Tbsp. all-purpose flour**
- 1¼ **cups reduced-sodium fat-free chicken broth**
- ½ **cup chopped green onions**
- 2 **garlic cloves, minced**
- 1 **Tbsp. fresh lemon juice**
- ¼ **tsp. table salt**
- ¼ **tsp. hot sauce**
- 2 **cups firmly packed fresh baby spinach**

1. Prepare Parmesan Grits: Bring ½ tsp. salt and 4 cups water to a boil in a medium saucepan; gradually whisk in grits. Cook over medium heat, stirring occasionally, 8 minutes or until thickened. Whisk in cheese and pepper. Keep warm.

2. Prepare Creamy Shrimp Sauce: Peel shrimp; devein, if desired. Sprinkle shrimp with pepper and ⅛ tsp. salt. Cook in a large nonstick skillet coated with cooking spray over medium-high heat 1 to 2 minutes on each side or just until shrimp turn pink. Remove from skillet. Reduce heat to medium. Add oil; heat 30 seconds. Whisk in flour; cook 30 seconds to 1 minute. Whisk in broth and next 5 ingredients; cook 2 to 3 minutes or until thickened. Stir in shrimp and spinach; cook 1 minute or until spinach is slightly wilted. Serve immediately over grits.

SERVING SIZE ½ cup grits and about ⅓ cup shrimp sauce CALORIES 235; FAT 6.1g (sat 1.9g, mono 2g, poly 0.6g); PROTEIN 19.1g; CARB 25.2g; FIBER 1.4g; CHOL 119mg; IRON 3.3mg; SODIUM 749mg; CALC 177mg

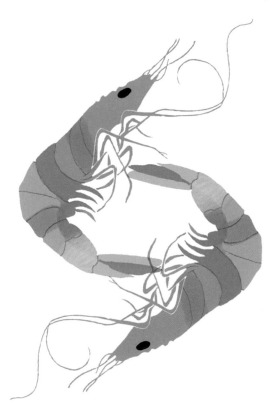

Avocado Fruit Salad

Technically speaking, avocados are a fruit. Loaded with fiber, vitamin K, folate, and vitamin C, plus healthy monounsaturated fat, they are a wonderful addition to salads. You can prepare this one day ahead, but don't cut up the avocado until just before you serve it.

MAKES 6 cups   HANDS-ON 15 min.   TOTAL 1 hour, 15 min.

1   **(24-oz.) jar refrigerated orange and grapefruit sections, drained, rinsed, and patted dry**

1   **(24-oz.) jar refrigerated tropical mixed fruit in light syrup, drained, rinsed, and patted dry**

2   **cups cubed fresh cantaloupe**

1   **medium-size ripe avocado, halved and cut into chunks**

¼   **cup chopped fresh mint**

2   **Tbsp. lime juice**

Garnish: mint leaves

1. Toss together first 6 ingredients. Cover and chill 1 hour.

Note: We tested with Del Monte SunFresh Citrus Salad and Del Monte SunFresh Tropical Mixed Fruit in Light Syrup With Passion Fruit Juice.

SERVING SIZE 1 cup CALORIES 166; FAT 4.7g (sat 0.7g, mono 2.8g, poly 0.6g); PROTEIN 1.9g; CARB 32.8g; FIBER 3.5g; CHOL 0mg; IRON 1.3mg; SODIUM 33mg; CALC 66mg

Brown Sugared Turkey Bacon

Sweet and salty with a hint of pepper, this crispy bacon is sure to please everyone at your breakfast table.

MAKES 12 servings   HANDS-ON 5 min.   TOTAL 19 min.

1 (12-oz.) package turkey bacon
Vegetable cooking spray
⅓ cup firmly packed light brown sugar
1 to 1½ tsp. coarsely ground black pepper

1. Preheat oven to 425°. Arrange bacon in a single layer in an aluminum foil-lined broiler pan coated with cooking spray. Sprinkle evenly with brown sugar and pepper.

2. Bake at 425° for 14 to 18 minutes or until done. Serve immediately.

SERVING SIZE 1 bacon strip (1 oz.) CALORIES 94; FAT 5.8g (sat 1.5g, mono 2.1g, poly 1.3g); PROTEIN 4.3g; CARB 6.5g; FIBER 0.1g; CHOL 26mg; IRON 0.6mg; SODIUM 346mg; CALC 17mg

Lime-Raspberry Bites

Everyone will love these luscious mini tarts, which blend sweet fresh raspberries and tangy lime flavors; light cream cheese keeps the calorie count low.

MAKES 28 tartlets   HANDS-ON 15 min.   TOTAL 15 min.

1 (8-oz.) container soft light cream cheese
½ cup powdered sugar
1 tsp. lime zest
1 Tbsp. fresh lime juice
2 (2.1-oz.) packages frozen mini-phyllo pastry shells, thawed
28 fresh raspberries
1 tsp. powdered sugar

1. Stir together light cream cheese, ½ cup powdered sugar, and next 2 ingredients in a small bowl. Spoon cream cheese mixture evenly into pastry shells. Top each with 1 raspberry. Dust evenly with 1 tsp. powdered sugar just before serving.

SERVING SIZE 1 tartlet CALORIES 47; FAT 2.3g (sat 0.9g, mono 0.6g, poly 0.2g); PROTEIN 0.8g; CARB 5.5g; FIBER 0.3g; CHOL 3.8mg; IRON 0.2mg; SODIUM 51mg; CALC 11mg

Tailgate Party

Tailgating in the South has its own very special set of standards. On any fall Saturday, you'll find more than 100,000 college football fans converging on tiny towns like Athens, Georgia, or Tuscaloosa, Alabama, all with one thing in mind: a premium, pregame tailgate complete with floral arrangements and flat-screen TVs under large tents, enough food to feed a small army, and everyone sporting school colors. Fitness tip: Get out of your team logo chair long enough to throw a football around or channel your inner cheerleader. Go team!

Menu for 6

Boiled Peanut Hummus

Coleslaw with Garden Vegetables

Spicy 3-Bean Chili

Pecan Sandies

Cajun Lemonade

Add the Light Cornbread on page 159 to complete your tailgate.

Boiled Peanut Hummus

Forget chickpeas: This hummus uses spicy boiled peanuts (a Southern specialty!) instead. If you can't find boiled peanuts on a stand near you, look for online purveyors.

MAKES 6 servings   HANDS-ON 25 min.   TOTAL 25 min.

Process **1 cup shelled spicy peanuts, ¼ cup water, 2 Tbsp. chopped cilantro, 2 Tbsp. lime juice, 2 Tbsp. olive oil, 2 Tbsp. creamy peanut butter, 1½ tsp. hot sauce, 1 tsp. minced fresh garlic,** and **¼ tsp. ground cumin** in a food processor 1 minute or until smooth. Spoon into shot glasses or small bowls, and drizzle with ½ **tsp. olive oil.** Sprinkle with pepper. Garnish with fresh cilantro leaves. Serve with **carrot** or **celery sticks.**

SERVING SIZE ¼ cup CALORIES 122; FAT 9.8g (sat 1.8g, mono 4.7g, poly 2.8g); PROTEIN 4.8g; CARB 4.3g; FIBER 2.1g; CHOL 0mg; IRON 0.5mg; SODIUM 327mg; CALC 2mg

Coleslaw with Garden Vegetables

Precut cabbage, such as thinly sliced angel hair cabbage slaw, cuts down on prep time and removes the "too-much-trouble" excuse for making salads. The red, green, and purple colors from other vegetables boost nutrition, eye appeal, and taste. Double the recipe for a tailgate crowd.

MAKES 4 servings   HANDS-ON 11 min.   TOTAL 1 hour, 11 min.

In a large bowl, stir together **¼ cup light mayonnaise, ¼ cup reduced-fat sour cream, 1 Tbsp. sugar, 2 Tbsp. fresh lemon juice, ½ tsp. celery seeds, ¼ tsp. table salt,** and **⅛ tsp. black pepper.** Add **¼ cup chopped red bell pepper, ¼ cup chopped green bell pepper, ¼ cup chopped red onion,** and **1 (10-oz.) package shredded angel hair slaw**. Toss well to coat. Cover and chill 1 hour.

SERVING SIZE 1 cup CALORIES 112; FAT 6.8g (sat 1.9g, mono 1.8g, poly 2.8g); PROTEIN 2.0g; CARB 12.2g; FIBER 2.4g; CHOL 10.7mg; IRON 0.6mg; SODIUM 274mg; CALC 60mg

Spicy 3-Bean Chili

This super-simple chili cooks relatively fast in just one pot. Leave the seeds and membranes in the jalapeño for those who like their chili spicy, or remove them for a milder chili.

MAKES 10 servings   HANDS-ON 20 min.   TOTAL 1 hour

2   **lb. extra-lean ground beef**
Vegetable cooking spray
1½ **cups chopped onion**
4   **garlic cloves, minced**
¼   **cup salt-free taco seasoning**
2   **Tbsp. fresh lime juice**
½   **tsp. black pepper**
¼   **tsp. table salt**
1   **jalapeño pepper, minced**
1   **(28-oz.) can crushed tomatoes**
1   **(15-oz.) can reduced-sodium black beans, drained and rinsed**
1   **(15-oz.) can pinto beans, drained and rinsed**
1   **(15-oz.) can kidney beans, drained and rinsed**
1   **(14.5-oz.) can reduced-sodium fat-free chicken broth**
Toppings: chopped fresh cilantro, chopped tomatoes, low-fat sour cream

1. Brown ground beef in a Dutch oven coated with cooking spray over medium-high heat, stirring often, 6 to 8 minutes until meat crumbles and is no longer pink. Drain in a colander. Wipe Dutch oven clean.

2. Add onion and garlic to Dutch oven; sauté over medium-high heat 5 minutes or until onions are tender. Return beef to pan. Stir in taco seasoning; cook 1 minute.

3. Stir in lime juice and next 8 ingredients; bring to a boil. Cover, reduce heat, and simmer, stirring occasionally, 30 minutes. Uncover and simmer 10 more minutes. Serve with toppings, if desired.

Note: We tested with Dei Fratelli crushed tomatoes, Bush's reduced-sodium black beans, and Frontier salt-free taco seasoning. Nutritional analysis does not include toppings.

SERVING SIZE about 1 cup CALORIES 240; FAT 5.8g (sat 2.4g, mono 2.1g, poly 0.5g); PROTEIN 26.1g; CARB 23g; FIBER 5.8g; CHOL 53mg; IRON 4mg; SODIUM 397mg; CALC 145mg

Pecan Sandies

Laced with crunchy chopped pecans, these small, sweet cookies use just five ingredients for an utterly simple treat.

MAKES 75 cookies   HANDS-ON 14 min.   TOTAL 2 hours, 20 min.

⅓ **cup finely chopped pecans**
1 **cup butter, softened**
½ **cup sugar**
2½ **cups all-purpose flour**
1 **tsp. vanilla extract**
Parchment paper

1. Preheat oven to 350°. Bake pecans in a single layer in a shallow pan 6 to 8 minutes or until toasted and fragrant, stirring halfway through.

2. Beat butter and sugar at medium speed with an electric mixer until fluffy. Gradually add flour, beating just until blended. Beat in vanilla. Stir in pecans.

3. Divide dough in half, and shape each half into a 12- x 1¼-inch log. Wrap each log in parchment paper, and chill 1 hour or until firm.

4. Preheat oven to 325°. Cut logs into ¼-inch-thick slices, and place ½ inch apart on parchment paper-lined baking sheets.

5. Bake at 325°, in batches, for 18 to 20 minutes or until lightly golden. Cool on pans 5 minutes; transfer to wire racks, and cool completely (about 20 minutes).

SERVING SIZE 1 cookie CALORIES 46; FAT 2.9g (sat 1.6g, mono 0.8g, poly 0.2g); PROTEIN 0.5g; CARB 4.6g; FIBER 0.2g; CHOL 7mg; IRON 0.2mg; SODIUM 22mg; CALC 2mg

Bring a Healthy Choice

MY STAY-SLIM SECRET
Mara Maddox, 38, special events planner

Don't leave food choices to chance when you're invited to a gathering. "My tactic is to always bring the vegetable or salad to a family dinner or potluck," says Mara Maddox, who organizes special events for Bloomingdale's in Atlanta. "Let someone else bring the bread or chips." Maddox loves Southern favorites but prefers fried chicken without the skin, okra broiled not fried, unsweetened iced tea, and whole pecans with no sugary coating. "I think the new South is ready for this type of eating and, especially, entertaining," she says. She's even convinced her Southern in-laws to enjoy spinach dip made with nonfat Greek yogurt instead of mayonnaise.

Cajun Lemonade

Give ice-cold lemonade a spicy jolt with a touch of hot sauce. Adding light rum gives the drink a grown-up kick. A tailgate tip: Be sure to pack a separate bag of ice for drinks.

MAKES about 8 cups   HANDS-ON 10 min.   TOTAL 10 min.

2 cups light rum
1 (12-oz.) can frozen lemonade concentrate, thawed
1 tsp. hot sauce
1 (1-liter) bottle club soda, chilled
Crushed ice
Garnish: lemon slices

1. Stir together first 3 ingredients. Add club soda just before serving. Serve over crushed ice.

Note: We tested with Tabasco hot sauce.

SERVING SIZE ¾ cup CALORIES 209; FAT 0g (sat 0g, mono 0g, poly 0g); PROTEIN 0g; CARB 20.5g; FIBER 0g; CHOL 0mg; IRON 0.1mg; SODIUM 53mg; CALC 6mg

Keep Moving, Eat Your Veggies, and Mix It Up

Whether she was paddling a canoe, riding a bike, playing softball with the neighborhood kids, fishing in the Gulf of Mexico, or hunting in the wilds of central Florida, fifth-generation Floridian Valerie Boyd Gargiulo grew up learning to love playing outside.

"I have to say I grew up eating a lot of fried foods, fried pork chops, fried chicken, and fried fish," says Gargiulo. "But after a meal, we'd go out and run around. As Southern girls, we were active."

Gargiulo, a slender brunette who has a degree in foods and nutrition and now co-owns a California winery, says she believes inactivity, rather than Southern cooking, is primarily to blame when the numbers on the scale climb too high.

She says she has never been on a diet, doesn't skip meals, and eats a little of everything in small portions, with extra enthusiasm for vegetables and fish. "Vegetables are a big part of my life, and I grew up eating a lot of them."

Gargiulo notes that the plant food focused Mediterranean diet is very close to the Southern diet, with lots of vegetables such as fresh tomatoes, okra, and corn.

Seafood is important in both diets, too. Fried mullet was often on the menu during her Florida childhood; fried calamari is now an alfresco indulgence

Valerie Boyd Gargiulo, Florida native, Napa Valley winery co-owner

she shares with her husband, Jeff (also a Floridian), at Gargiulo Vineyards.

"We entertain a lot with wine at lunch and wine at dinner," Gargiulo admits. But she says the energy-burning habits she formed as a child in the South keep her fit even in northern California. "You can't sit around at a winery."

"I grew up eating a lot of fried foods. But after a meal, we'd go out and run around."

Sunday Supper

Sunday supper is a chance for the family, and often the neighbors, to get together. Fine china and silver may make an appearance, or pretty paper plates might get the vote. But you can always count on too many people in the kitchen, children and pets underfoot, a table that celebrates comfort food, and everyone sharing funny stories—all elements of memories to remember for generations. Before or after the meal, how about a game of flag football on the lawn?

Menu for 4

Honey-Pecan Chicken Thighs

Sugar & Spice Acorn Squash

Gingered Green Beans

Buttermilk Biscuits

Peach-Rhubarb Crisp

Honey-Pecan Chicken Thighs

Chicken thighs are a bit higher in fat than chicken breast, but they're flavorful and tender. This recipe calls for thighs with the skin removed, an easy way to cut the saturated fat content. The pecan crust adds some crunch, along with heart-healthy fat and fiber.

MAKES 4 servings   HANDS-ON 15 min.   TOTAL 40 min.

½ **tsp. table salt**
½ **tsp. freshly ground black pepper**
½ **tsp. ground red pepper**
8 **skinned and boned chicken thighs (about 1½ lb.)**
6 **Tbsp. honey, divided**
6 **Tbsp. Dijon mustard, divided**
2 **garlic cloves, minced**
1 **cup finely chopped pecans**
Vegetable cooking spray
½ **tsp. curry powder**
Garnish: flat-leaf parsley sprigs

1. Preheat oven to 375°. Stir together first 3 ingredients; rub evenly over chicken in a shallow dish. Stir together 2 Tbsp. honey, 2 Tbsp. mustard, and garlic; brush over chicken.

2. Dredge chicken in pecans; place chicken on a wire rack coated with cooking spray in an aluminum foil-lined broiler pan. Bake at 375° for 25 minutes or until chicken is done.

3. Stir together remaining 4 Tbsp. honey, remaining 4 Tbsp. mustard, and curry powder in a small bowl; serve with chicken.

SERVING SIZE 2 thighs and 2 Tbsp. sauce CALORIES 412; FAT 24.1g (sat 2.8g, mono 12.7g, poly 6.9g); PROTEIN 22.5g; CARB 30.8g; FIBER 3g; CHOL 97mg; IRON 1.9mg; SODIUM 656mg; CALC 38mg

---

Explore Lighter Pairings

MY STAY-SLIM SECRET
Annette Shafer, 48, vineyard co-owner

Wines are usually paired with the meaty part of a meal, but Huntsville, Alabama, native and Napa Valley vineyard co-owner Annette Shafer enjoys matching wines with lighter fare. That way Shafer doesn't feel obligated to order steak or lobster just because of the wine. A Culinary Institute of America graduate, Shafer says the sweetness of vegetables like corn or sugar snap peas pairs beautifully with a well-balanced Chardonnay. She finds that grilled vegetables match deliciously with red wines such as Merlot, Syrah, Zinfandel, and even less-tannic Cabernets. And red wine with fish—a big red Shafer Vineyards Cabernet with salmon, for instance—can be terrific, too.

Sugar & Spice Acorn Squash

A small amount of nutmeg adds a nice hint of spice to this super-easy side dish. Acorn squash (and other winter squash) is often hard to cut because it's so dense. Microwave the raw squash for about a minute to soften it a bit.

MAKES 4 servings   HANDS-ON 5 min.   TOTAL 50 min.

1 **large acorn squash (about 1¼ lb.)**
¼ **tsp. table salt**
⅛ **tsp. black pepper**
2 **Tbsp. brown sugar**
⅛ **tsp. ground nutmeg**
4 **tsp. butter, melted**

1. Preheat oven to 400°. Cut squash lengthwise into 4 equal wedges; remove and discard seeds and membranes. Sprinkle flesh evenly with salt and pepper. Place, skin side down, on an aluminum foil-lined baking sheet.

2. Bake at 400° for 40 minutes or until squash is tender.

3. Combine brown sugar and nutmeg; sprinkle evenly over each wedge, and drizzle evenly with butter. Bake 5 to 7 more minutes or until sugar melts.

SERVING SIZE 1 wedge CALORIES 104; FAT 4g (sat 2.5g, mono 1g, poly 0.2g); PROTEIN 0.9g; CARB 18.1g; FIBER 1.7g; CHOL 10mg; IRON 0.8mg; SODIUM 186mg; CALC 43mg

Gingered Green Beans

Fresh ginger perks up green beans to elevate this simple Southern side to "company's coming" status.

MAKES 6 servings   HANDS-ON 16 min.   TOTAL 16 min.

3 **cups reduced-sodium fat-free chicken broth**
1 **lb. fresh green beans, trimmed**
1 **Tbsp. butter**
1 **cup vertically sliced sweet onion**
2 **Tbsp. minced fresh ginger**
2 **garlic cloves, minced**
½ **tsp. seasoned pepper**
¼ **tsp. table salt**

1. Bring broth to a boil in a large saucepan over medium-high heat. Add green beans, and cook 4 to 6 minutes or until crisp-tender; drain.

2. Melt butter in a large nonstick skillet over medium-high heat. Add onion, and sauté 4 minutes. Add ginger and garlic; sauté 1 minute. Add green beans, seasoned pepper, and salt; sauté 1 minute or until thoroughly heated.

SERVING SIZE about ⅔ cup CALORIES 55; FAT 2.2g (sat 1.3g, mono 0.5g, poly 0.2g); PROTEIN 2g; CARB 8.8g; FIBER 2.6g; CHOL 5.3mg; IRON 0.9mg; SODIUM 127mg; CALC 37mg

Buttermilk Biscuits

MAKES 16 biscuits   HANDS-ON 20 min.   TOTAL 35 min.

2   **cups all-purpose flour**
2   **tsp. baking powder**
¼   **tsp. baking soda**
¼   **tsp. table salt**
¼   **cup butter**
1   **cup nonfat buttermilk**

1. Preheat oven to 400°. Combine first 4 ingredients in a large bowl. Cut butter into flour mixture with a fork or pastry blender until crumbly; add buttermilk, stirring just until dry ingredients are moistened.

2. Turn dough out onto a lightly floured surface; knead 2 or 3 times. Pat or roll dough to ½-inch thickness; cut with a 1½-inch round cutter, and place on a baking sheet.

3. Bake at 400° for 15 minutes or until biscuits are golden.

SERVING SIZE 1 biscuit CALORIES 83; FAT 3.1g (sat 1.9g, mono 0.8g, poly 0.2g); PROTEIN 2.1g; CARB 11.8g; FIBER 0.4g; CHOL 8mg; IRON 0.7mg; SODIUM 135mg; CALC 43mg

Sweet Potato-Buttermilk Biscuits: Preheat the oven to 425°. Proceed with Step 1, increasing the baking powder to 1 Tbsp., omitting the baking soda, and increasing the salt to ½ tsp. Cut in the butter as directed. Decrease the buttermilk to ½ cup, and combine buttermilk with ½ cup cooked mashed sweet potato before adding the buttermilk mixture to the dry ingredients. Proceed with steps 2 and 3 as directed above.

SAVOR THE SOUTH LINGER LONGER INDULGE A LITTLE MAKE IT HAPPEN

Sweet Potatoes

The vibrant orange flesh of a sweet potato is a clue that it's loaded with the important nutrient beta-carotene, which plays a key role in both eye and skin health because our bodies turn it into vitamin A. In fact, it's considered a nutritional superstar because just one cup of baked sweet potato provides more than four times the vitamin A we need per day.

Sweet potatoes are also a good source of vitamin C, fiber, and vitamin B6. And you get all of this for a fairly low-calorie cost—100 calories per cup. Of course, that's before you add the butter, brown sugar, or marshmallows (as in the classic casserole), or toss them into the deep fryer. (Menu alert: At restaurants, sweet potato fries are sometimes actually higher in fat and calories than other fries because of how they absorb oil when fried.)

Better options: Try sweet potato wedges baked and sprinkled with a little salt, or baked and mashed sweet potatoes, which have a satisfying creamy texture and sweetness even without added butter or sugar.

Peach-Rhubarb Crisp

Rhubarb is high in vitamin C, B-complex vitamins, fiber, and calcium; team it with sweet peaches and sugar and you've got a zesty sweet-tart combination that's sure to please.

MAKES 10 servings   HANDS-ON 15 min.   TOTAL 1 hour

1 **(20-oz.) bag frozen peaches, thawed**
2 **(16-oz.) packages frozen sliced rhubarb, thawed**
1½ **cups granulated sugar**
3 **Tbsp. lemon juice**
1¼ **cups all-purpose flour, divided**
Vegetable cooking spray
⅓ **cup uncooked quick-cooking oats**
⅓ **cup firmly packed brown sugar**
⅓ **cup cold butter, cut into small pieces**

1. Preheat oven to 375°. Combine first 4 ingredients in a medium bowl; add ¼ cup flour, stirring well. Pour mixture into a 13- x-9-inch baking dish coated with cooking spray.

2. Combine oats, brown sugar, and remaining 1 cup flour in a small bowl; cut in cold butter with a fork or pastry blender until mixture resembles coarse crumbs. Sprinkle mixture evenly over fruit filling.

3. Bake at 375° for 45 to 50 minutes or until bubbly.

SERVING SIZE ¹⁄₁₀ crisp CALORIES 308; FAT 6.7g (sat 4g, mono 1.7g, poly 0.4g); PROTEIN 3g; CARB 61.9g; FIBER 3.2g; CHOL 16mg; IRON 1.4mg; SODIUM 59mg; CALC 189mg

Cocktail Party

Sure, you may associate a Southern cocktail party with classics like mint juleps and Sazeracs (the classic New Orleans beverage featuring whiskey, bitters, sugar, and a hint of absinthe), but down here we know how to mix a drink. From grapefruit margaritas to sparkling rum punch, bourbon-peach cocktails to a new take on the Old Fashioned, you'll find no shortage of inventions to imbibe. Party food is by nature bite-sized, making it easy to indulge just a little. If the music's playing, why not kick up those fancy heels and do some dancing to burn off a few of those cocktail calories?

Menu for 10

**Pepper Jelly Margaritas
OR
Fig-and-Bourbon Fizz**

Party-Style Pork Empanada

**Cracker Spoons with Creamy
Pimiento Cheese**

Mini Grits and Greens

Two-Layer Salted Pecan Bars

Pepper Jelly Margaritas

No need for a drink mix here: Green pepper jelly plays a starring role when stirred into lime juice, tequila, and orange liqueur.

MAKES 8 servings   HANDS-ON 10 min.   TOTAL 10 min.

1   **cup tequila**
1   **cup fresh lime juice**
½   **cup orange liqueur**
⅓   **cup powdered sugar**
¼   **cup green pepper jelly**
Garnish: lime slices

1. Stir together first 5 ingredients in a large pitcher, stirring until sugar and pepper jelly are dissolved. Fill cocktail shaker with ice cubes; pour desired amount of mixture into cocktail shaker. Cover with lid, and shake vigorously until thoroughly chilled (about 30 seconds). Strain into chilled glasses with salted rims and filled with ice. Serve immediately.

Note: We tested with Grand Marnier orange liqueur.

SERVING SIZE about ½ cup CALORIES 159; FAT 0g (sat 0g, mono 0g, poly 0g); PROTEIN 0.1g; CARB 17.8g; FIBER 0.1g; CHOL 0mg; IRON 0mg; SODIUM 1mg; CALC 4mg

Fig-and-Bourbon Fizz

Try using a Black Mission fig to give this drink a pretty tint. Put out plenty of figs and mint for guests to make their own drinks.

MAKES 1 serving   HANDS-ON 5 min.   TOTAL 5 min.

1   **fresh whole, ripe fig**
6   **fresh mint leaves**
1   **tsp. brown sugar**
¼   **cup bourbon**
Ice cubes
½   **cup diet ginger ale, chilled**
Garnish: mint sprig

1. Muddle fig, mint leaves, and brown sugar against sides of a cocktail shaker. (Fig should be fairly broken down.) Add bourbon and enough ice cubes to fill shaker (about 1 cup). Cover with lid, and shake vigorously until thoroughly chilled (about 30 seconds). Strain into a 10-oz. glass filled with ice cubes. Top with chilled ginger ale. Stir gently, and garnish, if desired. Serve immediately.

SERVING SIZE 1 drink CALORIES 183; FAT 0.2g (sat 0g, mono 0g, poly 0.1g); PROTEIN 0.4g; CARB 14g; FIBER 1.5g; CHOL 0mg; IRON 0.3mg; SODIUM 32mg; CALC 22mg

Party-Style Pork Empanada

Savory pastries stuffed with meat and seasonings, empanadas are popular in South America—and South Florida! These smaller versions are perfect party fare. To make ahead, prepare recipe as directed through Step 5. Cover with lightly greased plastic wrap, and chill 2 hours. Proceed with recipe as directed.

MAKES 10 appetizer servings   HANDS-ON 42 min.   TOTAL 1 hour

¼ cup slivered or sliced almonds

¾ lb. pork tenderloin (about 1 small tenderloin)

1 (1.25-oz.) envelope picadillo seasoning

½ medium-size sweet onion, chopped

1 small red bell pepper, chopped

1 Tbsp. olive oil

½ cup golden raisins

3 Tbsp. fresh lime juice

¼ cup chopped fresh cilantro

¼ cup light sour cream

½ tsp. black pepper

1 (11-oz.) can refrigerated French bread dough

1 large egg, lightly beaten

Vegetable cooking spray

½ tsp. cumin seeds (optional)

½ cup prepared refrigerated salsa

Garnish: lime wedges

1. Heat almonds in a large nonstick skillet over medium-low heat, stirring often, 4 to 6 minutes or until toasted and fragrant.

2. Preheat oven to 375°. Cut pork into ½-inch cubes. Toss together pork and picadillo seasoning.

3. Sauté onion and bell pepper in hot oil in skillet over medium-high heat 5 minutes or until tender. Add pork mixture, and sauté 6 minutes or until browned. Stir in raisins and lime juice, and cook 30 seconds. Remove from heat. Stir in almonds, cilantro, sour cream, and black pepper.

4. Unroll dough on a lightly floured surface. Gently stretch dough into a 14- x 12-inch rectangle. Spoon pork mixture onto dough, leaving a 1½-inch border. Lightly brush edges of dough with egg, and roll up, starting at 1 long side and ending seam side down.

5. Carefully place dough, seam side down, on a baking sheet coated with cooking spray. Bring ends of roll together to form a ring, pinching edges together to seal. Lightly brush top and sides of dough with egg. Sprinkle with cumin seeds, if desired.

6. Bake at 375° for 18 to 22 minutes or until golden brown. Serve warm with salsa.

Note: We tested with Nueva Cocina Picadillo Beef Seasoning and Pillsbury Refrigerated Crusty French Loaf.

SERVING SIZE ¹⁄₁₀ empanada and 2 Tbsp. salsa CALORIES 116; FAT 3.4g (sat 0.9g, mono 1.5g, poly 0.4g); PROTEIN 7.1g; CARB 14.9g; FIBER 0.8g; CHOL 27mg; IRON 1mg; SODIUM 190mg; CALC 16mg

Cracker Spoons
with Creamy Pimiento Cheese

Pimiento cheese and crackers are a Southern party staple. For less than $2, a teaspoon-shaped cookie cutter makes pimiento cheese party-ready.

MAKES 5 dozen   HANDS-ON 25 min.   TOTAL 1 hour, 20 min.

1½ (14.1-oz.) packages
    refrigerated piecrusts
1 large egg white, beaten
¾ tsp. seasoned salt
Parchment paper
Creamy Pimiento Cheese
Garnishes: diced
    pimiento, chopped
    fresh chives

1. Preheat oven to 400°. Unroll piecrusts; brush with egg white, and sprinkle with seasoned salt (about ¼ tsp. per crust). Cut dough into shapes using a 4½- or 5-inch teaspoon-shaped cutter. Place cutouts 1 inch apart on parchment paper-lined baking sheets.

2. Bake, in batches, at 400° for 9 to 11 minutes or until lightly browned and crisp. Remove from baking sheets to a wire rack, and cool completely (about 20 minutes). Store in an airtight container 1 day, or freeze up to 2 weeks.

3. Spoon Creamy Pimiento Cheese into a zip-top plastic freezer bag. (Do not seal.) Snip 1 corner of bag to make a small hole. Pipe pimiento cheese onto end of each spoon.

SERVING SIZE 1 cracker CALORIES 67; FAT 4.7g (sat 2g, mono 1.8g, poly 0.5g); PROTEIN 1.1g; CARB 4.9g; FIBER 0g; CHOL 6mg; IRON 0mg; SODIUM 116mg; CALC 34mg

Creamy Pimiento Cheese

MAKES 1¾ cups   HANDS-ON 10 min.   TOTAL 10 min.

Beat **1 (10-oz.) block sharp shredded Cheddar cheese, ½ cup mayonnaise, 1 (4-oz.) jar drained diced pimiento, 1 tsp. grated onion, 1 tsp. Dijon mustard, ¼ tsp. ground red pepper,** and **¹⁄₁₆ tsp. Worcestershire sauce** at medium speed with a heavy-duty electric stand mixer 1 minute or until creamy. Season with **¹⁄₁₆ tsp. table salt** and **¼ tsp. black pepper.**

SERVING SIZE 1 Tbsp. CALORIES 27; FAT 2.3g (sat 1g, mono 0.3g, poly 0.2g); PROTEIN 1g; CARB 0g; FIBER 0g; CHOL 5mg; IRON 0mg; SODIUM 46mg; CALC 34mg

Mini Grits and Greens

Warm the ceramic soup spoons in a 200° oven for 10 minutes before assembling to keep the grits at a serving-friendly temperature.

MAKES 3 dozen   HANDS-ON 45 min.   TOTAL 45 min.

1   cup chicken broth
⅓   cup half-and-half
¼   tsp. table salt
½   cup uncooked regular grits
½   cup (2 oz.) freshly shredded Cheddar cheese
¼   cup freshly grated Parmesan cheese
1   Tbsp. butter
½   tsp. hot sauce
¼   tsp. freshly ground black pepper
8   large fresh collard green leaves
2   small dry Spanish chorizo sausage links (about 2¾ oz.)
1   Tbsp. olive oil
2   tsp. apple cider vinegar
½   tsp. sugar
36   porcelain tasting spoons, warmed

1. Bring first 3 ingredients and 1 cup water to a boil in a medium saucepan over high heat; gradually whisk in grits. Cover, reduce heat to medium-low, and simmer, stirring occasionally, 15 minutes or until thickened. Whisk in Cheddar cheese and next 4 ingredients, whisking constantly until cheese melts. Keep warm.

2. Rinse collard greens. Trim and discard thick stems from bottom of collard green leaves (about 2 inches). Stack collard greens on a cutting board. Tightly roll up leaves, and thinly slice into ⅛-inch strips. Quarter chorizo lengthwise, and cut into small pieces.

3. Sauté chorizo in hot oil in a large skillet over medium-high heat 2 minutes. Add collard greens, vinegar, and sugar. Cook, stirring constantly, 2 minutes or until greens are bright green and just tender. Season with salt and pepper to taste.

4. Place about 1 Tbsp. grits onto each warm spoon, and top with collard mixture. Serve immediately.

SERVING SIZE 1 spoon CALORIES 37; FAT 2.5g (sat 1.2g, mono 1.0g, poly 0.2g); PROTEIN 1.5g; CARB 2.1g; FIBER 0.1g; CHOL 6mg; IRON 0.1mg; SODIUM 91mg; CALC 23mg

Two-Layer Salted Pecan Bars

This classic is updated with a sprinkle of kosher salt—a simple addition that's found in trendy sweet treats, from caramels to cookies to chocolate bars.

MAKES 20 servings   HANDS-ON 15 min.   TOTAL 55 min.

Vegetable cooking spray
1½ **cups finely crushed pretzels sticks**
½ **cup butter, melted**
3 **Tbsp. sugar**
1 **large egg white**
2 **Tbsp. fat-free milk**
40 **caramels**
1 **tsp. vanilla extract**
¾ **cup finely chopped pecans**
¼ **tsp. sea salt**

1. Preheat oven to 375°. Line bottom and sides of an 8-inch square pan with aluminum foil, allowing 2 to 3 inches to extend over sides; coat foil with cooking spray.

2. Stir together crushed pretzels, melted butter, sugar, and egg white; press mixture on bottom of pan. Bake at 375° for 11 minutes.

3. While crust is baking, combine milk and caramels in a medium saucepan. Cook over low heat, stirring occasionally, 5 minutes or until caramels melt. Remove from heat; stir in vanilla.

4. Remove crust from oven; pour caramel mixture over hot crust. Sprinkle with pecans and salt. Cool in pan on a wire rack 10 minutes. Chill at least 30 minutes. Lift mixture from pan, using foil sides as handles. Cut into 20 bars. Store in refrigerator up to 1 week.

SERVING SIZE 1 bar CALORIES 167; FAT 9.2g (sat 3.7g, mono 3.2g, poly 1.8g); PROTEIN 1.8g; CARB 20.8g; FIBER 0.5g; CHOL 13.7mg; IRON 0.3mg; SODIUM 175mg; CALC 34mg

Cook with Friends

MY STAY-SLIM SECRET

Ashley Christensen, 37, chef and restaurateur

With the current obsession with fast and easy cooking and 15-minute meals, chef Ashley Christensen thinks something has gotten lost in the shuffle. "Cooking has always been tremendously social for me," says Christensen, chef and owner of Poole's Diner and three other renowned restaurants in Raleigh, North Carolina. She savors the moments spent preparing meals for and with others, and says that when you cook with others you get more than physical nourishment. "There's something about shucking corn and shelling peas that forces you to sit down and engage," she says.

Chapter Eight

MAKE-IT-HAPPEN DAYS

Try as you might to choreograph a healthy week, you can never predict precisely what each day will bring. A last-minute work demand or a late invitation to a don't-miss party can interrupt your best cooking-at-home intentions. An unanticipated cancellation can leave you with a free morning, a growling stomach, and nothing healthy on hand for breakfast.

And, oh, don't I know it: Sometimes you pack the perfect lunch—only to leave it at home. And then there's how you feel: Some days you wake up ready to run five miles; others leave you craving a bacon cheeseburger and a nap. **There's really only one thing you can count on: change!**

So how do you incorporate healthy eating in your crazy-busy schedule? Apply the SLIM philosophy, of course! At their core, the SLIM principles are all about appreciating life: savoring your food choices, lingering for a few minutes to enjoy your meal and those you share it with, indulging a little in some of life's unexpected treats, and making good health happen with grit and grace, no matter what the day delivers.

The secret isn't changing your life to fit a completely new way of eating; it's learning how to adapt to life's changing demands and little surprises in healthy ways.

To help you visualize how the SLIM principles and the recipes in this book can work for almost any type of day, I've put together daily meal plans for seven different scenarios, or what I like to call "Make-It-Happen Days." Each presents its own eating challenges, but as you will see, the SLIM strategy helps you give your body what it needs to stay healthy, nourished, and satisfied.

Each of these seven menus totals less than 2,000 calories for the day, in keeping with the United States Department of Agriculture's dietary guidelines for moderately active females age 14 to 50. You may need to eat a little more or less depending on your gender, age, activity level, and goals (maintaining a healthy weight vs. losing a little).

Of course, this is just a sample of what you can do with the SLIM ideals and recipes. Whether you've got a sudden craving for chocolate, a crunched schedule that crowds out time for a walk, or a family request for buttermilk biscuits, rest assured that you can handle them in healthful ways.

Just take a deep breath, smile, and remember the word SLIM. Your secret to enjoying great food and good nutrition every day is embedded in each letter: Savor the South, Linger Longer, Indulge a Little, and Make It Happen.

Here's wishing you a lifetime of good eating and good health—no matter what kind of day you're having!

ROAD TRIP

Whether it's over the river and through the woods to visit Grandma or over to the airport and through the skies for a business trip, traveling takes you away from your regularly scheduled life. While your fridge and pantry at home may be stocked with healthy meal fixin's, nutritious options can be harder to find when you're out and about, and a day spent in the car or on a plane is a day with little or no physical activity. Use smart snacks, small portions, and a little planning to help keep you in the slim, Southern mind-set.

BREAKFAST: Kick-start your day with a healthy breakfast before you go. (Bonus points if you can slip in a brief walk or workout first.) A refreshing smoothie and a breakfast bread have protein and carbs to help keep your energy revved up on the road.

Blueberry Smoothie, page 42: 111 calories

Oatmeal Scone with Pecans, page 44: 238 calories

1 cup half-sweet tea: 30 calories

Sautéed green beans: 50 calories

LUNCH: Make a pit stop at a BBQ spot for a pulled pork sandwich, which offers down-home Southern flavor without weighing you down. Wherever you land for lunch, keep it under 600 calories by checking the menu, watching portion sizes, and avoiding smothered and fried options.

Pulled BBQ pork sandwich: 500 calories

¼ cup trail mix: 175 calories

1 banana: 100 calories

SNACKS: Avoid mindless snacking on chips or sweets by packing small portions of protein-packed trail mix and fresh fruit or veggies. (Solid foods such as these are allowed through airport security—and they're cheaper if you portion and pack your own.)

DINNER: Eating on the road? It's possible to have fast food that's not junk food. Reading the posted calorie counts can help at the drive-through.

Broccoli and cheese baked potato: 470 calories

Small chili: 210 calories

Total calories for the day:

1,884

BUSY WORK DAY

We all have busy days—the kind where you're on the run from sunup to sundown. It can be fun, and the time sure flies, but when your schedule is this crazed, you'll need energy to keep you humming. Skipping meals or snacks will leave you running on fumes, but don't grab just any ol' junk from the vending machine. It's important to choose foods with protein power and other nutrients that give you stamina. When you reach the finish line, enjoy an easy-as-pie dinner recipe and a beer. You've earned it!

Fruit Salad with Yogurt, page 36: 137 calories

12 oz. lemonade: 180 calories

BREAKFAST: A quick, protein-packed breakfast helps power you up for the tasks ahead.

1 fried egg made with cooking spray: 90 calories; 1 slice buttered whole wheat toast: 140 calories

LUNCH: No matter how busy you may be, don't skip lunch—that's a sure ticket to losing steam later in the day. A favorite sandwich on whole grain bread with some hummus and carrots keeps you going even when you're dining at your desk.

Ham and Swiss sandwich on whole grain bread with mustard: 260 calories

2 Tbsp. pimiento cheese with about 1 oz. pecan halves and 1 green apple, sliced: 360 calories

SNACKS: Keep your motor revved with an afternoon pick-me-up. Healthy snacks like fresh fruit with cheese and nuts are deliciously satisfying.

DINNER: Somebody cooked dinner for you! Oh, it was you! Throw this chili into the slow cooker before you leave the house, and it'll be waiting for you when you get home. Reward yourself with a glass of wine or light beer and a yummy (and pretty) piece of cornbread.

2 Lemon-Herb Cornmeal Madeleines, page 142: 116 calories

2 cups Slow-Cooker Veggie Chili, page 153: 322 calories

12 oz. beer (or 4 oz. wine): 120 calories

Total calories for the day:

1,725

WEEKEND WARRIOR DAY

Birds are singing, flowers are blooming, and you're waking up early to get in a brisk walk or a workout before the real world catches up with you. Take time for a quick pre-exercise snack; then enjoy a protein-rich breakfast after you've worked up a sweat. Keep your good-day feeling going with a light lunch, and finish with a deliciously healthy dinner that's worthy of any spa. Fresh fruit and vegetables add hydration to your body-beautiful day.

1 Corn Muffin, page 41: 129 calories; 1 boiled egg: 78 calories

BREAKFAST: Don't start exercising on an empty stomach: Simple carbs give you the fuel you need to power through, so grab a mini corn muffin and a glass of water to maximize performance. Post workout, refuel with rich and creamy Greek yogurt flavored with honey and granola. (The protein/carb combo helps with muscle repair and recovery.)

¾ cup Greek yogurt with 1 Tbsp. honey and ½ cup high-protein granola (such as Kashi GOLEAN Crunch): 290 calories

LUNCH: Bursting-with-flavor blueberries and protein-rich chicken served in a fiber-filled whole grain pita make a light yet satisfying lunch.

6-inch whole grain pita bread: 170 calories

1 serving Chicken Blueberry Salad, page 90: 201 calories

SNACKS: Juicy and refreshing, sweet watermelon is perfect for natural hydration! Peanuts give you protein for endurance and help fulfill that craving for a crunchy snack.

1 cup chopped watermelon: 50 calories

1 oz. peanuts: 160 calories

DINNER: A satisfying seafood dinner helps keep both mind and muscles strong. Pairing protein-packed catfish with some potatoes and broccoli helps you end the day on a nutritious note. Dessert comes in the form of a sweet treat made with frozen berries.

Roasted Red Bliss Potato Salad, page 150: 130 calories

Broccoli Slaw with Candied Pecans, page 134: 157 calories

Blackberry-Lemon Buttermilk Sorbet, page 201: 162 calories

Lime-Orange Catfish, page 163: 260 Calories

Total calories for the day:

1,787

FRIED-CHICKEN FIX

In the South, some days, you've just gotta have something crunchy, tasty, and fried. Embrace your craving and meet it smiling—it's possible to have your treat and eat it, too! The key is to keep the rest of your day light so you can fully enjoy that fried chicken special or whatever spells "splurge" to you. If you have to give in and have your fried treat at lunch, flip the lighter meal to dinner.

BREAKFAST: Even if your calorie count is going to be weighted toward your bigger meal, you need a baseline of good nutrition in the a.m. Fresh fruit and a satisfying frittata help start the day off right.

1 slice whole wheat toast with 2 tsp. butter: 160 calories

Zucchini-Onion Frittata, page 49: 219 calories

LUNCH: Who said salad has to be boring? This one sounds like a day at some sunny Southern beach. Yup, there's sweet tea in the dressing!

Grilled Shrimp Salad with Sweet Tea Vinaigrette, page 82: 356 calories

1 small dinner roll: 70 calories

1 cup sliced strawberries: 50 calories

1 cup sliced cucumbers: 15 calories; ¼ cup hummus: 120 calories

SNACK: Fresh vegetables and a creamy dip with a little healthy fat and protein offer a guilt-free midday pick-me-up.

DINNER: Nothing says Southern comfort like some fried chicken, cheesy grits, and greens. Take your time and savor every bite. And yes, you can have dessert, because this fried chicken recipe is lighter than the usual!

1 Mini Berry Cobbler, page 217: 210 calories

1 cup steamed collards: 100 calories

1 Skillet Fried Chicken breast, page 172: 467 calories

1 cup Baked Cheese Grits, page 52: 141 calories

Total calories for the day:

1,908

TIME FOR A PARTY

Every day's an excuse for a party in the South. To survive the celebrating and still slip into the season's fashions, you need a game plan. If you're at a buffet, circle the table first so you can see what's on the menu before you dig in. Make a pretty plate and take only what you really want. If it's a cocktail affair, lean toward the lighter side (fresh fruits and veggies, steamed shrimp, lean roast beef). And don't forget to slow down and socialize!

BREAKFAST: Don't save your calories for later just because you know you have a big bash ahead. A muffin and a spinach omelet fill you up without filling you out.

Omelet made with cooking spray, 2 eggs, 2 Tbsp. grated Parmesan cheese, and ½ cup frozen chopped spinach: 232 calories

1 oz. baked tortilla chips: 120 calories

LUNCH: Enjoy the barbecue! There's flavor aplenty to be had with Southwestern-style offerings.

Corn and Black Bean Salad, page 74: 69 calories

Grilled chicken breast with BBQ sauce: 275 calories

Carrot Cake Muffin, page 38: 128 calories

SNACK: Fresh fruit, veggies, and hummus offer fiber, which can help keep you from overdoing it at the buffet later on.

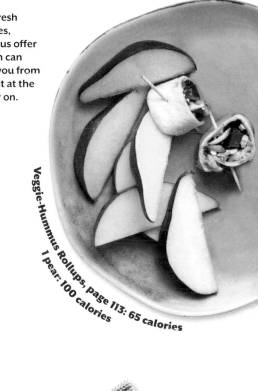

Veggie-Hummus Rollups, page 113: 65 calories
1 pear: 100 calories

DINNER: Now's the time to indulge a little. Reach for your favorites, but keep your portion sizes in check.

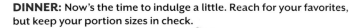

Pepper Jelly Margarita, page 260: 159 calories

1 serving Party-Style Pork Empanada, page 261: 116 calories; ½ cup grilled vegetables: 65 calories; 2 servings Marinated Shrimp & Artichokes, page 127: 141 calories; 1 Chicken and Mini Waffle, page 120: 101 calories

Total calories for the day:

1,571

SIMPLY DIVINE SATURDAY

Weekends are made for small indulgences. Wake up late and enjoy a lazy breakfast, kicked off with a mimosa toast! Then head to the farmers' market to browse for some local cheese and just-picked produce, visit with friends, and get some fresh air. Finish with a lovely dinner made with farm-fresh finds. Sit back, relax, and enjoy the day.

BREAKFAST: Hearty sausage and eggs set the tone for a relaxed atmosphere. Some bubbly with a splash of orange juice makes it feel like a real celebration.

Breakfast Sausage Tostada, page 56: 320 calories

LUNCH: Season's best peaches and tomatoes co-star in a delicious cold soup; serve with whole grain bread and a refreshing iced tea.

Peach-and-Tomato Gazpacho with Cucumber Yogurt, page 67: 150 calories

12 oz. sweetened iced tea with fresh mint garnish: 120 calories

Whole grain roll with butter: 125 calories

Mimosa
(2 oz. orange juice,
4 oz. Champagne,
and a splash of
orange liqueur):
120 calories

DINNER: The end of the day brings with it friends, family, and a supper that's worth remembering: a four-course meal with some of the South's biggest flavors, served with a cocktail to keep the weekend spirit going.

Grilled Green Tomato Caprese, page 137: 106 calories

Gingered
Green Beans,
page 255:
55 calories

Daiquiri
(1.5 oz. rum,
1 oz. lime juice,
1 tsp. sugar):
120 calories

½ cup cooked
couscous:
88 calories

Honey-Grilled
Pork Tenderloins,
page 183: 181
calories

Classic Strawberry
Shortcake, page 206:
200 calories

Total calories
for the day:

1,585

BEST BODY DAY

Whether you've got your eye on a pair of skinny jeans or need to squeeze into a new little black dress, sometimes you just feel a little more self-conscious about your appearance. Whatever your wardrobe motivation may be, it can help to follow a menu featuring foods that help beat the bloat. Choose lower-sodium foods, fresh produce, and lean protein keep you feeling full and looking your slimmest and trimmest.

BREAKFAST: Eggs and toast, sans butter, get you ready to take on the day without loading you down. Use pepper or salt-free seasonings to help minimize bloat.

LUNCH: Fill up with some soup and a sandwich. The healthy fats found in avocado and hummus are naturally satisfying so you don't feel the need to raid the fridge or pantry shortly after eating.

Baby Carrot Soup, page 68: 123 calories

2 hard-cooked eggs, 2 slices high-fiber wheat bread, 1 Tbsp. mayonnaise, 2 slices tomato: 300 calories

Unsweetened iced tea with sliced strawberries: 30 calories

Avocado Salad-Hummus Pita, page 92: 303 calories

6 oz. sparkling water with ¼ cup pomegranate juice and lime wedges: 35 calories

SNACK: There's no need for candy or other junk food when you've got sweet peaches to snack on! Add some protein with a handful of pecan halves.

¼ cup pecan halves: 170 calories

1 cup peach slices: 66 calories

DINNER: A fish dinner offers good-for-you fats and plenty of protein. Skip the salt, and season with fresh lemon juice and herbs. That leaves you room for a cocktail (or two!) in your hot new outfit.

¾ cup cooked quinoa: 170 calories

2 Cosmopolitans (1.5 oz. vodka, ¼ cup cranberry juice cocktail, 2 Tbsp. lime juice each): 280 calories

Glazed Salmon with Stir-fried Vegetables, page 164: 404 calories

Total calories for the day:

1,881

Nutritional Analysis

In Our Nutritional Analysis, We Use These Abbreviations

sat   saturated fat

mono   monounsaturated fat

poly   polyunsaturated fat

CARB   carbohydrates

CHOL   cholesterol

CALC   calcium

g   gram

mg   milligram

Daily Nutrition Guide			
	Women ages 25 to 50	**Women over 50**	**Men ages 24 to 50**	**Men over 50**
Calories	2,000	2,000 or less	2,700	2,500
Protein	50g	50g or less	63g	60g
Fat	65g or less	65g or less	88g or less	83g or less
Saturated Fat	20g or less	20g or less	27g or less	25g or less
Carbohydrates	304g	304g	410g	375g
Fiber	25g to 35g	25g to 35g	25g to 35g	25g to 35g
Cholesterol	300mg or less	300mg or less	300mg or less	300mg or less
Iron	18mg	8mg	8mg	8mg
Sodium	2,300mg or less	1,500mg or less	2,300mg or less	1,500mg or less
Calcium	1,000mg	1,200mg	1,000mg	1,000mg

The nutritional values used in our calculations come from either The Food Processor, Version 10.4 (ESHA Research), or are provided by food manufacturers.

Metric Equivalents

The information in the following charts is provided to help cooks outside the United States successfully use the recipes in this book. All equivalents are approximate.

Cooking/Oven Temperatures

	Fahrenheit	Celsius	Gas Mark
Freeze Water	32° F	0° C	
Room Temp.	68° F	20° C	
Boil Water	212° F	100° C	
Bake	325° F	160° C	3
	350° F	180° C	4
	375° F	190° C	5
	400° F	200° C	6
	425° F	220° C	7
	450° F	230° C	8
Broil			Grill

Liquid Ingredients by Volume

¼ tsp	=					1 ml		
½ tsp	=					2 ml		
1 tsp	=					5 ml		
3 tsp	=	1 Tbsp	=	½ fl oz	=	15 ml		
2 Tbsp	=	⅛ cup	=	1 fl oz	=	30 ml		
4 Tbsp	=	¼ cup	=	2 fl oz	=	60 ml		
5⅓ Tbsp	=	⅓ cup	=	3 fl oz	=	80 ml		
8 Tbsp	=	½ cup	=	4 fl oz	=	120 ml		
10⅔ Tbsp	=	⅔ cup	=	5 fl oz	=	160 ml		
12 Tbsp	=	¾ cup	=	6 fl oz	=	180 ml		
16 Tbsp	=	1 cup	=	8 fl oz	=	240 ml		
1 pt	=	2 cups	=	16 fl oz	=	480 ml		
1 qt	=	4 cups	=	32 fl oz	=	960 ml		
				33 fl oz	=	1000 ml	=	1 l

Dry Ingredients by Weight

(To convert ounces to grams, multiply the number of ounces by 30.)

1 oz	=	¹⁄₁₆ lb	=	30 g
4 oz	=	¼ lb	=	120 g
8 oz	=	½ lb	=	240 g
12 oz	=	¾ lb	=	360 g
16 oz	=	1 lb	=	480 g

Length

To convert inches to centimeters, multiply the number of inches by 2.5.)

1 in	=					2.5 cm		
6 in	=	½ ft			=	15 cm		
12 in	=	1 ft			=	30 cm		
36 in	=	3 ft	=	1 yd	=	90 cm		
40 in	=					100 cm	=	1 m

Equivalents for Different Types of Ingredients

Standard Cup	Fine Powder (ex. flour)	Grain (ex. rice)	Granular (ex. sugar)	Liquid Solids (ex. butter)	Liquid (ex. milk)
1	140 g	150 g	190 g	200 g	240 ml
¾	105 g	113 g	143 g	150 g	180 ml
⅔	93 g	100 g	125 g	133 g	160 ml
½	70 g	75 g	95 g	100 g	120 ml
⅓	47 g	50 g	63 g	67 g	80 ml
¼	35 g	38 g	48 g	50 g	60 ml
⅛	18 g	19 g	24 g	25 g	30 ml

INDEX

ISBN-13: 978-0-8487-4282-9
ISBN-10: 0-8487-4282-6
Library of Congress Control Number: 2013949076

Printed in the United States of America
First Printing 2013

Southern Living®

Editor: M. Lindsay Bierman
Creative Director: Robert Perino
Managing Editor: Candace Higginbotham
Executive Editors: Rachel Hardage Barrett, Hunter Lewis, Jessica S. Thuston
Deputy Food Director: Whitney Wright
Test Kitchen Director: Robby Melvin
Test Kitchen Specialist/Food Styling: Vanessa McNeil Rocchio
Test Kitchen Professionals: Norman King, Pam Lolley, Angela Sellers
Recipe Editor: JoAnn Weatherly
Copy Editor: Ashley Leath
Style Director: Heather Chadduck Hillegas
Director of Photography: Jeanne Dozier Clayton
Photographers: Robbie Caponetto, Laurey W. Glenn, Melina Hammer, Hector Sanchez
Assistant Photo Editor: Kate Phillips
Photo Coordinator: Chris Ellenbogen
Senior Photo Stylist: Buffy Hargett
Assistant Photo Stylist: Caroline Murphy Cunningham
Editorial Assistant: Pat York
Photo Administrative Assistant: Courtney Authement

Oxmoor House

Vice President, Brand Publishing: Laura Sappington
Editorial Director: Leah McLaughlin
Creative Director: Felicity Keane
Senior Brand Manager: Daniel Fagan
Senior Editor: Rebecca Brennan
Managing Editor: Elizabeth Tyler Austin

Slim Down South Cookbook

Editors: Nichole Aksamit, Shaun Chavis
Project Editor: Lacie Pinyan
Assistant Designer: Allison Sperando Potter
Recipe Developers and Testers: Wendy Ball, R.D.; Victoria E. Cox; Tamara Goldis, R.D.; Stefanie Maloney; Callie Nash; Karen Rankin; Leah Van Deren
Recipe Editor: Alyson Moreland Haynes
Food Stylists: Victoria E. Cox; Margaret Monroe Dickey, Catherine Crowell Steele
Photography Director: Jim Bathie
Senior Photographer: Hélène Dujardin
Senior Photo Stylist: Kay E. Clarke
Photo Stylist: Mindi Shapiro Levine
Assistant Photo Stylist: Mary Louise Menendez
Senior Production Manager: Sue Chodakiewicz
Production Manager: Theresa Beste-Farley

Contributors

Author: Carolyn O'Neil, M.S., R.D.
Writer: Alyssa Shaffer
Designer: Anna Christian
Illustrator: Claudia Pearson
Compositor: Frances Higginbotham
Recipe Developers and Testers: Marian Cooper Cairns, Jan Smith
Copy Editors: Donna Baldone, Julie Bosche
Indexer: Mary Ann Laurens
Nutritional Analyses: Keri Matherne, R.D.
Fellows: Ali Carruba, Elizabeth Laseter, Stayley McIlwain, Laura Medlin, Amy Pinney, Madison Taylor Pozzo, Jeffrey Preis, Deanna Sakal, Julia Sayers, April Smitherman, Tonya West
Photographers: Beau Gustafson, Becky Luigart-Stayner
Photo Stylists: Mary Clayton Carl, Anna Pollock, Leslie Simpson
Food Stylists: Erica Hopper, Ana Price Kelly

Time Home Entertainment Inc.

Publisher: Jim Childs
Vice President, Brand & Digital Strategy: Steven Sandonato
Executive Director, Marketing Services: Carol Pittard
Executive Director, Retail & Special Sales: Tom Mifsud
Director, Bookazine Development & Marketing: Laura Adam
Executive Publishing Director: Joy Butts
Associate Publishing Director: Megan Pearlman
Finance Director: Glenn Buonocore
Associate General Counsel: Helen Wan

ABOUT THE AUTHOR

Registered dietitian and award-winning Atlanta food and nutrition journalist Carolyn O'Neil, MS, RD, grew up along the Florida Gulf Coast and has tasted and reported on the best of Southern cooking—from down-home barbecue and finger-lickin' fried chicken to fancified restaurant fare and mile-high cakes and pies served on fine china under twinkling chandeliers.

O'Neil pioneered CNN's coverage of food and health, writes a weekly nutrition column for the *Atlanta Journal-Constitution*, contributes to WebMD, and appears as "The Lady of the Refrigerator" nutrition expert on Alton Brown's hit Food Network program, Good Eats.

A winner of the James Beard Foundation Award for best TV food journalism for her work at CNN, O'Neil is a member of the James Beard Foundation's Who's Who in Food and Beverage. Her work also has been recognized by the American Society for Nutrition, the American Heart Association, the Academy of Nutrition and Dietetics, and the National Restaurant Association.

O'Neil holds a master's degree in nutrition and communication from Boston University, and an undergraduate degree in foods and nutrition from Florida State University. She is the co-author of *The Dish on Eating Healthy and Being Fabulous!* (Atria Books).

ACKNOWLEDGMENTS

My mother says you can tell a lot about a person by their table manners. That always means saying thank you. I have many good people to thank for *The Slim Down South Cookbook*. First, thank you to the farmers who raise the fresh ingredients needed to create healthy and delicious Southern meals.

Thank you to all of the editors at Oxmoor House and *Southern Living* for shepherding this book from vision to reality. A special note of appreciation to Oxmoor House editorial director Leah McLaughlin for believing I was the right author for the job and to senior editor Rebecca Brennan and editor Susan Ray for launching me on the work. Many thanks go to my brilliant editors, Nichole Aksamit and Shaun Chavis, who helped me create the framework for it and brought the book to life, and to Alyssa Shaffer, who helped me write the manuscript.

Thank you to the talented Test Kitchen staff, the food photographers, the stylists, and the designers who helped make *The Slim Down South Cookbook* look and taste so delicious.

Thanks, too, to all the smart and savvy Southerners who shared their stay-slim secrets with me.

On a personal note, I'd like to thank Alison Lewis for first connecting me with Oxmoor House and Liz McDermott for helping me review hundreds of recipes to begin the selection for *The Slim Down South Cookbook*. Thank you to Mary Lalli for handling the business side of this publishing experience. Appreciation goes to all of my friends and to my children, Jack and Katie, who kept checking in on the progress of the book. You kept me focused.

Thank you to my mom, Jessie O'Neil, who is Scottish by birth but embodies the true spirit of Southern hospitality every time she sets the table and cooks a meal for family and friends. (Watch out! She *will* ask you if you want another biscuit and make sure you eat dessert.)

— Carolyn O'Neil